LATIN AMERICAN MISSION

An Adventure in Hemisphere Diplomacy

by

DELESSEPS S. MORRISON

Former U.S. Ambassador to the Organization of American States

EDITED AND WITH AN INTRODUCTION
BY GEROLD FRANK

SIMON AND SCHUSTER
NEW YORK

PUBLISHED BY SIMON AND SCHUSTER, INC.
ROCKEFELLER CENTER, 630 FIFTH AVENUE
NEW YORK 20, N. Y.

FIRST PRINTING

LIBRARY OF CONGRESS CATALOG CARD NUMBER: 65-11977
MANUFACTURED IN THE UNITED STATES OF AMERICA
BY THE BOOK PRESS, BRATTLEBORO, VERMONT
DESIGNED BY EDITH FOWLER

For Toni, Corinne and Randy

CONTENTS

About Chep Morrison—Editor's Note 9

An Introductory Note 21

BOOK ONE

1. I Am Asked to Be an Ambassador 27
2. My Road to Latin America: A Bit of Autobiography 42
3. First Exercises in Personal Diplomacy 60
4. Punta del Este—Birth of the Alliance 77
5. Behind the Curtain—Politics, Latin Style 93
6. President Kennedy Town 106
7. The President, the State Department—and Trouble in the Caribbean 112
8. The Legacy of Trujillo 129
9. Private Notes from an Ambassador's Notebook 144
10. Interlude: Two Mysteries 159

BOOK TWO

11.	Showdown	165
12.	Cuba Sí or Cuba No	177
13.	Some Thinking Aloud	198
14.	Kaiser—and Free Enterprise in Latin America	203
15.	The Critical Months	218
16.	L.B.J. and My Friends the Ambassadors	231
17.	Crisis	238
18.	The Men and the Problems of Tomorrow	252
19.	The Closing of a Mission	266
	Index	279

ABOUT CHEP MORRISON

DeLesseps S. "Chep" Morrison was by all tokens an unusual man. Former United States ambassador to the Organization of American States, four times mayor of New Orleans, three times candidate for the governorship of Louisiana, he was tragically killed with a party of six, including his seven-year-old son Randy, when their private plane crashed in Mexico in the spring of 1964. He was fifty-two, and in the prime of an extraordinarily vigorous life.

He had asked me to help him with the story of his experiences as President Kennedy's envoy to the O.A.S. and roving ambassador in Latin America. Chep's death came with shocking suddenness on Friday, May 22, 1964. He had been flying each weekend from New Orleans to Mexico; on this trip he was taking friends to inspect a cattle ranch at Tampico whose owner had evolved an ingenious plan for land distribution to peasants. In that plan Chep saw opportunities for United States private investment below the border, one of his favorite causes. On this flight, a short hop from the Mexican border to Tampico, the plane was caught in a sudden squall and crashed against a mountain. All aboard were killed.

At the time of Chep's death he had read most of these pages. What was not yet final, he had seen in rough form. On long trips

I made with him through Latin America, while he told his story to me, and through interviews with his associates, I began to understand the curious, engaging, sunny personality which made the story possible: a man always with a purpose, who took what he did seriously, but never himself.

Chep was, to be sure, a controversial man in some circles. A big-city Catholic attacked by Louisiana red-necks for everything from being "soft" on integration to the fact that he used cologne, a Kennedy Democrat denounced as a liberal by Southern conservatives, a lifelong foe of the Huey Long machine, he was nevertheless one of the most popular politicians in the South. He was the almost perfect political animal. He dealt in people. He affected others so that they felt immediately linked to him—indeed, as I saw repeatedly, actually grateful to him for allowing them to knock themselves out working for him.

These qualities showed themselves early in his life. At thirty-four he became the boy wonder of Louisiana politics by his election as mayor on a reform ticket—the first in fifty years. He was re-elected three successive times. He was "Mr. New Orleans" to much of the country. During his tenure he changed the face of downtown New Orleans. He engineered an $80-million construction and rehabilitation program, set into operation a $150-million transportation complex, and pushed the Port of New Orleans from seventeenth to second in the nation. In achieving this last he devoted much time and effort to Latin American relations—which ultimately led to his appointment by President Kennedy as ambassador to the O.A.S. in 1961.

The late A. J. Liebling wrote not long ago that Chep Morrison had been described by admirers as "a melange of Jimmy Walker for looks and manner, Fiorello LaGuardia for energy and probity, and Big Bad Bob Moses, the Builder, for getting things done."* Liebling, who had an unerring eye for the phony, began by taking a rather suspicious view of this high-powered and charming Louisiana politician, but ended by rooting for him.

Chep did that to people. He was almost too much to believe—at

* In *The Earl of Louisiana* (New York: Simon and Schuster, 1961), a brilliant study of the late Governor Earl Long. Visiting Louisiana while writing the book, Liebling became fascinated by Chep, the Long dynasty's perennial foe, who was then making his second race for the governorship.

first. Only as one grew to know him did one realize that here was a man of no subterfuge, for whom to think was to act—a supremely confident extrovert, whose carefree outlook, blindness toward any personal insult, genius for instantly erasing the memory of any setback, and unabashed friendliness toward the world were all slightly implausible.

Appointed an ambassador, surely Chep was among the least ambassadorial of diplomats. He marched into the formal world of Latin American protocol—next to the British, perhaps the most ceremonious—with a directness, a freshness, a complete lack of pretense, that overwhelmed his colleagues. Brash, unafraid, unorthodox, a bull in the china shop among the hairsplitting Latins, Chep made an unforgettable impression. But he liked them, he meant well for them, and they knew it. They responded, the vast majority of them, to their "Chepito" with the same open affection he exhibited toward them.

When word of Chep's death came, the first bulletins were heard over the radio below the border at 3 A.M. For some hours the fate of the plane and its passengers was uncertain; the suspense was harrowing. One Latin colleague in Rio de Janeiro was so agitated that despite the hour he began telephoning and awakening friends throughout Latin America. "I somehow wanted the whole world to know what was happening and to hear the scream I cannot produce," he wrote.

The wave of sorrow that swept New Orleans and the behavior of its citizens at the funeral a few days later were in this same grief-stricken key. Chep and seven-year-old Randy lay in state a day and a night in ancient Gallier Hall, which had been Chep's office when he was mayor. All during the day and night mourners filed past the two coffins, at the rate of 1,500 an hour. The line stretched out the door, across the street through Lafayette Square, and around the block. Chep was a major general in the United States Army Reserve; he was given a civil and full military funeral. Flags flew at half-mast; in the streets, people walked with tears in their eyes; men and women, white and Negro, who had never known him in person recalled stories about him. He had sent this student to Latin America; he had moved heaven and earth to bring together his Chinese laundryman and the latter's small son, then in Hong Kong; he had spent nearly an hour in the Mexico City airport helping a stranger—an inarticulate Mexican peasant—search for lost belongings. . . .

At the time of his death, Chep had been out of the mayor's office and not part of the New Orleans scene for nearly three years. As ambassador he had spent most of his time in Washington, or in Latin America, or speaking throughout this country. All the more impressive, therefore, this tribute to him.

The Chep Morrison who went to Washington in the summer of 1961 found his job anything but easy after New Orleans, where his unconventional, whirlwind political style was limited only by himself. Now, faced by checks and carefully spelled-out procedures, Chep simply forged ahead and let the chips fall where they would. As the reader will see, he broke protocol right and left. Were Chep a political philosopher—he was not, and he had little patience for theories or abstractions or indeed for any thought that did not result in action—he would have termed himself a pragmatist. If what he tried worked, if it enabled him to carry out his assignment as he understood it from Mr. Kennedy—who had brought him in "to get things off the ground"—it was right. Here he could be stubborn and single-minded.

Thus, he horse-traded votes with presidents, made private deals with ambassadors, listened in with them on their overseas calls to their foreign ministers, helped draft political documents for Dominican generals, wined and dined ministers of state, promised jobs to Latin delegates who risked dismissal if they voted with the United States bloc, rode herd on Congressmen, wangled a presidential plane to send home an ailing Brazilian diplomat or to carry two dozen Latin American ambassadors on a Morrison-conducted tour of grass-roots United States—the New Orleans Mardi Gras, Lyndon B. Johnson's LBJ Ranch, the Oklahoma-Texas football game.

In the State Department his method of operation often made him controversial. There were those who attacked him for not probing problems deeply enough, for being impetuous, for viewing intricate matters as either black or white. But the fact was that he could glance through a one-page memo—which he had demanded be reduced from half a dozen pages—and come to a firm decision which other officials, far more learned on the subject, had yet to reach after days of pondering over data. This some department technicians found infuriating, especially since Chep, as was pointed out to me by a knowledgeable Latin American observer, was proved right more often than not. Whatever it was—intuition, lightninglike mental calculations, an ability to grasp essentials—his method worked for him. He managed to cover a great deal of ground while involved in a great number of projects.

Nor did he hesitate to cross swords with presidential aides, State Department dignitaries and anyone else he thought mistaken. The reader will note how Chep repeatedly takes issue with Richard N. Goodwin and Arthur Schlesinger, Jr., two of Mr. Kennedy's top advisers, on the ticklish problem of how to handle Cuba in the O.A.S. Chep even points out indignantly that Goodwin went outside channels to obtain information—witness, among other things, Goodwin's secret, unauthorized meeting with Cuba's Major Che Guevara, Fidel Castro's economic adviser. Yet this was how Chep himself operated. When I commented on this fact, Chep grinned sheepishly, said, "You have a point there," and then, having instantly expunged this criticism, "drawn a blank on it," as one of his friends might say, went on to repeat the same charges in different words with the same indignation.

The reader will note, too, that Chep tells his story as one in the very center of history-making events. Others appear only on the periphery. Thus, you come upon him in a White House meeting, or with an O.A.S. investigating committee in the Dominican Republic, or in Costa Rica, and you realize that though other actors are on the stage, they are all but invisible. The extraordinary attention Chep could concentrate on a project—or a person—was, like the laser ray, so intense that it went directly to the heart of the target, touching nothing surrounding it, unaware of anything on either side. Chep reported best what he did, not in disparagement of others, for he lavishly praises many associates, but simply because the focus of his private camera is so sharp. At these high-level meetings he describes for us, did others besides Kennedy and Morrison speak? Perhaps it does not matter. For Chep, that was the meeting's essence and purpose: to know what Kennedy wished of him, and for him to go out and do it. All else was extraneous.

Chep gloried in politics. Everything about it excited him. He was gregarious, could not bear to be alone, liked making speeches, loved to be in the public eye, and was completely at home—indeed, at his best—at political analysis of the most minute nature. In New

Orleans recently someone mentioned the latest elections in Uruguay. That was all Chep needed. For a full ten minutes he descanted on the subject as if he were lecturing before a seminar, explaining the composition of the nine-man Council of State that rules the country, citing names (complete, in the Spanish fashion, with first, father's and mother's names), ages, month-by-month maneuvers by each of the nine, deals made not only by the major Colorado and Blanco parties but by half a dozen splinter groups, the *quid pro quos* exchanged, the strength of each man's constituency, its religious, social and ethnic composition down to half percentiles. It was an extraordinary exhibition.

I don't doubt that he could have delivered similar lectures on any of the other nineteen Latin states. His faculty for absorbing information from others made up for the fact that he read little—he would not take the time—and as he could extract from a memo what he had to know, so he could siphon from a conversation with an expert, from an embassy briefing, from exposure to a situation, an astonishing amount of knowledge, all of which stayed with him. It was one more cross to be borne by some of his State Department associates who could not believe this blithely confident Louisiana politician had actually picked up the essentials of a problem in so brief a time.

Chep was born to energy—and to enjoyment. Nearly six feet tall, solidly built, a handsome man with dark, penetrating eyes under a high forehead, his black hair beginning to show a bald spot, he kept in perfect physical condition. He seemed tireless. He was the kind of executive who could keep three secretaries constantly busy. He was never idle. I have watched him on planes, where most men may be forgiven if they doze off or relax. Not Chep. Time, which was so precious to him that he was always late for appointments—first, because he crowded so much activity into the day, and second, because he could not endure waiting for anyone—would not allow him to rest on a plane. The moment he strapped himself into his seat he began to work on his correspondence, which was truly enormous. This was his only writing-thinking time. He actually resented it if fellow passengers spoke to him then.

On long trips he usually traveled with Pat Mahony, his secretary, or some other associate, who brought along a series of manila envelopes each containing a strip of gummed labels such as magazine circulation departments use, the names and addresses already typed.

First, Chep got rid of routine mail—a scribbled note on each letter would be sent back to be typed, signed and mailed by his staff at home. Then, armed with some one hundred postcards, he would begin writing greetings on each; Pat would affix the labels; at the first stop, she would mail those that were done. In the airport she would purchase another one or two hundred cards. The same procedure, with a new strip of labels taken from another envelope, would be followed on the second leg of the flight; then, again, on the third—purchase, writing, mailing. Chep sent from four to six hundred postcards on each trip. It was impossible for his friends—private and political—not to be constantly reminded of him.

In his office these lists were kept in filing cabinets. In addition to "Campaign Contributors," "Press & TV," "Political Leaders," and the like, there was one large file headed "Women for Morrison." In each city in Louisiana, Chep had formed committees of civic-minded women who were among his most active political workers. But there was also a private file, which Pat Mahony had given the heading, "M.W."—"Morrison's Women"—to Chep's great delight. I do not know which file was larger. The first, to be sure, was limited to Louisiana. The second included nearly every large city in the United States and most of the capitals of the Western world. Chep must have flown hundreds of thousands of miles in his various capacities and, so far as I can determine, rarely if ever knew an evening on the ground when he did not escort, to use one of his favorite phrases, "a pretty lady." Chep, a widower, was an admirer of women, and they responded as a moth to the flame. Here his Latin temperament had perhaps its greatest play. I believe he knew well more beautiful women than any man of his age and generation, with perhaps the exception of the Aly Khan—and I would be inclined to give Chep Morrison the odds, because Prince Aly was more hemmed in by protocol. Chep's appeal to women and his success with them can only be described as extraordinary; it was one of the qualities highly respected by his Latin colleagues. He gave to each woman the same kind of concentrated, blowtorch attention that he gave to everything in which he took an interest—whether it was bringing water and electricity to an Uruguayan village, persuading Henry J. Kaiser to build an aluminum plant in New Orleans, or explaining the complex aims of the Alliance for Progress to audiences throughout the United States.

The women he knew in Latin America also served as a political touchstone for him. Through them he sensed the current climate of the country in which he found himself, and often received briefings on issues and personalities such as no United States embassy aide could give him. From them he learned, too, the intricate family and class loyalties, the rivalries and antipathies, which gave him such a familiarity in the field as more experienced diplomats might never attain.

Any assessment of Chep's service as ambassador—and it is essentially his service as ambassador that is the province of his book—must take into account the value of the person-to-person diplomacy in which Chep was endlessly engaged. Yet this is most difficult to measure. His personal contacts in Latin America, cultivated in more than sixty trips *before* Mr. Kennedy appointed him, and considerably expanded in some twenty-one trips in as many months after, were probably at least as numerous as those of any other North American. Add to this that he rarely forgot a name or a face and his genuine liking for Latins, who in turn liked and trusted him. His effectiveness among them was not so much a matter of persuading them to our view through logic; he rarely attempted to convince a man, point by incontrovertible point, so as to prove the other wrong and himself right. He was too much of a Latin himself not to understand that loss of face could outweigh even the heaviest evidence. Rather, it was a matter of intuition; he sensed people, their strengths and weaknesses, he could manage to get inside their will and, like a Judo wrestler, use their thrust to bring them to his side. I find this quality difficult to explain, but it was part of Chep and was frequently remarked upon by those who knew him well. Others might have thought him naïve in his approach, only because at the moment Chep was not concerned about the aspect of the problem visible to them, but was concentrating on another phase; in the end it developed that he had made progress where he wanted to make it, and it was this phase which turned out to be important.

By the same token, he could get his aides to do things that experience told them simply could not be done. "I'd go through the motions just to satisfy him," one told me. "I'd make the telephone call I knew would not get what we wanted—and, by God, it *would* work out. I would say, 'Mr. Ambassador, you just don't *do* things that way!' But he'd already be calling Pat, or dialing someone, or dictating a note to someone else—sometimes all at the same time—and we'd be off and running."

His greatest vindication as ambassador and chief of the United States delegation to the O.A.S. came little more than two months after his death, when economic and diplomatic sanctions against Cuba were voted by the O.A.S. foreign ministers in Washington on July 27, 1964. This had been one of his major goals; he had fought for it, he had insisted it could be done without splitting the hemisphere—and in the end, it was.

Chep decided to write the story of his experiences as ambassador toward the close of his campaign for the governorship of Louisiana, in late 1963. He had resigned his Washington post on September 13 to make the race. His election could only strengthen Kennedy in the South; and Chep, as everyone knew, despite two successive defeats still wanted to be governor with all his heart. "He would rather sit in the Governor's Mansion in Baton Rouge than in the White House," a close friend had told me.

As the campaign ended in early 1964, every poll, every newspaper predicted a landslide victory for him in the Democratic primary, which in Louisiana is tantamount to election. His opponent, Public Service Commissioner John J. McKeithen, running on a rabid segregationist platform, was comparatively unknown.

With victory assured, Chep decided to take off two weeks, beginning the day after election, to start work on this book. To think was to act. He immediately telephoned a friend, former President Miguel Aleman of Mexico, and five minutes later had the use of Aleman's showplace beach home in Acapulco, a regal, four-level, fifteen-room villa complete with staff of ten. A second call, to another friend—a private plane and pilot would pick up Chep and his party in New Orleans at nine o'clock the morning after election and fly us direct to the Mexican resort. The party consisted of Chep; his three children (Toni, twenty; Corinne, seventeen; and Randy, seven); two secretaries, Pat Mahony and Peggy Baudreaux; his aide, Winston Lill; myself; two electric typewriters; and huge packing cases of documents, biographical material, O.A.S. reports and office supplies.

To everyone's astonishment, when the election returns came in, the night before our departure, John J. McKeithen had defeated deLesseps Morrison. It was one of the major political upsets of 1964.

The manner in which Chep took this blow is still talked about. A friend happened to look out of his hotel window at about ten o'clock election night, to see Chep and three of his principal backers crossing the street to his campaign headquarters to concede defeat. Chep was in the lead, the three behind him, their faces drawn, walking heavily, almost dazed, as at a wake; but Chep, smiling, head up, strode forward vigorously, nodding cheerily at friends. He had already dismissed the defeat, erased it, drawn a blank. It was behind him now, and he would never turn his head. He was walking away from it, swiftly, his mind already teeming with what he would do tomorrow, next week, next month. Ambassador to Mexico, perhaps? Run for Senator? Try again for the governorship? Three times, why not a fourth?

Perhaps a final clue to Chep, the man, lies in his one sport—water-skiing. He did not smoke; he drank sparingly; food and sleep were unimportant to him; he spent no time on cards, golf, tennis, swimming or boating. Dancing he delighted in, and could not get enough, but his supreme enjoyment was water-skiing. Like dancing, it was action, and in action he fulfilled himself. Wherever he went, if at all possible, he water-skied. Friends teasingly accused him of planning the numerous good-will tours he led throughout Latin America to include places of interest only to water-skiers; then of arranging for the sightseeing buses to carry his tour members past the bay at the very moment he was performing on skis, so that he could have what he dearly loved—an audience. True or not, Chep reveled in this sport, its recklessness, its driving forward—if there was an operative word in his life, it was *go, go, go!*—and its speed. Few motorboats pulled him fast enough, he complained. He had taught skiing to every friend who allowed him, as well as to his sons and daughter as soon as they were old enough to manage.

I remember Chep, in Mexico, the day after his defeat. We had arrived in Acapulco, and the staff was setting up for our work. Chep, with his characteristic distaste for inaction, was already water-skiing. I had come along, to sit in my bathing suit next to the Mexican youth at the wheel of the speedboat towing Chep behind us at a breakneck pace. It was a little after midday. The night before, in New Orleans, at six o'clock, Chep had believed himself the next governor of Louisiana. Only a few hours, really, had passed. He was alone now, on the wide bay. No audience to cheer him, no one to see him. No need here to pretend, to hide his disappointment.

We were far from shore now. The Mexican boy and I faced forward, bracing ourselves against the pounding of the water against the hull, the sharp salt spray roaring blindingly back at us. On impulse I turned in my seat, to catch the expression on Chep's face as he rode the water, some seventy feet behind us. I looked. The three-times-defeated candidate for the governorship of Louisiana had attached the rope to his waist so that his arms were free, and there, on the skis, the spray rising majestically on either side of him like twin geysers, he was dancing the twist, singing, having a wonderful time.

So Chep Morrison lived his life, working, playing, and unabashedly enjoying every minute of it.

—Gerold Frank

AN INTRODUCTORY NOTE

This is, I should like to think, a different book on Latin America—different in two ways: First, it is a highly personal report of a mission which began with my appointment as United States ambassador to the Organization of American States by President Kennedy on June 13, 1961, and ended with my resignation on September 13, 1963, to campaign for the governorship of Louisiana. It therefore tells the story of a personal experience—for me, memorable and enormously rewarding—during that historic twenty-six-month period. It was a historic period because it saw the birth of the Alliance for Progress, our vast, cooperative, hemispheric effort to improve the social and economic lot of more than 200,000,000 people of Latin America. It is historic, because in that span of time we, the American family of nations, finally faced up to the fact that Cuba was indeed a Soviet satellite; in that period we closed ranks and ousted Cuba from the inter-American society; and in that period, part and parcel of what went before, came the great confrontation that brought the United States and the Soviet Union to the brink of war over the missile crisis. From the unique experience of these months I emerged not only wiser, I think, in the complexities of Latin America (though I began serenely confident that I knew a great deal), but I also gained a knowledge of American diplomacy in action, a glimpse of the power struggle and play of personalities behind the scenes in the White House and the State Department. Thus, for me, duty and education went hand in hand, and I am grateful for the opportunity to have benefited from both. And I am proudest of the statement of appreciation from a man who was perhaps more deeply loved south of the border than any American, John F. Kennedy:

> . . . You have performed most capably and with tremendous devotion and enthusiasm for the cause of our nation in Latin America. After twenty-six months of extensive duty, you leave the government with the respect, admiration and friendship of your fellow U.S. officials, as well as the deep affection of your Latin American colleagues. You have been truly an able diplomat and a champion for the cause of democracy and freedom in this hemisphere.

No award in my lifetime could possibly give me greater consolation or satisfaction.

By vocation I am a lawyer and politician; but my avocation has been and is Latin America. I was born and grew up in the deep South. For fifteen years I was mayor of New Orleans, our nation's second port. I could look north and see all the United States before me; but I found myself time and again turning south, south to Central America, to South America, to the warm, beautiful lands of warm-hearted people, deep-feeling, emotional, perhaps—is it a dangerous word today?—*innocent*; people seeking in the shadow of the Colossus of the North, their powerful and for so long feared neighbor, to grow into maturity with self-respect, to achieve liberty, to realize the completion of the revolution begun by their great spirits but never brought to fulfillment, as was ours.

Spiritually, I consider myself a Latin. On my mother's side I am of French extraction. My great-granduncle, for whom I was named, was a French engineer, Ferdinand de Lesseps, who built the Suez Canal and attempted, but failed, to build the Panama Canal. So I have both spiritual and physical ties to the Latin world. But more than that, I have made the countries of Latin America my home away from home. In more than eighty trips to the southern part of the hemisphere I have sought to acquaint myself with its people, their problems, their hopes, their fears. During my service as ambassador to the O.A.S., that smaller United Nations of Latin America, I tried to translate not only my personal affection, but also my fellow Americans' warmth and respect, for our friends below the border, and at the same time to hold firm against the menace of Communism emanating from Cuba.* Because Cuba is a Latin American country, this was for me a difficult and, at times, sad assignment. The story I tell, therefore, is the story of one man's attempt to understand, to report, to put a measure of light on, one of the most complex and vital areas of our world today.

But I would be less than honest if I did not speak of the second way in which I believe this may be different from other books on this much-belabored subject of Latin America. I write as an optimist. A columnist once commented—perhaps after I had lost two consecutive attempts to be elected governor of Louisiana and thereupon announced I would make a third—that "Chep Morrison could find a ray of sunlight in a coalbin in a dark cellar at midnight." I don't know that I could *find* it; I do know that I would *look* for it.

Much that I have read in recent months and years on Latin America, beginning long before our disastrous Bay of Pigs invasion of Cuba in the spring of 1961, has been written in accents of doom. Do only Cassandras write of Latin America? For I read: We shall lose Latin America to the Communists; Latin America will go the way of China; the Alliance for Progress is a failure; the United States, in spite of its twenty-billion-dollar commitment to Latin America in the next decade, in spite of the billions of dollars it has already poured in loans, credits and outright grants into Latin America since President Kennedy launched the Alliance three years ago, in spite of its vast investment of human energy, talent and intelligence in this tremendous self-help effort which is the Alliance —in spite of all this, the United States reaps not friendship but hate, and not only is "Yanqui go home!" scrawled on buildings, but it also would be sounded loudly on the tongue of every *campesino*, every peasant, every exploited peon who identifies the United States

* I note that Mr. Carleton Beals, a prolific writer on Latin America, in his recent book, *Latin America: World in Revolution*, credits me with having "been responsible in good part for punitive measures and for the Punta del Este deal against Cuba." He has unforgivably slighted the two-thirds majority of Latin American foreign ministers who voted with the United States in that "deal."

with the oligarchies of his own land, if he but dared speak up. . . . In short, there is (say these prophets of despair) a hard, irreducible core of distrust and hostility toward the United States that can only grow, not diminish. In the end Latin America will be convulsed by a bloody revolt that will mark the beginning of the end of all our hopes and will perhaps take us—in our conceit, our arrogance, our greediness—down with it to catastrophe.

I do not believe this.

At the same time, I do not shut my eyes to the enormous problems that face us: our frequent inability to communicate our true attitude, and to the degree we fail in this, the existence of suspicion as to our motives; the reluctance of entrenched privilege, almost feudal in nature, to yield up its prerogatives; the deep-rooted factors, based on Latin American history, politics, economy and racial backgrounds, which present their special obstacles to the speedy growth of democracy as we understand it; the shockingly disparate distribution of wealth, power and literacy in a continent where in some countries five per cent of the population controls ninety-five per cent of the wealth—these are staggering to contemplate.

But Latin America *is* awakening. Its people are seeking to leap from the seventeenth century to the twentieth. Because they are, Latin America is a continent in turmoil. It is awakening with such power, to quote a Peruvian friend of mine, "that if we cannot control that power, if we cannot channel that energy, it will unbalance the world."

The optimist in me says we can control, we can channel, this energy. We can do it together, the United States and all the freedom-loving nations of the hemisphere. We are already doing it. We began it when together we signed the Charter of Punta del Este, on August 17, 1961, which brought a brand-new concept into the thinking of the hemisphere, and which, in President Kennedy's words, "laid down a new principle of our relationship—the principle of collective responsibility for the welfare of the peoples of the Americas." We continued it when together we took action on Cuba, first placing her outside the O.A.S. in January 1962 at Punta del Este, and then, because of that same sense of collective responsibility, joining as one in unanimous support of President Kennedy's quarantine of the Soviet's attempt to send offensive weapons to Cuba in October 1962. We are continuing it today when American youths from Connecticut and Texas feed milk to Indian school children in the remote villages of Peru and Guatemala, when United States Army officers teach Colombian soldiers not how to use bayonets but how to build roads and clear swamps, when young New Yorkers and Californians in the Peace Corps plow the fields of Chile and Venezuela side by side with farmer and peasant, and schools are built, housing projects flourish, and endemic diseases are wiped out thanks to United States money and Latin American money pooled together in a true alliance for progress.

Not long ago Galo Plaza, former President of Ecuador, one of Latin America's most distinguished leaders and political philosophers, wrote:

"You in the United States had your war of independence more than 180 years ago. It was a complete revolution from the President down to the humblest farmer, who not only participated in your war for independence but subsequently enjoyed the fruits of victory. *Your* revolution represented a complete change, politically, socially, economically.

"In Latin America, however, it is different. Our revolution began shortly after yours; it continued until 60 years ago. We, too, threw off the yoke of the mother countries—Spain, Portugal and France. But many of our revolutions were incomplete: the political change simply substituted domestic tyrants for foreign tyrants. The lot of the rank and file of our people was unchanged: they continued to know poverty and misery as they had for centuries.

"Today a vast ground swell of tremendous desire, of passionate determination to complete the incomplete revolution of years ago sweeps all Latin America. Our people want the economic and social changes which you in the United States have enjoyed for well over a century."

I say to my friend Galo Plaza: Today the incomplete revolution is being completed. We believe we can help complete it through the Alliance for Progress, an *alliance*, a *partnership*, between us and you. The Communists say they can do it better. I believe that all Latin Americans, given a chance to see what it is we wish to do, propose to do, are doing, will make their choice with us.

—deLesseps S. Morrison

New Orleans, Louisiana
May 1964

BOOK ONE

1. I AM ASKED TO BE AN AMBASSADOR

It began with a telephone call. I was in Fort Buchanan, Puerto Rico, in my capacity as brigadier general in the United States Army Reserve, addressing an officers' luncheon one Saturday in May 1961. In the midst of my speech the loudspeaker suddenly boomed: "The White House wishes to speak with General Morrison on the telephone."

There was a moment of confusion, even in that disciplined company; in the century-old history of the Fort there had never been a call put through from the White House. When I picked up the telephone, at the other end was Secretary of State Dean Rusk, whom I had known—not well—when he was president of the Rockefeller Foundation.

"General," he began, without preface, "could you come to Washington to talk to me on Monday?"

I said of course. I did not ask why. I suspected that it might have something to do with Latin America. I was known in Washington as a mayor obsessed with the subject, forever selling Latin America to anyone who would listen; and at the moment our entire Latin American policy was a matter of great debate in the public mind, especially after the Bay of Pigs disaster a few weeks before.

As it turned out, Latin America was the subject on Secretary Rusk's agenda when I saw him in his office two days later. A tall, husky, balding man with a courtly Southern manner, he came quickly to what he wanted to say. "A great number of people have been talking to me about your coming into the Latin American field for us. Senator Smathers, Senator Long, Congressman Boggs—they all say we ought to have you aboard."

There had been much in the press assailing the alleged confusion in our policy toward Latin America. President Kennedy had taken office in January 1961. In March he had announced the first major project of the New Frontier—his Alliance for Progress, a vast, far-reaching partnership between ourselves and the American republics to satisfy the basic needs of their 200,000,000 people for "houses, work and health, land and schools." He had called upon our neighbors to join us in "this great ten-year plan for the Americas, a plan to transform the 1960's into a historic decade of democratic progress." I thought the Alliance a tremendous idea, not only because it meant attacking ancient evils by building up the economies of these countries, but because we would also be building a bulwark in our hemisphere against Communism, which fed on poverty and social injustice.

But though the world had been told about the Alliance, the key men to direct it had yet to be chosen. For months the position of Assistant Secretary of State for Inter-American Affairs had been left unfilled, and President Kennedy had still to appoint the United States Delegate to the Organization of American States, the man who would deal directly with the twenty republics on the new program. Latin American affairs in Washington were handled on a day-to-day basis by a three-man task force. Adolf Berle, former Assistant Secretary for Inter-American Affairs, was chairman, assisted by two White House aides, Arthur Schlesinger, Jr., and Richard N. Goodwin. Both had worked closely with Kennedy during his campaign, advising him and writing speeches for him, and he brought them into the White House with him. Schlesinger, a Harvard historian in his early forties, was a redoubtable and brilliant man, and Goodwin, a twenty-nine-year-old lawyer, was already recognized as a kind of budding Harry Hopkins. But neither one had any previous experience in Latin America.*

* I had been told that so improvised, so Alice-in-Wonderland were those first New Frontier days that Goodwin was quite taken aback to find himself a Latin American expert helping to make policy in a part of the world he had never visited. Shortly after coming to the White House he had accosted a newspaperman. "I'm going to be appointed to a high Latin American post,"

As if voicing my own thoughts, Rusk said, "We need to move on Latin America, we especially need someone vigorous to get the Alliance off the ground." I could have my choice of either job: Assistant Secretary of State or O.A.S. delegate. Was I interested? Was I free to consider these?

Yes and no, I said, a little vaguely. My fourth four-year term as mayor of New Orleans had a year and a half to go. I could not succeed myself, thanks to a measure I had introduced in the early fifties, which prohibited anyone from serving more than two consecutive terms after 1954. However . . .

"If you're agreeable in principle," the Secretary was saying, "I think you'd do best pushing the Alliance—working with the O.A.S. We're going to upgrade the post not only to ambassadorial status, but to make it subject to Senate confirmation. That means you would rank with the Assistant Secretary, though nominally you'd be working through his office." I would have freedom to do a creative job. When the O.A.S. was not in session I would be, in effect, a roving ambassador to Latin America. The only comparable post in the State Department was that held by Adlai Stevenson as United States ambassador to the United Nations. Rusk smiled. How did I feel about this?

I could not make a final decision then. "I'll think it over, Mr. Secretary," I said, and flew back to New Orleans with his promise that I might have time to decide. There was much to consider. Two years before, my wife, Corinne, had died at the tragically young age of thirty-seven. My three children—Toni, sixteen, Corinne, thirteen, and little Randy, four—were very much on my mind. To leave New Orleans for Washington would involve many changes in my personal life. Was I ready to make them? And as to my career, was I prepared to turn my back on a political future, after two near-misses at the governorship, and trade that for diplomacy, even though in an area very exciting to me?

The cab that took me from the State Department to the airport passed the Pan American Union, the home of the O.A.S. It was a beautiful spring day. I looked at the magnificent gray-marble struc-

---

he told him. "Can you suggest some good books I ought to read?" That week the President's Special Advisor on Latin American Affairs began to take lessons in Spanish.

ture with new interest. I had gone there often to attend glittering, Old World receptions. Every Latin American country sent an ambassador to the O.A.S., as they did to the UN; but the O.A.S. was far older and had a far more colorful background. As early as 1826, Simon Bolivar, the great Venezuelan liberator, called upon the former colonies of European powers to unite as a hemispheric group for their mutual benefit. Each country had its own tortured history of oppression, exploitation and misrule; each had fought for its freedom and won it at bitter cost. Now Bolivar sought to bring them together at the Congress of Panama and sign pacts of mutual help and collective security. But his dreams did not come true until 1890, when the International Union of American Republics was founded. In 1910 this became the Pan American Union; and after World War II, in 1948, it grew into what is now the Organization of American States. The Pan American Union Building, dating back to 1910, had kept its old name. Fronting on the same grass ellipse bordered also by the White House, the Washington Monument and the Treasury and Commerce buildings, the majestic structure had always seemed to me a bit of Latin America transported to the United States—its gracious patio, its fountain, its macaws and other exotic birds, its tropical plants, its great, high-vaulted halls, its muraled corridors, its marble busts of fiercely mustached and noble-browed Latin American heroes and liberators . . .

Back in New Orleans I asked the advice of my former law partner, Representative Hale Boggs, Democratic whip of the Congress. Hale was one of those who had spoken about me to the Secretary. He is married to my cousin Lindy and thus is part of my family; he and I began our political careers almost at the same time, and he has been my confidant ever since we worked together in our twenties. He could be forgiven for lauding me to Mr. Rusk.

"Take it, Chep," he said enthusiastically. "You've been talking about Latin America for fifteen years. Now's your chance to do something about it."

But Hale's advice was completely the opposite of that of my political constituents and my City Hall advisers. I wanted to run for the governorship of Louisiana again in 1964, although no Catholic had been elected to that office in eighty years. I had lost twice; in 1956 to Earl Long, Huey Long's brother; and in 1960, by a hairline margin, to Jimmie H. Davis. I knew that I could have any number of executive positions in New Orleans after I left City Hall, and so be able to prepare for my campaign on home grounds. If I took a post that kept me in Washington or Latin America, how would this affect our political hopes? Would not "out of sight" mean "out of mind"? As mayor I had managed to keep squabbling political factions together, so that we won our elections by two-to-one majorities in New Orleans; together we had put through reforms and civic construction programs that had changed the face of New Orleans. We had a good administration. I was proud to have won the National Junior Chamber of Commerce Award in my first term as one of the ten outstanding young men of the country, and in my second term, the LaGuardia Award as the outstanding mayor in the United States. Decent people in New Orleans feared that if I left, the heirs apparent would fight among themselves, there would be a breakdown in the reform administration built up since 1946, and a return ultimately to the kind of corruption that had plagued New Orleans for half a century.

I was tugged at from both sides. The New Orleans *Times-Picayune,* a highly respected force in the community, declared editorially that I had a moral commitment to serve out my term. An emergency meeting of city officials passed a resolution calling upon me to decline the offer. I began slowly to conclude that I must say no to Mr. Rusk.

I did not underestimate my country's problems in the wake of the disastrous attempt to invade Cuba. I had hoped ardently that we would succeed. When we failed, I was sick at heart. The door of my office at City Hall was always open to Cuban exile leaders; they confided in me, and I was at one with their cause. Our failure struck me almost like a personal blow. I knew how Latin Americans think. United States prestige was at a dreadful low. Any job dealing with Latin America would be most difficult. Yet every day made the need for direction and action more imperative.

A few days after my talk with Rusk—I was still pondering what to tell him—I picked up *The New York Times* to read a "dope" story from Washington. It painted a shocking picture. Even louder were charges of confusion in our foreign policy. Cuba and Laos were both critical. Kennedy, it was alleged, was acting as his own foreign minister. He had surrounded himself with his brain trust—McGeorge Bundy, Goodwin, Schlesinger, Walt Rostow—and they all now had their hand in foreign policy. The worst confusion existed in the Bureau of Inter-American Affairs. Here conditions were "chaotic." The Berle-Goodwin-Schlesinger task force was very much in evidence. Instead of reporting to Dean Rusk, they reported to Mr. Kennedy. Latin American ambassadors were complaining privately they did not know to whom to bring their problems—the task force or the State Department. If Berle and Goodwin were the door to the President, why go to Mr. Rusk? In any event, there was still no Assistant Secretary for Inter-American Affairs or Chief Delegate to the O.A.S. to go to. Both Senator Wayne Morse, chairman of the Senate Subcommittee on Latin American Affairs, and Representative Armistead I. Selden, chairman of the House Subcommittee on Inter-American Affairs, were perturbed. They had charged that they were not being consulted about Latin American policy, that Mr. Kennedy's advisers were handling matters by themselves.

I put down the newspaper, thinking, Why go into this? Why walk out on New Orleans, why jeopardize my political future to go into this barrel of worms? I had virtually made up my mind to decline the offer when a call came from Secretary Rusk. Last time he had traced me to an Army installation in Puerto Rico. Now he found me at home, studying a prospectus for a new bond issue I hoped to sell to the people of New Orleans.

"Well, Chep," he said, in his hearty voice, "what's the status of our discussion?"

I replied honestly, "I'm very much in doubt, Mr. Secretary. I'm trying to mesh everything together—"

"You're not turning me down, are you?"

When it was put that bluntly, I hadn't the courage to say yes. I heard myself say, "No, I'm not turning you down, but—"

"Good," he said. "I've made an appointment for you to see the President. He wants very much to talk to you. Ten A.M., June ninth —is that O.K.?"

I hung up and turned to little Randy, who was insisting he was a demon radio interviewer and had held the microphone of a toy tape recorder under my nose while I talked to Rusk. "Randy, old pal," I said, "I think they've got your dad."

John F. Kennedy is the only man I ever knew who, sitting in a rocking chair, gave you the impression he was made of steel springs, held under restraint, ready at any moment to leap into action. When I called on him that June morning, the White House buzzed with activity, but in the President's sunlit office, with its great, ceiling-to-floor windows overlooking the rose gardens, the mood was one of relaxation. "Chep, I'm delighted to see you . . ." and Kennedy was out of his rocking chair, with its pile of papers beside it, shaking my hand, with that wonderfully contagious grin on his boyish face.

My relations with the President were cordial and highly informal. He had been my guest in New Orleans several times; our paths had crossed often. Our friendship dated back to the Democratic National Convention in Chicago in 1956, where Kennedy had been a dark-horse candidate for the vice-presidential nomination, and I had been a delegate from Louisiana. I had brought the young Massachusetts Senator to our Louisiana breakfast and introduced him about, and we had all gotten along handsomely.

Now, as he excused himself for a minute to sign letters and hand them over to Mrs. Evelyn Lincoln, his secretary, I thought of the last time I had been in this office. In February, a few months before, I headed a committee of New Orleans business leaders which called upon the President to discuss a plan to combat the recession. We were already putting it into effect at home: we advanced all our public works one year. "If every city, every county, every state would do this, Mr. President," I had said, "we'd put a tremendous number of people to work right away."

Our delegation was imposing. It included our two Senators, Allen J. Ellender and Russell B. Long, our two Representatives from New Orleans, Hale Boggs and F. Edward Hebert, the head of the Port of New Orleans, several bank presidents, labor leaders and half a dozen industrialists. I was talking, seated across the desk from Mr. Kennedy, making an out-and-out sales pitch, when he opened a drawer in front of him and solemn-faced, pulled out a copy of *Time* magazine, folded back to an inside page, and slid it across the desk to me. "Mr. President," I was saying at that moment, caught up in my own eloquence, "We're going to push our Port work a little faster, move our homebuilding programs a little faster, make our road construction go a little faster, and if we could only get a green light from the Federal Mortgage people—"

Suddenly the room was full of laughter. Staring up from the page at me and my—until then—extremely dignified colleagues ranged on either side of me, was a photograph showing me dancing amorously cheek to cheek with Zsa Zsa Gabor. It had been taken a few nights before at the Stork Club in New York.

I paused in mid-sentence, my mouth open. For one of the few times in my life I was at a loss for words. I felt myself reddening.

Mr. Kennedy gave that puckish grin of his. "What's the matter, Chep, did I startle you?"

Over the laughter I said lamely, "Well, Mr. President, at least I can see you're human." I couldn't help admiring him as a man who despite the cares on his shoulders couldn't resist the chance to have a moment of teasing fun.

But now we had little time for pleasantries. He had already begun to speak with great seriousness. He and Mr. Rusk agreed they wanted me with them. They also agreed that my best contribution could be made as United States delegate to the O.A.S., where, working closely with the Latin American ambassadors, I could promote the Alliance for Progress.

I spoke of my difficulties at home if I took the position. As a practical politician and head of my party, Mr. Kennedy could appreciate this.

The President stopped rocking and leaned forward. "Chep, what I'm asking you to do is far more important than being mayor of New Orleans or governor of Louisiana. We're talking about the security of our hemisphere. This is the fight against Communism." He spoke frankly. We had been badly hurt by the Bay of Pigs. Not only the failure was disastrous, but also the loss of face among the Latin Americans, who place tremendous value on strength successfully used and cannot forgive a show of weakness. We were in a serious way throughout the entire hemisphere. He wanted me to serve, and if I feared attack at home as an elected official who ran off to garner titles and honors, and left a task unfinished, "I will issue a statement saying this is a critical assignment at a critical time and I have asked you as a good soldier to take it on now."

He stressed the significance of the job. In doing so he gave me a succinct briefing on the almost revolutionary change he was making in our traditional American policy toward Latin America, and the role of the O.A.S. in that change. He said, in substance:

A. Until now the United States had placed its principal emphasis on bilateral diplomacy in inter-American affairs. That is to say, we had dealt as between ourselves and an individual

Latin American country. From now on the United States would engage in multilateral diplomacy. We would act in concert with other Latin American countries, one partner among equal partners, in all matters relating to the hemisphere. This meant that so far as Cuba was concerned, or the threat of direct or indirect aggression, we would act in consultation with our neighbors, and always through the Organization of American States. Latin Americans bitterly resented and would always resent patronage by this country. Every vestige of Uncle Sam's big-stick policy must be eradicated. It was not our purpose to dictate solutions. We must work together as equals—fight Communism, poverty, ignorance, hunger, disease; labor for land reform, tax reform, social justice; but all within the framework of the O.A.S. For this purpose he had already asked Congress for $600 billion as the first step in the Alliance for Progress.

B. The Alliance for Progress was not an almsgiving program by the United States. It was a cooperative effort between the nations of the hemisphere in which the United States, as the most developed, offered capital and technical assistance to help them to help themselves. Its success would depend as much upon them as upon us. We would make use of all the instrumentalities available: our AID program, the Export-Import Bank, the World Bank, the Inter-American Development Bank, the Food for Peace Program.* Fully 80 per cent of

* AID is the Agency for International Development, a United States agency through which the United States carries on its foreign-aid program. It makes loans and grants (usually in the form of technical assistance) to less developed nations—to governments, to private firms, to development banks in the interested countries—to carry out projects for which loans usually can't be obtained from other sources. The loans carry a low rate of interest and may last as long as forty years. The Export-Import Bank, also known as EX-IM, grants long-term loans for larger development projects and is the principal United States agency devoted to international financing and promotion of export-import activities between the United States and foreign countries. The World Bank, also known as I.B.R.D.—International Bank for Reconstruction and Development—finances public and private projects to develop the productive facilities and resources of more than eighty countries who belong to it. The Bank obtains its funds from member countries, from subscriptions, and from sale of bonds. The projects it is interested in are such as electric generating plants, transportation facilities, heavy industry, irrigation projects. The Inter-

Alliance money would be given in credits and loans, *which had to be repaid*; these were not handouts, which often resulted in antagonizing and humiliating those forced to accept them.

C. For the first time we were doing something to *latinize* a program dealing with Latin America. They would call the shots—not us. The obligation taken by the individual American republics was part and parcel of the deal: they must submit blueprints for long-range development and social reforms, they must mobilize their resources, enlist the energies of their people. It was their program in which we, as partners, would work together for our own self-interest and theirs—for the self-interest of the hemisphere, and peace.

"This is the theme I want stressed," the President said. "We are carrying out our policies as one member of the family of hemispheric nations. That is why the O.A.S. is so important—and your job, to get in there and get it off the ground, is so important."

Weeks before, Kennedy had announced he would ask the finance ministers of the twenty-one American countries to gather at Punta del Este, Uruguay, to launch the Alliance—to draft its charter, set up its budget and work out its massive social and economic blueprint for action. Secretary of the Treasury Douglas Dillon would lead our delegation of some thirty-five experts to this O.A.S. conference, and my first major job would be to attend it as one of Mr. Dillon's principal advisers. Here the President confirmed Mr. Rusk's promise: he would elevate my post to a position requiring Senate confirmation and carrying the rank of ambassador. This would show Latin America the increased importance we attached to the O.A.S. He would raise the salary to be commensurate with the task in-

American Development Bank—also known as I.D.B.—focuses exclusively on the American republics and loans to governments and to private enterprise, and also seeks to finance projects in housing, land improvement and reform, higher education, health and sanitation. The Food for Peace Program devotes itself to providing food for poverty-stricken peoples of the world. But in addition to all these, departments of the United States government—Agriculture, Commerce, Treasury, Health, Education and Welfare, Labor, Defense, the Bureau of the Budget, Bureau of Public Roads, Federal Housing Administration, Census Bureau—all were to help, lending their specialists and their experience.

volved. I would have a clear road: Adolf Berle was leaving; there would be no conflict of authority. The President would appoint an Assistant Secretary of State for Inter-American Affairs, with whom I would work. "I will back you," he said. "If you have any problems, any difficulties, I want to resolve them."

I knew what he meant. I was not a State Department career man. I was coming from the outside, into a State Department building of some seven thousand employees who naturally protected their own. I would have to depend on them, the technicians, for everything—briefing, technical help, advice. The role of an outsider in the tightly knit United States Foreign Service was not always an envious one. What Kennedy was saying, was: Don't worry about this. Move, act, do—cut red tape. "I want the O.A.S. revitalized," he said, "and Chep, you're the fellow who can . . ." Here he used a colorful, locker-room expression that I can best paraphrase as "put steel in their backbone." He did not anticipate difficulty in getting Senate approval for my appointment. He would submit my name; a few weeks would pass before the Senate Foreign Relations Committee acted; and this would give me time to go back home and stitch up any loose ends that still troubled me. As for my desire to run for the governorship two years hence—if I accepted the ambassadorship and served until I was ready to make my campaign, he would then accept my resignation with sincere thanks. I would have done my country a great service.

Mr. Kennedy sat in his rocking chair looking at me, very relaxed, very convincing. He had all the answers. He was determined to make this sale this morning—and he made it. I think I knew in the first few minutes that I would take the appointment.

"What can I say, Mr. President," I said, finally. "I accept, and I'm very honored that you have such confidence in me."

"Fine," he exclaimed. We shook hands, and a moment later Richard Goodwin, whose office was a few doors away, came in to draft the statement announcing my appointment. I greeted him with considerable interest. I was meeting for the first time the young man who was to play a more important role in my ambassadorship than I could have anticipated. He was solidly built, of medium height, with dark, darting eyes that gave him an impatient, self-confident air. He had curly black hair, a rather swarthy complexion, and an ever-present cigar.

In the few minutes we chatted together, I had the impression of a lightning-quick mind—an ability to grasp and absorb facts almost instantaneously—and a striking facility with words.

"Dick," President Kennedy said, "here's what I'd like to say." Rapidly he outlined the tenor of the statement. "Make it strong," he said. "Say I'm asking Mayor Morrison to assume this critical post at this critical time as a service to his nation and the hemisphere." Goodwin should stress the "importance and difficulty" of the post; the future of the hemisphere, the very maintenance of freedom, would largely depend on how vigorous the O.A.S. became. (I knew the reputation of the O.A.S. as a debating society rather than a body given to action; and that on Castro Communism, it was reluctant to move effectively.) "Point out that he has the experience and ability to help build an effective O.A.S., that he's been active in Latin American affairs, is well known down there and we're very gratified that he's coming aboard."

Goodwin and I went into his office, and he worked out a press statement which we brought back to the President to read. "Fine," he said, and added one sentence with his pen: I would be one of the leaders of the American delegation to the forthcoming Punta del Este meeting.

I came away from the White House excited, thinking, He's absolutely right in his appraisal of Latin America. He's confirming what I've argued all the time with anyone who would listen. For too long we had taken Latin America for granted. In less than half a dozen years we had spent more than $48 billion in the Marshall Plan to help European countries to recover from World War II, whereas in Latin America in a period of nearly twenty years we had spent less than $4 billion—and that as a result of our world-wide Point Four program.* It had not been specifically earmarked for Latin America. All one could say was that Latin America had routinely received a share. Even our diplomatic posts in Latin America suffered in comparison to Europe. Our ambassadors below the border were frequently purely political appointees, businessmen who

* Our Marshall Plan aid was equal to something like $30 per year to every Englishman, $22 to every person in West Germany. Today (1964), after more than three years of the Alliance for Progress and the billions we have spent and are spending, our per capita aid is about $3 to every Latin American.

had contributed handsomely to political campaigns but often did not speak Spanish and more than once had never heard of the country to which they were accredited until the day of their appointment.

Our program in Latin America all too often had been a crisis-to-crisis affair, inadequate, lacking over-all planning, lacking a real realization of what was needed. Yet, how quickly we moved elsewhere! The enormous sums we poured into Italy and France, fearful that they might go Communist, while we ignored our own backyard! It was inconceivable to us that our neighbors might not always sleep lazily in the shadow of our might. They were our friends, they had supported us in the past, and though many were politically unstable, one *coup d'état* following another, we took all this as a matter of course.

We had begun to awaken toward the end of Mr. Eisenhower's administration, thanks to the surveys in Latin America his brother Dr. Milton Eisenhower had begun to make for him in 1953. Then Castro shocked us into action. His Communist take-over shocked us into the realization of how enormous Latin America's problems were—and how infinitesimal, compared with the need, were the limited amounts of money, energy, thought and analysis we devoted to the Southern part of the hemisphere.

To me all this was an enormous challenge. I was at last in a position where I could do something about what I had long complained about. And I had a President who would back me. There were many things I wanted to do. Adlai Stevenson was now visiting Latin America as President Kennedy's emissary on a ten-nation tour to assess their political stability and their ability to cooperate in the Alliance. So far his trip had come off rather badly in the press. He was well received in many places but in some I would have acted differently. For example, when he met General Alfredo Stroessner, the strong-arm President of Paraguay, the latter attempted to give him an *abrazo*. Stevenson backed off sharply and, instead, extended his hand. I assume Stevenson didn't care to be photographed in a back-slapping bear hug with a dictator. But when you call upon a Latin American chief of state, representing your own chief of state, and under friendly auspices, you greet with an *abrazo*. It is the custom; it means nothing; it is comparable to a cordial handshake.

One visits a foreign country in order to create a good impression. I thought this a tactical error on Stevenson's part.*

I believed I could bring to the job a more intimate understanding of the people and their countries. I was convinced that I had the feel of the Latin American. Either one communicates with them, or one doesn't.† I enjoyed the challenge presented to me. It was sufficient for me to leave my home and my three young children, who certainly needed me, for they had no mother. I could not bring Toni, Corinne and Randy to Washington. I would not be there enough. I would have to find some way to care for them. Fortunately, my mother lived four blocks away from me, in New Orleans; my father-in-law lived with me. I would ask my mother to be in my home as much as possible. They would take over in my absence. Guiltily I promised myself I would visit New Orleans on every trip to and from Latin America. I would also come down from Washington every weekend possible. Nonetheless I would still be separated from my children in their growing years, and I felt badly about this.

In addition, I realized as I turned these matters over, even as I still glowed from the Kennedy interview, that this job was financially disadvantageous. I must maintain two homes, no matter how little I lived in each. My mayoral salary had been $25,000 plus a $5,000 contingent nontaxable fund. That of the United States Delegate to the O.A.S. was $20,000. President Kennedy had raised it to $25,000, though I did not discuss it with him and did not know it at the time. Twenty-five thousand dollars with two homes to maintain and three children to educate would not go far. Had I not a modest independent income supplemented by my military active-duty pay, I could not have considered the job.

I had no idea that before I finished my mission, I would fly hundreds of thousands of miles, that in the next twenty-six months I

* In justice to Mr. Stevenson, it should be pointed out that the State Department had proposed that democratic leaders should be given *abrazos*, while dictators should be given no more than a formal handshake. A dubious technique, in my opinion, and signifying nothing—except the curious impracticality one often finds in State Department directives.

† I confess that I was gratified when I was told by a Latin American at Punta del Este some weeks later, that when I entered a caucus of Latin American diplomats, they continued their discussion as though one of their own number had entered; but when other foreign diplomats appeared, even members of the United States delegation, they immediately changed the subject.

would make twenty-one tours or visits to Latin American countries, deliver nearly five hundred speeches explaining the Alliance for Progress here and below the border, find myself caught up in at least one Latin American riot, read at least three "informed" newspaper articles confidently predicting my imminent dismissal and—perhaps the most bizarre—be accused of accepting a bribe from a Dominican Republic secret agent allegedly to persuade the Organization of American States to lift the crippling diplomatic and economic sanctions it had imposed on that unhappy country.

2. MY ROAD TO LATIN AMERICA: A BIT OF AUTOBIOGRAPHY

Three weeks were to elapse before the Senate met on my appointment; but, as an optimist, I took it for granted I would have no trouble and moved at once to Washington to the Willard Hotel, a few minutes from the State Department, where a temporary office was given me and the staff of two I had brought from New Orleans. I began to immerse myself in my job, to be briefed each morning on developments, and especially to visit the Operations Center of the State Department where every day—often, every hour—arrived the latest confidential cables from our ambassadors abroad.

As I read the cables from Latin America, as I boned up on my duties,* as I contemplated the ramifications of this job, so important to me but so little known to the general public—if the people knew

* My titles were to become so numerous as to be bewildering: Ambassador to the O.A.S.; Chief of the United States Mission to the O.A.S.; Delegate to the Inter-American Economic and Social Council; Chairman of the Inter-American Institute of Agricultural Sciences; Chairman of the Public Information and Cultural Affairs Committee; Member of the Inter-American Peace Commission; Member of the O.A.S. Special Subcommittee on the Dominican Question—all phases of our involvement, through the O.A.S., in Latin America.

hardly anything about the United Nations, how much less they must know, or care, about the Organization of American States—my mind began to swim. Yet, there was a poetic justice about it. For in this direction, looking back, it seemed I was aiming all the time.

I considered my assets and my liabilities. I knew Latin America well. I was in friendly touch with most of the chiefs of the Latin American states, for reasons I shall explain in this chapter. I had visited them in their home countries, or entertained them in New Orleans. I was eager to do a good job. I felt they liked me. As a politician I was gregarious, I enjoyed people, I felt at home in this world.

My liabilities? I was a singleton. I was not a career man. I had no party or clique backing me. I had no group of State Department aides who had been working with me for a long time. I was moving as an individual in what was really a large group enterprise.

But I had the advantage of a unique experience in New Orleans, where for nearly fifteen years I had conducted a kind of private Latin American foreign service of my own. For New Orleans, commerce with Latin America was all-important. Our port competed directly with New York and Miami. During World War II, it had been second to New York. When I was elected mayor in 1946, a year after the end of World War II, I discovered we had dropped from second to seventeenth place. With the backing and stimulation of civic leaders in New Orleans, I determined to make the New Orleans port as busy in peacetime as it had been in wartime, and second again only to New York.

We launched an international-trade development program, in which I headed delegations of forty-five to eighty persons on sixty different trips to Latin America. Nearly all were under auspices of two nonprofit organizations, our International House and our International Trade Mart. International House had been founded a few years before, as a home away from home for Latin American visitors, and to promote trade and good will with their countries. It was supported by dues from members here, in Latin America, and in the rest of the world. Today the two institutions spend considerable sums of money selling nothing but good will, understanding and contact with Latin America and the world.

In addition, when I received especially distinguished visitors in certain fields, each time we gave them a key to the city, I appointed them honorary representatives of New Orleans in their home cities. As a result, nearly a hundred honorary consuls general of New Orleans are to be found in Latin America, most of whom are not political figures, but prominent editors, publishers, industrialists—men who for emotional, intellectual or economic reasons are genuinely interested in helping us. We keep in touch with each other. Thus, by visits, by constant social intercourse, by the endless links of trade and industry, I was, when the President called on me, virtually as immersed in Latin American affairs as in Louisiana politics. I was forever selling Louisiana—and the United States—to my Latin American friends, and selling Latin America, its needs, its potentialities, to my own country.

The job President Kennedy had now given me was, in essence, as much salesmanship as diplomacy. For, I thought, what is diplomacy but selling, more or less subtly, and according to well-established protocol, a point of view, an approach, a policy?

Now, as I prepared to take my new post, I thought to myself, I am a good salesman; I can sell a project, an idea, a cause. I had had to sell eight difficult bond issues to the people of New Orleans, asking them to obligate themselves for many millions of dollars. One, the Union Station project, had been highly controversial. Indeed, more apparently had been against it than had been for it. Yet I had proposed it and defended it, and in the end the people had supported it. During my term of office I had built twenty-four overpasses and underpasses, erecting a new consolidated terminal, and rearranged the entire transportation system of our city—a major project involving over $57,000,000. I had been able to sell it to the public. I had confidence, therefore, that I could sell Latin America and the Alliance for Progress. For my job would be not only to convince Latin Americans of the importance of the Alliance, and their part in it, but also to convince the American people, for it was they who would support the Congress, which had to vote the money for the Alliance.

Behind my salesmanship in New Orleans had also been something of a reformer's zeal. I am a stubborn fellow, and when it is necessary, I have a one-track mind. This last can be a blessing for it results in getting things done, sometimes new things not done before; but it can also force one to follow the track to wherever it leads, regardless of consequence.

In my case I was the man who broke the political machine, the gang and spoils rule in New Orleans after nearly half a century of uninterrupted power. So *Time* magazine characterized me in a cover story in November 1947, summarizing my first year in office. Out had gone bookies, illegal pinball machines, clip joints, prostitution, gambling; in had come playgrounds, boys' clubs, a new fourteen-acre civic center—a completely new approach to commerce and industry and to the development of the city.

As to why I was a reformer—why I was stubborn and refused to follow beaten paths—this goes back to my early days and essentially to my father, the late Jacob H. Morrison, and to the kind of man he was.

Even as a student at Louisiana State University in the early 1930's I had fought the regime of Huey Long, the "Every Man a King" governor of Louisiana. Along with most Louisianians, I was fascinated by his political style, but I opposed his methods vigorously. My father, our family, all we stood for, were in opposition to the state machine. We felt that the machine was corrupt, and we fought it; and in the years that followed I continued to find myself on the opposite side of the fence from the Long dynasty in Louisiana.

For most of his adult life my father, living in New Roads, Louisiana, had been the political leader of our home district. For twenty-one years he was the District Attorney. He was an honest but a poor man. He made a salary, and that was it. He had no use for dictatorial government or for crookedness in government, or anywhere else for that matter, and I grew up reflecting my father's attitude. He would come home from Baton Rouge, the capital, furious over the graft and chicanery he found there. I still hear his voice. "Everything has a price," he would storm bitterly. "If you want to get a man out of jail, there's a price. If you want a pardon, you pay a price—everything has its price!" He had labored to send a guilty man to jail only to discover the man had walked out scot free. Some politician somewhere had paid some money to someone.

I admired my father with all my heart. He was one of the most popular men in the state. He possessed a faculty I lack—his political enemies liked him. He had constant success at the polls and carried the three parishes of West Baton Rouge, Pointe Coupee and Iberville as long as he lived. Relatives told me, years later, that I had his persistence, his stubbornness. One of my earliest recollections goes back to an outdoor rally my father led. I was about eight, and I sat in the front row, and when he appeared on the platform I began shouting, "Hurray for Papa!" so loud and so repeatedly that the only way they could silence me was to halt proceedings and lead me to the lemonade barrel.

My father committed suicide at fifty-three, when I was seventeen, the summer after my freshman year at Louisiana State University. He suffered from cancer of the liver; he had had several expensive operations; and on the day before he took his life he had borrowed a thousand dollars from his law partner, Judge Calvin Schwing, a wealthy man, to enable him to go to the Mayo Clinic, in Rochester, Minnesota, for still another operation.

On the morning of August 14, 1929, we both rose before dawn. I was to drive him to the train, at a junction outside our home town of New Roads, that would take him to Rochester; then I was to go on to my summer job, working as a road laborer not far from the station.

On the way to the train, he had said, "I want to stop for a minute at the office." It was just before 6 A.M. I waited downstairs, at the wheel, the motor running. I heard a shot. I ran up. It was a sight I hope I never see again: my father lying on the floor, dead, with blood seeping from the bullet hole in his temple.

I had had no idea how ill he had been; it was not a subject he talked about. But he had been sick and constantly worried, and many nights I had heard him pacing the floor. Now, without any other word, he had left us, suddenly and forever.

His death was a tremendous blow to me, for we had been very close. I believe that I had more to do with him than anybody. He and I went everywhere together; he followed my athletic career with great excitement; when I played football, he was there; when I played basketball, he was there. He lived my life at L.S.U. Although he got companionship from all of his children—my brother, Ben, who was nineteen; Jake, who was twenty-three; my sister, Virginia, who was twenty-six—I, the youngest, took him as my hero. I wanted to be like him, to become a lawyer, to join him in his law office when I received my degree.

Now he was gone, and I felt alone, although my mother and all of us were together in our grief. To have lost my father was somehow the greatest loss I could have had. Almost overwhelmed, I returned to school for my sophomore year the month after his death. My grades, for the first time, fell very low.

In my freshman year I had been the top student in my class. I have always regretted that the letter from the registrar, citing me as having the best grades in the class, arrived the day after my father's death. He never had the satisfaction of knowing that. But he knew I was a good student, for I had been valedictorian at Poydras High School, in New Roads. He had coached me in my speech. I see him sitting in the back row now, holding his hands to his ears, indicating that I must speak louder.

The year after his death was difficult not only because of my emotional state but also because of lack of money. The Depression was upon us. The stock market crashed five weeks after my father's funeral.

At my high-school graduation, our Congressman, who delivered the commencement address, had asked me if I wanted an appointment to West Point or Annapolis. I had not thought seriously about the offer then and enrolled at Louisiana State University. But now a free education became important. I obtained an appointment to Annapolis, dropped out of L.S.U. the second semester, and took and passed the examinations for Annapolis.

But by this time, the spring of 1930, my grief had somewhat subsided. I was able to see things in brighter perspective. I was now working at two jobs. My mother also worked. She had taken a position as hostess at the Baton Rouge Country Club, while I obtained one there as swimming-pool manager and lifeguard. At the same time I was selling Realsilk Hosiery house to house at night.

I came to a decision. I would resign my appointment to Annapolis and work my way through L.S.U. and the law school. If I continued at Annapolis, though my education was free, it meant being in school and the Navy for the next seven years. If I worked my way through university and law school, I'd have my LL.B. in five years and be standing on my own feet so much sooner.

Stubbornly, I did that. For the next five years I hoed potatoes and cotton on a farm before and after classes, sold hosiery at night, was a lifeguard during the summer, and managed somehow to study when I had a free moment. For five years I had little sleep. My father would have been proud to know that nonetheless I graduated *summa cum laude* from the university in 1932 and *summa cum laude* from the law school in 1934. In those years I discovered two things: the value of a dollar; and that that which I thought I had to have, I did not have to have.

My decision had been a good one. Within four years, I was a practicing attorney, and since I had continued my R.O.T.C. duties, I was also a second lieutenant in the Army Reserve. So I hastened my maturity. Struggling through those years on my own was, I think, better training for me than a routine life in a peacetime Navy.

In 1934 I went to New Orleans and opened my law office. I had just turned twenty-two, but I was appointed junior assistant N.R.A. trial attorney at $1,800 a year. Two years later, in the 1936 primary election campaign,* I had my first brush with politics when I was named an election commissioner, by the reform party fighting the Long machine. One twenty-four-hour experience fixed me in politics forever. The only real competition to the Long machine at this time came from the New Orleans political ring. It was as corrupt as he, but Huey, a political genius, had used their corruption against them, forcing them to join him. The combination was unbeatable.

Under his law, his Board of Supervisors appointed three election commissioners at each polling place, and allowed the opposition—which meant us—only two. Even with this advantage, the Board stacked the cards, for they themselves chose the two from a list of twenty submitted by their opposition. In this instance they picked me—because, at twenty-four, I was the youngest; the other was one Lafayette Keller, seventy-two, the oldest on the list, who was known to be very grateful for his $39-a-month W.P.A. job.

On election day Mr. Keller and I showed up at the polling place—a garage—to find it filled with Long people. There were the three election commissioners, plus "watchers," strong-arm goons on hand to beat up anyone who might prove difficult. We began to have trouble at once. By 1 P.M. Mr. Keller, tired, went home. I was left to guard the sanctity of the ballot. I took my job very seriously, fighting every inch of the way to prevent the three commissioners

* In Louisiana, political activity is virtually monopolized by the Democratic party. As a result, the only real election contests are the primaries, wherein opposing groups of candidates seek the party's nomination as its representatives in the interparty elections in November. Victory in the primaries is, then, tantamount to victory in the general election.

from stuffing the box or voting dead people—the so-called graveyard votes. And all day long they were saying to me, "Look, bud, we're in charge here, to hell with you."

I'd retort, "Dammit, I'm a lawyer, I'm a notary public, and I'm telling all of you I'm going to sign affidavits against you and do my best to send you to jail, because you're violating the law."

The policeman on duty was a Long man. He saw nothing. I was beside myself as the day wore on. "You can't vote this man!" I'd shout, when they produced a derelict who didn't even know his precinct. "I'm making a note of this, I'm putting an affidavit in court tomorrow. . . ." The legal terms I flung at them tended to frighten them. The commissioners were, after all, $15- and $20-a-week clerks in some city office, and here I stood, using these impressive words, all righteousness and indignation. . . .

The polls finally closed. We began counting ballots. Now I was even busier than before. A commissioner would take a ballot, call out the vote—"One, two, three, four, tally." But since I did not trust him I insisted on examining each ballot; then I'd tally to see if my count was right. To foil them, to prevent them from slipping phony ballots into the box, I ran a threaded needle through each counted ballot and then pushed it carefully down the thread into the box. Any ballots found in the box that were not on the thread would obviously be illegal. To be doubly sure, I sat on the ballot box.

Presently the returns started coming in over the radio. My man was beaten; in short order, he conceded. My three opposition election commissioners and one watcher pulled out several bottles of whisky and began to celebrate. They grew nastier and nastier. Finally the watcher approached me, where I sat on the ballot box, stubbornly guarding it. "Go home, kid," he said, and straight-armed me, knocking me off the box. I said nothing but picked myself up, brushed myself off, and sat down on the box again.

He pushed me off again. I got up from the floor. "All right," I said, my voice trembling, "Someday you're going to pay for this. I don't know when, but someday you'll see." I sat on the box again, my arms folded, glaring at my enemies.

This incredible contest went on from 8 P.M., when the polls closed, until nearly 1 A.M. They grew drunker, more nasty, manhandling me a little more each time. The election was over; why I remained there, I don't know. But I was determined to get the correct count and turn that count into the clerk's office myself. They beat me, they knocked me off the box time and again, they attempted at one point to arrest me—and I kept repeating, "Someday you're going to pay for this. You'll see."

Finally they all reeled out drunk. I tallied up the vote, took the ballots down to the clerk's office and made out the full return. Next morning I marched into the United States Attorney's office and signed affidavits against each of the four. I was fortunate to be able to file a Federal charge, since a Senatorial contest was involved that year. Had it been limited to state contests, I would have been able to file only a state charge and the Long machine would have simply dismissed it.

That night when I got home, my four tormentors were waiting for me in the living room, meek, apologetic, literally hat in hand. "Look, Mr. Morrison, we don't want any trouble. We're sorry about what happened. We're too old, we'll die in jail if we're sent there. We didn't realize you were going to the U.S. Attorney. Can't you forget about this?"

I said, "No, now it's my turn. You're going to pay for this." I showed them to the door.

They were arrested; they made bond, and I waited for their case to be called.

Two weeks later I woke one morning to read that a fire of "unexplained origin" had broken out in the Customs House. By a strange coincidence all affidavits charging election irregularities—there had been many others—had burned to ashes.

I am a determined fellow. I promptly went down and made out new affidavits.

Once more I was foiled. Governor Richard W. Leche had made a deal with President Roosevelt to deliver the Louisiana delegation—whereupon all prosecutions growing out of the 1936 Louisiana primary elections were canceled.

For the third time I walked into the United States Attorney's office and signed new affidavits. "Roosevelt be damned," I said. "I have a right to insist upon a prosecution, and I want them prosecuted."

I was shouting against the wind. One postponement led to another, and in the end nothing was done.

In the next four years my political education continued swiftly. In 1940 I joined the gubernatorial campaign of Sam Jones, a reform candidate sworn to defeat Earl Long, Huey's brother. I admired Sam; and though my law practice, mainly civil law, was flourishing and could take all the time I could give it, politics excited me. I was Jake Morrison's son, out to send the rascals scrambling. And I still had scores to settle with the Long dynasty.

Sam Jones, older, fatherly, gave me the task of choosing a number of promising young lawyers to run on his ticket for the Louisiana Legislature. My first choice was Hale Boggs, then alumni secretary of Tulane University, later to be a Congressman from Louisiana and one of my champions before Dean Rusk. Hale, his wife (my cousin Lindy) and I boarded with my aunt, Mrs. E. S. Morrison, at 4023 St. Charles Avenue, in the Twelfth Ward.

However, Tulane University officials frowned on Hale's candidacy. If he publicly opposed the Long machine, the university might suffer. At the last moment Hale reluctantly dropped out. Unable to find anyone to replace him on short notice, in a kind of desperation I wrote my own name in for his and forgot about it. I was fighting for Sam Jones and for good government in Louisiana.

I threw myself into the election. Day after day I toured the Twelfth Ward in a sound truck, damning the Long candidacy, urging our people to fight. It was a hell-bent-for-leather election. If the 1936 campaign had been rough, this in 1940 was even worse. Our reform movement was growing, and the Long forces grew bolder in their attempt to intimidate anyone who dared fight them. They deputized "yellow badge" election commissioners and gave them revolvers; and we had the spectacle of armed goon squads roaming the city beating up the opposition. Out of this violent year 1940 came prosecutions for ballot-box stuffing, switching of boxes, terror and brutality, that continued for years afterward. Scores were sent to the penitentiary. My own sister-in-law, Mary Morrison, a high-spirited woman married to my brother Jake, was forced to go out of town in fear that she might be harmed in the aftermath of her appointment as an elections commissioner for our reform party.

What had happened was this. While guarding a polling place, she was beaten over the head with a pocketbook by a member of a gang led by Captain Nino Patorno, who directed the Long forces in the Fifth Ward, the heart of the French Quarter, where Mary lived. Not only Mary but others were beaten. Charges of assault and battery were brought against Patorno: he was tried and convicted. Shortly after his conviction he walked into the Fifth Ward Athletic Club and blew out his brains. That night Mary fled the city. Word had reached us that the Mafia was out to get her. The Latin Quarter buzzed with laments for Nino and threats of vengeance—"a life for a life."

The state, faced with growing irregularities, called out the National Guard. I was a second lieutenant in the National Guard; and as candidate for the Legislature, I was also a political leader. When the call came at 4 A.M. on election day, I put on my uniform and went on duty, determined that I would especially watch matters in the Eighth Precinct. Here, in the past, the majority of voters supported us; but the opposition always carried the precinct by the simple expedient of turning the lights out just before the votes were to be counted and in the darkness switching the ballot boxes. We had only one commissioner assigned to the Eighth Precinct. I promised myself I would be on hand to back him up. I would stick by that box all day and prevent any sleight of hand.

In those days a United States Army officer had an elaborate uniform—Sam Browne belt, boots, spurs, leather trappings—that made one look like General George Patton. This is how I dressed, and with all my gear no one could tell whether I had sidearms. In my back pocket, however, I carried a flashlight.

At 6 A.M. I approached the house used as a polling place. Only later did I learn that three men were lying behind a high hedge a half block before the place, waiting for me. They were going to beat me up. I had caused them enough trouble with my sound truck and my obstreperousness in the first primary. The opposition had made up its mind: *We're going to get rid of that son-of-a-bitch Morrison. We'll pass the post on him. Put him in the hospital for a few days and maybe he'll tone down.*

They saw me approach, in full uniform. They had not expected me to be in uniform. They did—nothing. They did not dare do anything. I walked by unharmed. At about noon I learned that the opposition had formally protested to General Fleming, head of the Louisiana National Guard. I was taking unfair advantage of my uniform; they wanted me out of the ward. General Fleming, who happened to be a good friend of mine, refused. "No," he said.

"Lieutenant Morrison is an officer in the National Guard. He may be called to a trouble spot at any moment."

The voting ended. At 8 P.M. I found myself on the steps of the house where the voting had taken place. Inside, Long's henchmen were about to count the ballots. Since I was not an election commissioner, I could not be present in the room where the counting took place, but it was my legal right to remain immediately outside it. I took up a position on the top step and stood there.

Suddenly, the lights went out. I pulled my flashlight out and trained the beam on the box—and kept it there. Just as a pair of hands reached out to snatch the box, the rays of my flashlight struck it.

One of the election commissioners strode up to me. "You have no right to have a flashlight!"

"Who says I haven't?" I demanded. There was nothing they could do; I was legally allowed to be where I was.

Three minutes later the lights went out again. Again I threw my flash on the box. It remained there, untouched.

Finally a big fellow with a yellow badge walked up the steps to me, and put his nose to my nose. I suddenly realized I was surrounded: standing on either side of me were two other yellow-badge officials, and behind me, breathing down my neck, a policeman. The big fellow spoke. "You're a yellow son of a bitch," he said distinctly, his nose to my nose.

I said, "Sir, I know you want me to slug you and then this cop will haul me off. I'm not going to raise a hand to you. I'll take your abuse right now. But I want to make a challenge to you. Tomorrow morning at eight o'clock I'll meet you at the New Orleans Athletic Club, without your gun or my gun" (I had no gun) "and I'll beat the hell out of you." I said, "Is that a date?"

The crowd that had gathered by this time to see the fun, began to laugh. Somebody called out, "He's got you there!" The big fellow hurried down the steps and consulted with his friends. It was obvious they didn't know what to do now. After their huddle, he strode up the steps again, and his nose to mine again, tried once more to provoke me.

My eyes were practically crossed staring at him, and his breath was anything but pleasant. But I did not move. I said, "Tomorrow morning, eight o'clock, at the Athletic Club. We'll strip down and I'll just beat hell out of you, sir."

He finally gave up and walked away. I did not stir from the spot. I stood on the step from 8 P.M. until midnight. The opposition made no attempt to count the ballots, knowing the result would be against them. Meanwhile, city-wide returns started to come in over the radio. My man was winning. Now they became worried. I gloated. "Boys, you're marked. You know what I did four years ago. I had those fellows in hot water and only Mr. Roosevelt got them out of trouble. Nobody's going to get you fellows out of trouble. This time you're all going to jail. I swear it on my mother's life that you're going to jail."

At 6 A.M. they finally left. My lone election commissioner began to count ballots. Then I went home to get ready to go to the Athletic Club. I had a date with this fellow and I was going to keep it. I wasn't looking forward to it. He was bigger than I, and I had little heart for a fist fight after such a wearying day and night.

When I reached home, a telegram was on my table. It was from the man I had challenged. "Dear Chep, congratulations on a great race. Your friend, Mike."

It was the first word that I had been elected to the Louisiana Legislature, as Representative from the Twelfth Ward, New Orleans. I had almost forgotten my own candidacy. The duel of honor was off; I was twenty-six and a lawmaker.

My election, a surprising thing in itself, was all the more astonishing in view of the fact that Sam Jones, although he won the state, failed to carry New Orleans. As it was, only four others and myself —of twenty candidates running for election in New Orleans—were successful.

Sam Jones soon designated me a floor leader. I was able at Baton Rouge to put through a number of reform measures, including the introduction of voting machines and several changes in the election laws, about which I understandably felt quite strongly. In the middle of my legislative career I went off to duty in World War II as a reserve officer. I entered as a first lieutenant; I emerged, five years later, as a colonel. I considered those to have been valuable and productive years. I had begun with the Infantry, had then been transferred to the Transportation Corps, and in 1943 went overseas, where I helped to set up ports in England and in France. I had fought in the Battle of the Bulge, and with British forces that took Bremerhaven, Wilhelmshaven and Bremen. Toward the end of the war I was Chief of Staff of the Bremen Port Command and, in effect, acting mayor of the German seaport. I had no idea how soon this experience would be important to me.

When I returned to New Orleans on December 9, 1945, I found myself literally thrown into the mayoralty race. A group of citizens had formed the Crescent City Democratic Organization, pledged to reform city government. They asked me to be their candidate. Forty-five days later, in January 1946, I was elected mayor. I was thirty-four, a colonel still in uniform, holding the Bronze Star and the Legion of Merit—and I was mayor of New Orleans. In a six-week, fourteen-hours-a-day campaign I had defeated a political machine entrenched for more than fifty years, whose principal interest was to remain in power and perpetuate the spoils system.*

I would not take office until May 1, 1946. As I was casting about, familiarizing myself with my new job, I was invited to lunch one day by Rudolph Hecht. That afternoon my foot was placed directly on the road to Latin America. Hecht was that rare citizen—dynamic, creative, civic-minded, a man combining vision and leadership—who appears once every few decades in a city. I was fortunate that he was part of the New Orleans scene when I took on the job of mayor. Then chairman of the board of the powerful Hibernia Bank of New Orleans, Hecht had organized the giant Mississippi Shipping Company and had founded International House, a private, nonprofit organization established a few years before to act as a center for Latin American visitors.

Over the luncheon table, he spoke persuasively. "You have a terrific challenge before you," he began. "For half a century we've suffered from a corrupt regime. It had no interest in the city, its people or its future. New Orleans has been asleep for all that time. We haven't had a new industry in twenty years. Our port has dropped from second to seventeenth. We're considered outside the mainstream of American business and industrial activity.

* The graft was appalling. One example: checking through the payroll of the Port of New Orleans, I discovered 3,000 men employed as rat-catchers. To the opposition, 3,000 votes was 3,000 votes.

"You can reverse all this. You can whip this city around 180 degrees, Chep Morrison. Your election has awakened the business community. Now you go ahead and keep it awake—and I'll back you every step of the way!"

He emphasized the importance of the Port of New Orleans. This was the key to our future. Since war cargo no longer moved through it, we needed new thinking, new vigor, new programs. One way to start things humming—to increase Latin American trade through the port—was to launch an international program aimed at Latin America, making use of International House.

Mr. Hecht excited me. I had always liked Latin America, but as I listened to him, new vistas opened. I would develop an international program. I would establish an International Relations Office at City Hall and provide an attractive reception room there. When distinguished visitors arrived from Latin America, International House would make them feel at home; they would have an office, a secretary and a car at their disposal.

He introduced me to Mario Bermudez, at that time Director of Latin American Relations at International House, and later International Relations Director for the city, for International House and for International Trade Mart. Bermudez was a Colombian, a man of fertile ideas and great energy. Later Charles Nutter, former Associated Press correspondent and bureau chief in Latin America, joined International House as Managing Director. Together we worked out a program to bring Latin America to New Orleans, and sell New Orleans to Latin America.

When governments below the border learned of our interest, I was invited to visit Guatemala, El Salvador and Nicaragua. Since there was a four-month interim before I took office, I accepted the invitations. When my wife and I returned, I threw myself into my new job.

I had to look for key personnel. The only people I knew in the last five years were my military colleagues. When I announced my appointments, my chief of police was a Marine colonel, Colonel Adair Waters; my sanitation director was a tank commander, Colonel Nathan; my city attorney, Henry Curtis, was a colonel in the Army. It did not occur to me then that I had so many colonels on my staff. My only purpose was to select the most competent persons I knew.

Then I opened my International Relations Office at City Hall. This ancient building, though considered one of the finest examples of Greek Revival design in the nation, for years had been peopled by typical, old ward politicians with bulbous red noses and pot-bellies, men who spent much of their time in bookie shops and bars, which crowded the tiny streets about City Hall.

Now the new Morrison administration took over. First, I declared a nine-to-five workday. This shocked everyone. Since time immemorial, City Hall personnel began leaving at three o'clock—including the mayor.

Then I moved in with my band of colonels, my newly decorated Office of International Relations, complete to chandelier, pastel-colored walls and sumptuous carpets. My assistant was Rafael Urruela, my adviser was Mario Bermudez. At City Hall the word was: If you want a job with Morrison's outfit, you have to be a colonel or have a Spanish accent.

So, we got the Spanish look.

My visits to Latin America, before taking office, had made me even more pro-Latin. The reception my wife and I were given, the warmth and friendliness, overwhelmed me. I was not accustomed to it: the Chief of Protocol waiting at attention at the airport; the Marimba bands playing the "Star-Spangled Banner," then launching into "Yankee Doodle" and "God Bless America"; the flower girls waiting to decorate us; the speeches of welcome; the cavalcade of limousines taking us to meet the chief of state; the motorcycle escorts with screaming sirens; the cheering crowds; the mayor of each capital as my personal guide. . . . They liked me, they liked my pretty, blond wife, they took us to their hearts, the papers were full of our doings; my most faltering speech in my beginning Spanish was a triumph, I thought.

When I was sworn in, immediately on returning, among the guests of the City of New Orleans were seventy-five dignitaries whom I had invited from Latin America—the first time such a gesture of friendship had been made by my city to our friends below the border. Shortly after, I had International House and the city sponsor a tour of the major Caribbean ports to encourage trade with us. I led the delegation of forty-five businessmen to Puerto Rico, Colombia, Venezuela, Haiti and the Dominican Republic.

Before leaving the Dominican Republic, word came that we

would be received by Generalissimo Rafael Leonidas Trujillo, the dictator. I was intrigued. He was the key to increased trade with the United States. But I was curious, too, to meet this man, the closest approximation to an absolute monarch in the Western world, who ruled his country of nearly three million as though it were his private plantation. I wanted to see how such power was exercised.

At the sumptuous Palacio Nacional we waited half an hour in the thickly carpeted reception room, soldiers everywhere on guard, motionless as statues, before El Jefe appeared. He was a stocky, handsome man in uniform, with an erect bearing and the aura of an emperor, out of the Orient; and he received us as might an emperor accepting homage that was due him—grand, remote, his face inscrutable, not a single play of expression on it. I could believe the stories I had read of his ruthlessness, his cruelty to enemies, his jails full of political prisoners, as his black eyes flicked over us and he gave us a cool, limp hand. Later, he sat on a sofa with me. I was still in my colonel's uniform, not having been officially discharged from the service, and he asked me about my war experiences. He was interested in military maneuvers, especially the pincer movement engineered by General Omar Bradley in the Ruhr area of Germany, and since I had taken part in that, I could talk about it.

Meanwhile, I realized, the great man was beginning to unbend. He was actually selling the Dominican Republic to me. "Puerto Rico is two hundred miles away," he said. "It is run by the great United States. Look at conditions in Puerto Rico* and at conditions here, then tell me how bad a dictatorship is." We had gone about the country swiftly; there was progress—new buildings, new port facilities, new hospitals, new roads—but in our brief mission there was little I could learn about the true situation in this long-misruled country. No one came forward to speak to us; obviously no one dared. Yet we knew we were in a dictatorship. Our cars sped through streets completely cleared of people; armed soldiers were everywhere; every detail of our program proceeded without a single interruption, the result of a perfect and rigid regimentation. And everywhere were signs proclaiming "The Era of Trujillo," expressing thanks to Trujillo, paying tribute to El Benefactor Trujillo.

* This was before Operation Bootstrap, Puerto Rico's social and economic program which achieved such remarkable results.

At one point sitting with me, he said, "There is only one sailing a month from your port to Ciudad Trujillo. Before the year is out, you will have ten or fifteen a month."

This was what I, as mayor of New Orleans, had wanted to hear. For this reason we had come here. Generalissimo Trujillo was the man who could say it—and do it. I thought, wryly, In a democratic country you might make fifty calls before finding anyone who could promise to change the *status quo*—and had the power to do so.

Next afternoon we were all invited again to the Palacio Nacional. El Jefe wanted to decorate the leaders of our party. I consulted our embassy. Was this wise? They told me to accept; this did not mean I endorsed his government. Presentation of decorations was standard operating procedure in Latin America. To refuse would be considered an insult and destroy the purpose of our visit.

A few hours later El Benefactor, with a rare smile, pinned the Order of Duarte, Sanchez and Mello—named for the Dominican Republic's three national heroes—on my uniform. I thought, Here I am, the new reform mayor, fighting dictatorship in my own state and now I can very well be criticized for consorting with dictators!

I was—as it turned out so many years later—far more prophetic than I knew.

3. FIRST EXERCISES IN PERSONAL DIPLOMACY

Presidents may appoint ambassadors, but the Senate has the last word; it must confirm the appointments. Usually this is done routinely. One's name is submitted, it is accepted, the appointment goes through. But if one Senator has questions to ask, a public hearing must be held.

When Dean Rusk first talked to me, the thought flashed through my mind: Was there anything in my background that might rise to plague me? I pushed the thought aside. But in the wake of Mr. Kennedy's press release, it developed that Senator Wayne Morse, Chairman of the Senate Subcommittee on Latin American Affairs, wanted a hearing. A "number of matters" concerned him.

I knew that he would be a formidable opponent. Two years earlier he had prevented Clare Boothe Luce's appointment as ambassador to Brazil, after she had made a splendid record as our first woman ambassador to Italy. President Eisenhower had been forced to withdraw her name. In my case, I learned Senator Morse's points of doubt were: First, the New Orleans branch of N.A.A.C.P. had sent a letter protesting my appointment. (Ironically enough, I had just been defeated for the governorship of Louisiana because my opposition accused me of being the N.A.A.C.P. candidate.)* Second, it was alleged that I was the friend of dictators. Had I not been decorated both by the late General Trujillo of the Dominican Republic—Trujillo's name was in the news because he had been assassinated only a few weeks earlier—and by Juan Peron, former dictator of Argentina?

Over the telephone, Dean Rusk said to me: "I canvassed the entire Senate Latin American Affairs Committee when I submitted your name. Senator Morse will pursue these issues, but he is the only one. I advise you to be prepared to answer them."

When I walked into the Senate hearing room and shook hands with Senator William Fulbright, chairman of the Senate Foreign Relations Committee, I was armed with photostats of twenty-nine newspaper editorials endorsing my appointment. I looked forward to clearing up the record, but I was red-eyed from lack of sleep. The hearing had been postponed; then, at the last moment, it was put on the agenda of July 11, with less than twenty-four hours' notice to me. In the days before, I had been very busy. I was going to the State Department at 8:30 A.M. daily to be briefed and to familiarize myself with my duties; I was making two and three calls a day on my opposite numbers, the ambassadors to the O.A.S. from the various Latin American countries, who had read of my appointment and might take it amiss if I failed to make my protocol calls on them; and I was already on a merry-go-round of speechmaking, for until now, no one had been available—and all this despite the fact I was not yet officially in the job and might never be, if Senator Morse or any of his colleagues seriously opposed me. I came to the hearing without sleep. The night before, I had addressed the 20-30 International Clubs in Tucson, Arizona, and had flown back, to arrive in Washington at 8:30 A.M. just in time to walk into the hearing.

Both Democratic Senators from Louisiana were on hand, Allen J. Ellender and Russell B. Long, and in accordance with protocol, both made statements. Senator Long, whose family, as the reader knows, I had been fighting through the years, was magnanimity itself. He brought smiles when he observed, "Mayor Morrison owes none of

* Just for the record, since I am on this subject, I lost the race for the governorship again in January 1964, after my opposition warned the people of Louisiana: "You elect Chep Morrison and you'll have Lena Horne and Sammy Davis, Jr., in the Governor's Mansion."

his success, I can assure you, to my efforts." He added: "He has been an outstanding administrator and a real get-it-done mayor, and the people think he has done a magnificent job for them. I heartily commend him for your consideration for confirmation in this important position." Senator Ellender, a man of blunt speech, said: "The Mayor is not only a good politician but a man of the people. He gets around and he can sell them a bill of goods, and that is what we need for South and Central America."

Was there anything I wanted to say, Fulbright now asked, about being decorated by Trujillo in 1946 and by Peron in Argentina in 1949? Behind this lay the question: How could I equate these with the post of a United States ambassador, one who would have a hand in policy-making in the hemisphere?

I pointed out that I had received some seventeen decorations from Latin American governments, of which these were two. In both cases I had gone as mayor of New Orleans on good-will missions. The Argentine trip was made also in my capacity as president of the Inter-American Municipal Association, conducting a group of fifty-four other mayors through eight countries, including Argentina. I had never accepted a decoration from any chief of state, I went on, without first receiving the approval of the American ambassador on the scene. "As to the medal from Peron, Ambassador James Bruce not only wanted us to maintain good relations with Argentina but asked me to ask President Truman to invite Mr. Peron to the United States. Ambassador Bruce told me to accept the decoration as an act helping establish understanding and good will between our two countries."* I did not endorse either Peron or Trujillo simply because I was decorated by them. The purpose of our 1946 Caribbean tour was to increase trade relations between New Orleans and the ports of the Caribbean, including Ciudad Trujillo—capital and chief port of the Dominican Republic. In that sense it had been most successful.

Senator Morse ruffled through his papers, then, with a smile, looked up. "We have some communication in the file that your wife received a valuable ruby ring from Mrs. Evita Peron. First I ask the question whether or not it is true."

* Ambassador Bruce had been sent to Buenos Aires two years earlier by Mr. Truman with the order to "make friends with these people."

I must have looked a little nonplused. I am accustomed to all kinds of accusing letters, but who would have remembered that little incident of twelve years ago—I had quite forgotten it—and thought it significant enough to write a letter to the Senate Foreign Relations Committee? It seemed utterly absurd that we should have to devote time to something like this.

"Senator, it is true," I said. "But as I remember it, it was not a valuable ring—it was more costume jewelry. A nice-looking ring, one of those large affairs that are easy to see, but not an expensive ring. Perhaps less than two hundred dollars, I should say, though I never had it appraised. The ring meant nothing to my wife, but she thought if she refused it they would be offended. As a matter of fact"—I suddenly remembered—"it came in a little box sent to our hotel. We didn't know what it was until we opened it, and then it turned out to be the ring."

Something else popped into my head. If they had so complete a file, they undoubtedly had a news story that once accused me of naming a New Orleans street "Trujillo Drive," in honor of General Trujillo. I wanted to scotch this. I pointed out that the street was named for the capital city of the Dominican Republic, that we already had a Havana Street, a Panama Street, a Mexico Street and many others. "We did so because after one of our trade missions to the Caribbean, General Trujillo named a street in his capital 'New Orleans Avenue' and when the mission returned, they suggested that our City Council reciprocate."

Senator Morse cleared his throat and came to the most troublesome item: the N.A.A.C.P. letter. I was charged with refusing the local branch, a year before, permission to use the Municipal Auditorium for an unsegregated meeting. I did not prohibit the meeting, I explained, but I could not permit the use of the auditorium, because the laws of Louisiana prohibited mixed meetings in a municipal hall. (The meeting was held elsewhere.) I had also acted in conformity with the opinion of the City Attorney, to whom I took the matter. Morse, listening, nodded. But the letter, he said, also charged that I had allowed the segregationist White Citizens Council to meet there.

"That is true," I said. "The laws of Louisiana did not forbid that. But I'd like to point out that the Citizens Council used the auditorium that night to denounce me, and to urge the people to put picket lines around City Hall. They booed my name because I placed Negroes on the police force for the first time in our history, and because the Negro vote in New Orleans was cast principally in my favor—a fact that was later used by my opposition to defeat me when I ran for governor."

Thus, question after question and finally Morse posed an over-all query the burden of which was: How could I properly represent our nation in Latin America when I came from the deep South, from a region which practiced racial discrimination and customs repugnant to the Latin American people?

I did not think this a subject to treat with levity, yet I tried to leaven my answer with humor. I prefaced it by saying that the question of civil rights was a desperately difficult one in the South, and men of good will were doing their best, within the framework of the customs of their society, to find an answer. I could point out that New Orleans was the only Southern city in the United States where the State Department would schedule a tour for prominent colored visitors such as the Emperor of Ethiopia or the President of Liberia. When President Eisenhower invited President William V. S. Tubman of Liberia, an American Negro born and raised in Decatur, Georgia, New Orleans was the one Southern city Mr. Tubman visited in this country. I was convinced that basically every public official in the South carried out as best he could the customs that existed there. I had been accused of being pro-Negro again and again, and I had even defended that, saying I was attempting to do good things for the Negroes but that I had never recommended the breaking of the customs; these were matters for the courts, and when the courts decide, I would comply. It was as simple as that.

"Mr. Senator," I went on, "when you think about the deep South, I wish you would also think about the good things. For example, we are geographically close to Latin America. I like to think that we are linked emotionally and sentimentally with these wonderful people. But we have another asset. I notice that when many of our prominent Americans travel to Latin America they suffer bad receptions. Take the case of Vice-President Nixon, a Republican. He went to Latin America. His trip was greatly publicized. Eggs and tomatoes were thrown at him; he was insulted; and wherever he went, these ugly signs confronted him, 'Yankee Go Home.' The same thing happened to Adlai Stevenson, a Democrat. He visited Latin America and had the same reception—more tomatoes, more eggs and more ugly signs, 'Yankee Go Home.' I am sure that when I go, I too will have my share of bad receptions. I'm sure that I'm going to be confronted with these signs—'Yankee Go Home'—but coming as I do from the deep South, I can look up and truthfully say, 'They're not talking about me.' "

This brought laughter and the tension eased. Senator Morse turned to the reporters:

"I want to say for the benefit of the press that on the matter of the decorations and the matter of the racial problems about which I have interviewed Mayor Morrison, I feel that he has responded in an admirable and commendable manner, with a forthrightness that is a tribute to him and, in my judgment, leaves no question as to his ability to perform the work of the ambassadorship to which he has been appointed in so far as any charges that have been brought against him either on the decoration item or the race item. . . ."

Then, in what I considered a significant promise, forecasting problems we would meet together in the future, he addressed himself to me:

"It is the policy of my subcommittee on Latin American affairs to stand ready and willing to consult and be helpful if we can, and we want you to know that that will be our attitude toward any duties you perform for this government in the position of ambassador to the Organization of American States. . . . Only in a teamwork relationship between the Congress and the State Department and the White House do we have much hope of developing a program in Latin America, and that will permit us to save it in time—and I do not think we have got much time.

"I have no more questions."

I was unanimously approved.

From the Senate hearing room I telephoned my staff: Winston Lill, who had been writing my City Hall speeches and would help me prepare those I would make (in some months, almost one every other day), and my secretary, Pat Mahony, both of whom were waiting to hear from me in New Orleans. They could arrange to move to Washington, I said; we were coming aboard. Later a second secretary, Rosalie Grad, who had been with me for many years in New Orleans, joined my Washington staff.

Now matters went swiftly. Five days later I was sworn in by

President Kennedy at a ceremony in the Cabinet Room at which my four-year-old Randy stole the show. He greeted the President with a cheerful, "Hi, where's your little girl?" and when the ceremony was over, Mr. Kennedy scooped him up and held him in his arms, while Randy gleefully accepted congratulations on his father's behalf.* Sworn in at the same time was the man to fill the other long-vacant post, the new Assistant Secretary of State for Inter-American Affairs. This was Robert F. Woodward, fifty-two, until now our ambassador in Chile, a tremendously capable career officer, with some thirty years of experience in Latin America. The State Department had been reluctant to bring Bob from Santiago; but, as I heard it, nearly twenty candidates had been canvassed for the assistant secretaryship and rejected it because of the interoffice difficulties involved. Woodward, as a career diplomat, had no choice but to accept a position whose authority was compromised because the White House advisers on Latin America were closer to Mr. Kennedy's ear than the State Department. This dilution of command was to plague both Bob and myself—me far less than him, because my authority came from the President himself. My problem would be to make my advice to Mr. Kennedy prevail over that of Dick Goodwin and Arthur Schlesinger where their view differed from mine.

I flew home that night and formally resigned as mayor of New Orleans. Four days later, on July 21, I was introduced at a meeting of the Organization of American States in the Pan American Union Building and made my first ambassadorial speech in Spanish and my duties began in earnest.

The O.A.S. is composed of the twenty-one republics of the Western Hemisphere, each of whom is represented by an ambassador.† As is the case with the United Nations, most countries also have an ambassador to Washington. The O.A.S. ambassadors customarily meet, in permanent session, at the Pan American Union, in Wash-

* I cannot forbear telling another story on Randy. My fifty-second birthday arrived as I was working on this book. Randy, now seven, tiptoed up to me and handed me a little note elaborately wrapped in a pink ribbon. It read: "Dear Dad: My birthday gift to you is one full day of silence. Love, Randy."

† Cuba is still a member of the O.A.S. However, its government, since its exclusion, has had no Cuban ambassador to the O.A.S., and its seat at the Council table is empty. The story is told in Chapter XII.

ington, as the Council of the O.A.S. Each country's delegation includes economic, political, military and legal advisers, as well as a technical staff. It is the Council that executes policy and carries on O.A.S. activities.

On special occasions the Council may meet under another name. For example, in an emergency, when a member nation demands a special meeting at the highest (foreign minister) level, the ambassadors may meet in place of their foreign ministers. When there is time, the foreign ministers may arrive from their home countries to take the front chair at the O.A.S. table, while their ambassadors sit behind them. Such a meeting was to occur in January 1962, when the O.A.S. decided to have a Meeting of Consultation of Foreign Ministers on complaints that Cuban agents were intervening in the internal affairs of member nations and voted to oust the Castro regime from the inter-American system.

If the problem is one of economic and social importance, the finance ministers of the member nations may meet as the Inter-American Economic and Social Council of the O.A.S. This would be the nature of the forthcoming conference at Punta del Este. In such instances each O.A.S. ambassador becomes an adviser to his finance minister and sits with him at the Council table.

The essential purpose of the O.A.S., as stated in its charter, is clear: a) to strengthen the peace and security of the continent; b) to prevent possible causes of difficulties and to ensure the pacific settlement of disputes that may arise among the member states; c) to provide for common action on the part of those states in the event of aggression; d) to seek the solution of political, juridical and economic problems that may arise among them; and e) to promote by cooperative action their economic, social and cultural development.

It is easy to see how smoothly the Alliance for Progress—the program to stimulate social and economic reform in Latin America, with the collateral hope, for the United States, of achieving Western-oriented political stability—would mesh with the purposes of the O.A.S.

In my first speeches to my fellow ambassadors I stressed that the United States was going full steam ahead with the Alliance, as would be seen when we met at Punta del Este some ten days later, and that we would take a very strong stand on Castro. This, I felt, was one of the most important contributions I could make—taking a hard line toward Castro Communism wherever it and the United States collided in the O.A.S., and this would fully reflect the wishes of President Kennedy.

I soon learned that such collisions occurred almost daily in the Council meetings. Cuba's Ambassador Carlos Lechuga, a former newspaper political writer and clever phrasemaker, rarely let an occasion pass without denouncing the United States in violent, intemperate, but I must say often effective, language. For weeks he had done this. The Bay of Pigs had given him considerable oratorical ammunition. Arturo Morales-Carrion, a Puerto Rican diplomat whom President Kennedy appointed Deputy Assistant Secretary of State for Inter-American Affairs, had been doubling in brass as interim United States delegate to the O.A.S., pending my appointment; but since his O.A.S. situation was temporary, he had not replied to Lechuga. So clearly had the Cuban delegate hewed to the Communist line in denouncing us, while insisting he was not a Communist,* that the Guatemalan Ambassador, Carlos Urrutia Aparacio, once turned on him: "Mr. Ambassador, your name is Lechuga but I say to you, sir, you are not a lettuce [*lechuga* is Spanish for "lettuce"] but a beet, red on the outside, red on the inside, and red all over."

At my first staff meeting I discussed Lechuga with Ed Jamison, Director of the Office of Inter-American Political Affairs, a career State Department officer with wide Latin American experience, and my alternate at the O.A.S. "Ed, I've been reading this man's speeches," I said. "They're vitriolic and I want to answer them. I'd never let a political opponent get away with these lies." We agreed that I would reply to Lechuga each time he attacked us, and immediately. If his diatribes went over the wires to the entire Latin American press, why shouldn't the United States Delegate's equally vehement countercharges appear in the same dispatch? Until we

* This, it must be remembered, was before Castro's famous statement, made in a TV address December 2, 1961, that he was a "Marxist-Leninist and would remain a Marxist-Leninist to the last day of my life." The Cuban line until then had been to explain Castroism as a wide-ranging social revolution to correct the inequalities and oppressions of the Batista dictatorship, which he overthrew. To the rest of Latin America Castro had painted himself as a Robin Hood taking from the rich to give to the poor.

left for Punta, thanks to my excellent staff, working even as Lechuga spoke, I was able repeatedly to hurl his words back into his mouth. The Voice of America reported that I was now a prime target of Radio Havana, denounced as "the ex-Mayor of New Orleans who practiced segregation and slavery."*

My first act as ambassador a few days later was hardly world-shaking. But it was typical of the kind of behind-the-scenes activities I was to engage in—by themselves anything but dramatic, yet when taken together, cumulatively effective in building up support for the United States position on the various issues that came up for decision by the O.A.S.

Ambassador Fernando Lobo of Brazil, Chairman of the O.A.S., had just suffered a stroke. He lay paralyzed. His family was desperate. They wanted to return him immediately to Rio by jet, but he was too sick to use the regular commercial airline facilities, and I could find no authority for arranging United States government transportation for a sick diplomat. Ironically enough, if he died there was authority to fly his remains home.

Ambassador Lobo had been a good friend of the United States, often more inclined to support us than his own foreign office, and I was convinced that every means should be taken, even outside channels, to prove we appreciated his friendship. I decided to take the bull by the horns. I telephoned the White House and spoke with General Godfrey T. McHugh, Air Force Aide to the President, and an old friend. We had to help Lobo, I said; not only should we provide transportation at once, but first-class transportation. "Let's do it right, Godfrey; let's send Ambassador Lobo and Mrs. Lobo to Rio in the President's own jet, Air Force One, complete with doctors, nurses and aides. This will go straight to the heart of the Latin American people. And we owe it to Lobo."

"Well—" said General McHugh; then, "Wait a minute. The door is open to the President's office. I'll ask him." A moment later he was back on the phone. "Done!" he said. The President was all for it. He had authorized the plane, a staff, security officers, stewards, and was sending along, as well, his personal physician, Dr. George Burkley, and Godfrey himself.

* This was mild compared to Radio Havana's later strictures. By November I had become "the lynching advocate of the Kennedy party," and, even more colorfully, "the remarkable cretin . . . who brays in the O.A.S."

I've never been too bashful to press my luck. "Godfrey," I said, "would you go back to the President's office and tell him if he wants to do something really sensational, let him take off twenty minutes and drive to the Brazilian Embassy with me and personally extend this invitation to the family?"

Godfrey went back again and returned to the phone to say this was impossible: the President was about to receive President Ayub Khan of Pakistan; but Mr. Kennedy was at this moment writing Mrs. Lobo a letter in longhand, making the offer; Godfrey would bring it to me, and we were to call on Mrs. Lobo and present it to her, saying the President would have come in person but was unable to do so.

In half an hour we were at the Brazilian Embassy and Mrs. Lobo, a regal woman in her fifties, was sitting in a chair, letter in hand, weeping with emotion and gratitude. "I never dreamed anything like this could happen, that the President of the United States himself—" She could not go on.

At dusk that evening Air Force One took off from Andrews Air Force Base. All the Latin American ambassadors were present. I had invited them to see Ambassador Lobo off on what may have well been a life-saving flight.

The day before our departure for Punta del Este, our delegation called on Mr. Kennedy to talk over final plans. The telephone rang just as we had completed our discussion. "Yes, Governor," Kennedy was saying into the mouthpiece. It was a call he had placed earlier to Governor Nelson Rockefeller of New York. He made no attempt to conceal his conversation. He was urging Rockefeller to persuade Senator Kenneth B. Keating, Republican, of New York to vote against the Byrd amendment which, if passed, would pretty well gut our entire foreign-aid program. The President had enough votes to pass the foreign-aid bill, but the amendment, sponsored by Virginia's powerful Senator Harry F. Byrd, Chairman of the Senate Finance Committee, troubled him. He wanted it defeated.

When he hung up I ventured, "Mr. President, it looks as though you're mighty hard up when you have to go to your prospective opponent to get a rock-ribbed Republican to support you. You're scratching pretty deep for those votes."

He nodded, concerned. "We're right on the edge with this. It's just a matter of one or two votes."

I took a long breath. "Mr. President, there is one Senator from Louisiana, Senator Long, who urged me to take this post and stressed its importance. I've talked to him about the bill, and though he's opposed foreign aid in the past, if you need votes that badly, I think we may get him to come along with you. But you've got to do something material for Louisiana."

Kennedy's eyes lit up. We were talking politics now, and he was intrigued—and hopeful.

Not long ago the Army had closed Fort Polk, Louisiana—to the dismay of our state—and transferred the troops to Fort Hood, Texas. As the Army's representative in Louisiana, I had helped to sign up seven million acres of maneuver rights in the vicinity of Fort Polk. To get the leases signed, we had promised that it would be reopened. It had been reopened, only to be closed again. Now, with the Berlin crisis—in these last days of July 1961 Khrushchev was stepping up his campaign to drive us out of West Berlin—Mr. Kennedy had just increased the Army's strength from 875,000 to 1,000,000 men, and military posts were being reopened throughout the country. But Fort Polk was still closed down. "This isn't playing fair with the people of Louisiana," I said to the President. "If you could find your way clear to reopen Fort Polk, I think Senator Long would vote against the Byrd amendment. At least, I will talk to him about it."

It was not necessary for me to explain Fort Polk's importance to the Louisiana economy. The Fort had virtually supported western Louisiana, now a hard-hit area.

The President picked up his phone and got McGeorge Bundy, his Congressional liaison assistant, on the line. "See General Taylor [his Special Military Representative] and ask him what's involved in reopening Fort Polk. If we can do so, let's let Ambassador Morrison try to get that vote for us."

Our delegation was to leave at daybreak next morning. During the day I telephoned Senator Long. His re-election was to come up next year. He had voted against foreign aid in the past because he believed that we should not send dollars abroad when we could not care adequately for our own poor in Louisiana. I said, "Russell, you know what reopening Fort Polk would mean to the folks in that area. If you can bring this about, I think you have a moral justification to support foreign aid this time and vote against the Byrd amendment. . . ."

That night I was summoned back to the White House. I had seen Kennedy in the morning, talking briskly on the telephone, energetic, quick-witted, joking with his Republican opponent; now, as I walked toward his office shortly after eight o'clock, I saw him escorting the Prime Minister of Tunisia to the elevator. He turned from the elevator, obviously tired, saw me, and all but sighed. On my own, far lower level, I knew exactly how he felt. How many times I had stayed late at City Hall, and ready to leave, exhausted, looked up to see still one more customer, and groaned to myself, "Oh, my, I've got another one!"

I said, hastily, "Mr. President, you asked me over, but you look tired and I don't want to keep you—"

"Yes, yes, Chep," he said. "I'll tell you what I wanted to see you about. I talked with General Taylor. He's not in favor of reopening Fort Polk."

"Mr. President, this is a vote for you—"

"I know," he said. "And I need that vote badly."

Why, I asked, was General Taylor against reopening the Fort? The President replied, "Fort Polk is listed as an armored post."

"Oh," I said with relief. "I think I can straighten that out." The Army at this time wished to reopen infantry posts. Fort Polk had always been an infantry post. Two years before, in order to conduct maneuvers there, the Engineers had gone in and strengthened the bridges so they would support tanks. As a result, Polk was thought of as a post made to handle heavy armor. I said, "Mr. President, I know Fort Polk. I've crawled over every inch of it in maneuvers. It's perfectly wonderful for basic infantry. That's what it was used for all through the war. Just because they strengthened the bridges, that doesn't mean trucks can't roll over those bridges, jeeps can't roll over them, troops can't walk over them. It's still perfect for infantry."

I must have spoken with considerable emphasis—for the moment not as Ambassador Morrison but as Brigadier General Morrison.* The President looked at me. "You have a point there," he said.

* I had been promoted to brigadier general in 1955; I made major general in 1963.

"You need that vote," I said.

Mr. Kennedy nodded wearily. "I sure do." Then: "O.K. We have a deal."

A moment later we shook hands. I went down the elevator. I telephoned Senator Long. Now he had a coup.

"Russell, you have a 10 A.M. appointment with the President. I'm leaving for Punta del Este at 6 A.M. We stop for refueling about midday in Surinam, and I'll call you from there to see if everything went all right."

At 1 P.M. next day our plane—Air Force One, the Presidential jet that a few days earlier had taken Ambassador Lobo to Brazil—stopped for an hour at Surinam for refueling. I put aside papers I had been studying, on an ingenious plan to bring water and electricity to backward Latin American villages, and went to the nearest phone. I managed to get through almost at once to Senator Long in Washington. Fort Polk, he told me, would reopen in two weeks. All went well.

When, sometime later, I read that the Byrd amendment had been narrowly defeated, I was gratified. In the list of Senators who had voted No was "Long (D), Louisiana."

Between Surinam and Punta del Este came a fantastic two-day interlude in Brazil, when we called upon President Janio Quadros in the exotic, still-unfinished new capital, Brasilia, 600 miles from nowhere in the interior of that vast country. I still do not know which was more bizarre—Brasilia or President Quadros. Brasilia, a strange, futuristic city that might have come out of Aldous Huxley's *Brave New World*, or George Orwell's *1984*, was the creation of Quadros's predecessor, President Juscelino Kubitschek, a man of vision, the originator of "Operation Pan-America," which evolved into the Alliance for Progress.* From the air, Brasilia looks as though it were constructed with child's blocks and an erector set, on a vast, uninhabited plain—strange, soaring buildings; an underground cathedral, whose only evidence is a block-size iron crown of thorns showing above the red, tortured earth; endless cloverleafs of empty roads; grotesquely beautiful structures of aluminum, steel, glass, concrete—rectangular, square, oval, some looking like inverted

* In 1956, Kubitschek, then newly elected, proposed his "Operation Pan-America," a wide-ranging plan calling for an international fund to help develop the economies of the Americas.

bowls, others like enormous drying dishes set in the sun. Kubitschek wanted to develop the interior of Brazil. Approximately 90 per cent of Brazil's population, its trade and its industry are concentrated along its coastal area; Kubitschek decided that the best way to popularize the all but empty interior was to build a new capital there.* The site he chose was on a plateau some 600 miles by air from Rio, nearly 1,300 miles by road; the architect he selected was the Brazilian Oscar Niemeyer, a brilliant, avant-garde leftist, and one of the architects of the United Nations building in New York, to whom Kubitschek gave free rein. As a result, Brasilia is the only city most of whose architecture reflects the ideas of one man, one of the few completely planned cities in the world, the design being that of another ultra-modern architect, Brazilian city-planner Lucio Costa. It has been widely praised—and as widely damned, as "Kubitschek's Folly," and the "newest ruins in the world."

As strange as Brasilia struck me, even stranger was President Quadros. On the agenda of our meeting at Punta del Este were such problems as placing a floor under raw-material prices. Among Latin America's principal exports are coffee, bananas, sugar, oil. Chief among these is coffee, and we wanted to discuss an international coffee agreement with President Quadros.

I had read and heard a good deal about this man as an eccentric. He was unpredictable, politically as well as personally. Adolf Berle had called on him a few months earlier, seeking to persuade him to join the anti-Castro bloc, and when, at the end of their fruitless meeting, he wanted to shake hands with him, Quadros deliberately turned and walked away. He looked like a larger Groucho Marx, with heavy black shell-rim glasses, and he acted like Groucho in some of his more zany films. When he campaigned, Quadros—a spellbinding speaker—carried a salt shaker in his pocket; now and then he took it out to shake salt on his shoulder, to show that he had dandruff—he was an ordinary fellow, he said. During a speech he might suddenly produce a paper-wrapped sandwich from his

* The idea of moving the capital from Rio had been talked about for more than a century. When work finally began on Brasilia, it was at a tremendous pace, with day and night shifts. Today, however, construction has halted, though many buildings are still uncompleted, some little more than steel-and-concrete skeletons. The effect is truly weird: perfection in one plaza, frozen chaos in the next.

pocket, say, "I've been so busy I haven't had a chance to eat today," take a bite, replace it in his pocket, and go on with his speech.

Yet he had been elected President seven months before, with 6,000,000 votes—the highest ever given a presidential candidate in Brazil. A onetime schoolteacher, as governor of São Paulo, the great industrial state of Brazil, he had apparently worked wonders. He had cleaned out graft—his campaign badge was a miniature broom—and his reforms were immensely popular with the people. Like Castro, for whom he had immense respect (Quadros characterized himself as a "neutralist," but on the eve of his election he paid a highly publicized call on Castro), he was famous for lengthy, dramatic television appearances. These matched the man. He appeared usually late at night, even midnight. The camera opens on him sitting alone in a chair, smoking his pipe, in a small, austere room dominated by a huge map of Brazil on the wall. He sits, smoking, meditating, saying nothing. Sometimes he rises, paces the floor, deep in thought, then returns to his chair, still without a word. Minutes pass. Quadros sits, in a brown study. The members of the TV audience might be forgiven if, lying in bed, watching, they dozed off. Suddenly, with an electrifying shout, Quadros leaps to his feet, dashes to the map, snatches up a long wooden pointer, and begins to lecture: "This is what we are going to do here"—using the pointer to indicate the area—"and this is our problem here"—again using the pointer. He speaks rapidly, eloquently, at tremendous speed, with great excitement; then he concludes his lecture as abruptly as he began it. The screen goes dark. The President has spoken.

As we drove through the long, empty avenues of Brasilia to government headquarters—Brazil's Congress is in two white concrete buildings which from the distance appear to be two gigantic bowls, side by side, one inverted, one right side up—my aide, Winston Lill, said, "Kubitschek spent something like six hundred million dollars to build this city, and I'm told that Quadros has added only one structure—a movie house that specializes in American Westerns. He's wild about them. He sits in the audience, and each time there's an Indian raid, or a settlers' fight, he takes part in it—sits there pretending he's one of them, pointing the index finger of each hand alternately at the screen—as though he had a pistol in each hand—and shouting 'Bang! Bang!' "

Quadros, when we met him, turned out to be the bouncingest

man I ever saw. He greeted us effusively, all personality, wrung our hands, said to me swiftly, "Ah, yes, Ambassador Morrison, we all appreciate what you did for Fernando Lobo, he's quite comfortable now," and for the rest of our meeting was a jumping bean. We had walked in to find him seated behind his desk. A moment later—even as we were talking with him—he had bounced off to a corner to pick up a stray bit of paper. He tossed it into a wastebasket, turned suddenly, and began speaking again with the same rapidity and excitement he must have exhibited on television. We were able, however, to discuss the coffee question with him; and Secretary Dillon and Michael Blumenthal, our coffee expert, found him alert and knowledgeable. He said he looked forward to the conference; his country would cooperate; his finance minister, Moreiro Sales, was on his way to Uruguay now; he wished us all success. He flashed his quick smile, and bid us goodbye.

As we left his office, I looked back. He was no longer at his desk. He had bounded out of the room through another door.

An hour later we were high above the incredible city of Brasilia and were bound for Punta del Este.

4. PUNTA DEL ESTE—BIRTH OF THE ALLIANCE

Punta del Este—the name means "Eastern Point"—is a tiny finger of land in Uruguay, between Argentina and Brazil, sticking out into the Atlantic Ocean. It is a rich man's playground, a seaside summer resort where wealthy Argentinians and Uruguayans maintain villas so they can boat, water-ski, swim, gamble (at either of two casinos) and dance (at a luxurious country club). Sixty-five miles from Montevideo, the Uruguayan capital, via a single, paved road, Punta del Este has been the scene of many international congresses, and for good reason.

First, Montevideo is easily accessible to the rest of the world, with a first-rate airport. Second, Uruguay, one of the most advanced of Latin American countries, is comparable in its neutrality to Switzerland. The most stable country in Latin America, it has never had a revolt or a *coup d'état*; it rarely becomes involved in wars; it acts as a buffer between the two great powers on either side; and it serves ideally as a meeting place for Latin American countries in whatever state of belligerency or instability they may be. Third—and this is sometimes the most important—it is almost impossible to carry out riots or disturbances there, such as have disrupted international congresses in New York, Paris and Geneva, and in other Latin

American capitals. At some places the peninsula is less than three city blocks wide; from the point of security, it is only necessary to station a company of soldiers across the base of the finger, like a band about a cigar, and would-be pickets, troublemakers and student rioters cannot get through. Or, once through, they cannot escape capture.

When Air Force One reached Montevideo we found ourselves in the midst of extraordinary air traffic. Carrasco Airport was as busy as New York's Kennedy International Airport. Nearly two thousand persons were converging upon this little country. In addition to the delegations there were nearly a thousand members of the communications media from all parts of the world, as well as hundreds of observers, including Cuban exiles. As our plane was about to make its approach, the tower radioed our pilot. The plane from Havana, carrying the Cuban delegation, was about five minutes behind us in the pattern—did we wish to allow them to go in ahead of us? A crowd of some fifteen hundred persons, waving pro-Castro banners and placards, was waiting on the airport apron. Ought we allow them to land first so they could have their reception, go off to Punta del Este, and be out of the way when we landed? Or ought we go in first?

It was decided that we would go in at once.

Looking out my window, as we approached the runway, I saw the waiting crowd. They seemed surprisingly youthful. Then it came to me. These were students, obviously from the University of Montevideo, which had a history as a left-wing concentration point. Off in the distance, in a street beyond the airport, I could make out a string of parked buses. Here was confirmation. They had been brought to the airport en masse. This was not a spontaneous outpouring of pro-Castro supporters. It had been arranged.

All at once I remembered. These students had caused trouble before. Both President Eisenhower, in 1960, and Vice-President Nixon, in 1958, had had a bad time with them. Nixon had been heckled unmercifully in what turned out to be the forerunner of the stoning attack on him in Caracas, Venezuela, a few days later; and though President Eisenhower had received a hero's welcome throughout Brazil, Argentina, Chile and Uruguay, here in Montevideo, the Uruguayan capital, among the thousands cheering him had been a group of nearly a hundred students from the university armed with Castro banners and even tear-gas bombs.

I was a little tense as our plane landed, then taxied slowly toward a roped-off section about a hundred yards ahead. I could see the assembly of Uruguayan government and United States embassy officials, the microphones set up where Secretary Dillon would extend an official greeting on behalf of our delegation. As our plane glided forward, we had to pass the mass of students waiting for the Cubans; and as we did so, we were treated to a remarkable and, were it not so regrettable, ludicrous scene. Suddenly, as we were almost opposite them, with one accord, as if a command had been given, the entire crowd of students turned their backs on us. Silently Air Force One, the Presidential Seal gleaming brightly on either side, slid by fifteen hundred backs. One didn't know whether to burst into laughter or grit one's teeth.

We came to a halt. A score of police and soldiers, rifles at the ready, immediately surrounded our plane. It was several minutes before our door was opened. As it did so, we heard a tremendous shout, then deafening cheers. The Cubans had arrived, some forty of them. There was a paroxysm of flag-waving as the plane began discharging its passengers, all in uniform, bearded, shirts open at the necks, berets on their heads, and led by bearded Major Ernesto "Che" Guevara, Cuba's minister of industry, the Marxist mastermind behind Fidel Castro. Guevara, who was to be the star of the show during our eleven days at Punta del Este, was almost engulfed, uniform, beret and all, in the press of students.

We arrived, presently, in Punta del Este.

Later, Secretary Dillon and I sat in the villa of President Eduardo Victor Haedo of Uruguay, host to our conference. I had wanted Dillon to meet Haedo informally, in the latter's summer home, a charming lodge with stone fireplaces, swimming pool, enormous outdoor barbecue and private chapel, almost lost in the thick pine woods not far from the Edificio de las Americas, where our sessions would be held. Nearby, at the luxurious Cantegril Country Club, were a number of cottages. Because of lack of hotel accommodation, one of these—Cottage No. 50—was taken by Mario Bermudez, International Relations Director of International House, New Orleans, and Cottage No. 50 became our own little International House in Punta del Este, a social headquarters for Latin American colleagues and friends.

President Haedo, a chubby, jovial man, was wearing a gay, bright-colored lumberjack shirt and a beret perched on his curly gray hair as we drove up. He advanced upon us with a cry, "Chepito! Chepito!" and as Dillon looked on with some amusement, the President and I pounded each other on the back in an old-fashioned *abrazo*. We had known each other since 1952 when, as president of the mayors' organization, I had brought fifty-four American mayors to Uruguay for the Fourth International Municipal Congress. I introduced Haedo and Dillon, and we sat down together on a sofa before a crackling fire. Drinks were served.

The Uruguayan President, puffing on a long, gnarled pipe, glanced at me, then at Dillon, then back at me. "I understand you were given something of an unpleasant reception."

Dillon said, with a smile, "Well, some of those who greeted us appeared rather cool."

"You must accept my apologies for their bad manners," Haedo said. "But it has no significance. That demonstration was put on by the Communists. I consider it a failure. They wanted to make a much bigger show. My people tell me those fellows expected a crowd of five thousand, but their buses arrived half filled. They did not do well by themselves."

He went on to talk about the conference. He had hoped that President Kennedy would come to lend his personal prestige to the occasion. The entire country was excited. On the other side of the equator the seasons are the opposite of ours, and though this was mid-August, it was winter in Punta del Este, and the resort was all but closed, but many prominent Argentinians and Brazilians had already come down and reopened their houses in our honor. The Alliance had captured Haedo's imagination. "My friends, you will make history here," he said. Punta del Este was a little town, unknown to most of the world, yet it already had a place in history. In World War II a decisive victory over the Nazis had taken place here. A few miles away, in the bay of Montevideo, the great German battleship *Graf Spee* sank. He, Haedo, had been among the thousands who stood on the beach and watched the battleship, sunk by its own captain to avoid capture by the British, slowly go down. Now, he was sure, a second and greater victory—this over poverty, misery and hunger—would be marked here. He had highest hopes for our success.

Next morning, as I breakfasted in the dining room of the San Rafael Hotel, the waiter brought me the morning newspapers. I stared at the headlines over a story reporting our arrival: YANKS JEERED, CUBANS CHEERED! Failure (as my good friend Haedo called it) or not, that was the story given to the world on our opening day, and it was small solace that we knew the truth.

Under these auspices, while reports filtered through of American planes hijacked by Cuba, of growing concern over the Berlin crisis, the twenty-one finance ministers of the Americas, assisted by some four hundred experts on coffee quotas, price stabilization, bank credits, tariffs, taxation, land reform, education, health and sanitation, met to forge the charter of the Alliance for Progress.

The technical task before us—to work out formulas for social and economic change, the size of loans, at what interest and for what purpose, the allocations of money to be pooled—was difficult enough; but the problems we sought to attack by these means were staggering—politically, economically, socially.

We were faced by a continent in upheaval, plagued by the fact that a majority of its 200,000,000 people were poverty-stricken, some living in conditions beyond the comprehension of any United States citizen who has not seen them. Hunger—actual hunger—had driven peasants, not in China or Korea, but in Brazil, so rich in natural resources, to riot for food, pouring into towns and attacking storekeepers with rakes and sticks. In the northeast section of Brazil, the largest country in Latin America—one out of three Latin Americans is a Brazilian—one found areas where a family's income was less than $23 a year, where life expectancy was thirty years, where one out of two babies died before its first birthday.

In neighboring Peru, virtually half the population of 11,000,000 never saw or used money. They lived outside the money economy, neither buying nor selling, but trading. In Panama, one per cent of the landowners owned half of all privately owned land. The majority of the countries had no middle class: what one found was a small thin crust of land-rich upper classes, literate, confident, masterful, generally healthy—and a vast, impoverished lower class, illiterate, defeated, resentful, chronically ill. There was little between. The gap between haves and have-nots was enormous. Of all the countries, only Argentina and Mexico could be said to have a sizable middle class. In Venezuela, which received hundreds of millions of dollars in oil royalties, seven out of ten persons could not read or write. In Mexico, where social-reform programs have been in effect longer than anywhere else on the continent—more than fifty years—six out of every ten families still lived in one room. In Bolivia, one half the houses in the capital, La Paz, were without water. Of the 35,000,000 Latin Americans living in cities of over 200,000, one fourth—nearly 9,000,000—lived in slums, in caves, in roofless lean-tos, in shantytowns of tobacco and gasoline tins, of packed mud and reeds, in hovels without water, gas, electricity or sanitation facilities.

Economically, countries suffered. In fourteen republics, the economy depended essentially on one crop, coffee. (Sixty per cent of Brazil's earnings came from coffee.) In Bolivia, it was tin. The fate of one commodity in the world market dictated the financial health of these countries. In others, there was virtually no industry at all to depend upon. In Argentina, the cost of living had risen five times in as many years. Many countries were in such great debt that simply to pay interest on their loans would use up most of the profits from their export earnings.

Politically, the scene was equally overwhelming. Argentina, second largest country in Latin America, in eighteen months had had three presidents, seven foreign ministers, one hundred cabinet changes, and six revolutions. In twenty-five years Ecuador had had thirty presidents. In Colombia, because of a political assassination in 1948, some 200,000 persons had been killed in merciless internal warfare; the violence, banditry and murder still continued in 1961. In Guatemala, in thirty years, not one president had escaped assassination or exile. In Paraguay, in Haiti, in Nicaragua, thousands of political prisoners languished in jails or had taken refuge in friendly embassies; in the Dominican Republic, riots and terror still marked the aftermath of Trujillo's assassination; and in Cuba, threatening all Latin America, was Castro Communism—Fidelismo, whose signs we saw everywhere—the Kremlin's bridgehead to the new world.

It was this intense and troubled panorama south of our border, and the tremendous challenge it posed, that led President Kennedy, carrying out the promise of the Act of Bogotá,* moving with style and vigor, to launch the Alliance. He had requisitioned the first 600 million dollars. He had given a point-by-point outline of what was needed: to support economic integration, so one country would not compete destructively with another; to examine commodity-market problems; to step up our Food for Peace program so children would have school lunches and farmers in stricken areas would receive food grains; to start new projects in medicine, to expand technical training programs and to aid universities and research institutions; through the Peace Corps to assist peoples directly; and finally, to come to the defense of any American nation whose independence was in danger.

It was an over-all blueprint to build Latin America from the ground up. It formed our terms of reference as we sat down in the great hall of the Edificio de las Americas to hear President Haedo open the conference with words echoing his informal remarks of the day before:

"Gentlemen, you have a meeting with destiny."

We began work at once, encouraged by a message from President Kennedy which brought a wave of applause: The United States would allocate more than one billion dollars to the Alliance during its first year, from March 13, 1961, the day he announced the Alliance in Washington.

Our problem was to draft a ten-year economic agreement, involving virtually every financial and banking institution dealing with Latin America, and the resources of every country in the Western Hemisphere, and spelling out precisely what the country would be called upon to accomplish. This meant getting commitments in writing from every Latin American government that it would carry out an enormous complex of reforms—land, tax, social—and earmark a certain amount of their resources for these. In

* In 1960 President Eisenhower, in one of the last great achievements of his administration, brought together the American republics in an O.A.S. conference in Bogotá, Colombia. Here was drafted an international agreement, which used Kubitschek's earlier "Operation Pan-America" as a basis, aimed at bringing social reform to Latin America. This was the Act of Bogotá of September 12, 1960, signed by all American republics, save Cuba. Our spokesman at Bogotá was Douglas Dillon, then Undersecretary of State for Economic Affairs. Now, in Punta, he would complete what began in Bogotá.

education, for example, the commitment we sought was that within ten years every child in Latin America would have at least six years of schooling. This was an almost astronomical objective, since Latin America today is 50 per cent illiterate, and some countries, even more: El Salvador, 60 per cent, Guatemala 70 per cent, and Haiti, 89 per cent. The illiteracy went hand in hand with social, economic and political conditions.

We were asking, in short, that every nation pledge itself to change a way of life that had existed for centuries. We were pushing land reform in a part of the world where 5 per cent of the people owned 70 per cent of the arable land.* Making matters even more difficult, the very delegates seated about the conference table, Latin Americans of wealth and property, belonged principally to that 5 per cent. We were demanding tax reform—which meant increased taxation, or the imposition of income taxes where such taxes were rarely if ever paid. Once more, the very delegates to whom we appealed were those at whom it was aimed.

Yet it had to be done in this fashion. Simply to pour billions into Latin America without bringing about reforms—to leave the monopolies and oligarchies untouched, to do nothing about the structure of a society with the few rich and the many poor—would succeed only in making the rich richer and the poor poorer.

As I sat in the various committee meetings, now discussing his speech with Secretary Dillon—the most important address of the Conference, for it would reveal the full extent of the United States commitment—or listening to the droning voice of an expert on coffee prices proving that a one-cent drop in the price of raw coffee could wipe out a year's loans to a coffee-producing country—or making notes on the splitting up of land holdings in Peru—it seemed impossible to me that we could emerge with a document agreeable to everyone. We were touching on so many sensitive areas!

Some months later I was to find myself arguing with a wealthy industrialist who belonged to one of the "Fourteen Families" which, it is said, rule El Salvador. He had with him the text of a new tax law proposed in his country, and he was furious. He showed it to me accusingly. "And your ambassador, sir, is pushing this bill."

"That's correct," I said. His government had obligated itself at

* The disproportion of owners and ownership was only one aspect. Of this 70 per cent, only one fourth was under cultivation—and this while people starved!

Punta del Este to pass a tax-reform law. We naturally wanted it passed so we could add our assistance, according to the self-help requirements of the Alliance.

"But look at the taxes I shall have to pay!" He pointed to the last line of a bracket which read, "Those with income over $1,000,000 a year . . ." the class to which he belonged. The tax opposite the figure was 55 per cent. "That is confiscatory!" he exclaimed. "It is Communistic! And your country supports it!"

I smiled. "I'm far from a Communist," I said, "but do you know that if you were in that bracket in my country, the capitalistic United States, you would pay ninety per cent in taxes? And in Great Britain—conservative, Anglo-Saxon Great Britain—ninety-five per cent?" I tried to point out that the American people were being taxed to furnish the money we contributed to the Alliance. Surely it was only equitable that the Latin Americans tax themselves, too.*

But as we sat in the Edificio de las Americas, it seemed almost impossible that we would succeed.

Yet a treaty was worked out. The terms of reference set by President Kennedy were followed. The final document, which runs more than eight thousand words, was hammered out, but not without dramatic moments.

The drama began soon enough. It had been keyed by the jeering on our arrival. We woke the second morning to new headlines. Soviet Cosmonaut Titov had orbited the earth 17½ times, making our achievements—we had so far sent up small animals, the Soviets had now orbited a man on two separate occasions—seem almost amateurish. It was another blow to Western prestige, and it cast a pall over us. One Argentine delegate summed up the general Latin American feeling: "This flight emphasizes, as no amount of talk ever could, the progress in science and technology made by the Soviet Union." It was obviously a tremendous Soviet propaganda gain. But when, a few days later, a new series of headlines assailed us—Khrushchev had begun to build the Berlin wall—this public admission that the Communists literally had to imprison the people of East Germany, helped to restore the balance.

One fact was clear from the beginning: the Cubans were out to

* This gentleman, who so vehemently opposed the tax reform brought about by the Alliance, later agreed, at my request, to serve on the National Commission for El Salvador—one of the committees set up to publicize and bring the story of the Alliance to the people of the country!

sabotage the conference. Che Guevara, their spokesman, handsome, dashing in his olive-green uniform with scarf tied ascot fashion, with dark flashing eyes, distinctive black mutton-chop beard and an infectious smile, immediately began talking about the "Alliance for Exploitation." Alone of the delegates, he had refused to applaud Kennedy's message. He and his *barbudos* ("bearded ones") stole every scene, coming to and from the Edificio de las Americas in a cavalcade of shiny cars that sped by, sirens screaming, and came to a halt with shrieking brakes. "Like a bunch of teen-age delinquents," one of our secretaries commented, but it was obvious that Che himself was not easily downgraded. He lobbied for Cuba and against the United States wherever he could. Most of the delegates shunned him religiously—simply to be photographed with Che would have caused them considerable trouble at home—though newspapermen and the curious followed him about as though he were a Hollywood celebrity. He played this role well, signing autographs with a flourish,* accompanied everywhere by an armed bodyguard and, reportedly, even a food taster. In private conversation he was reported to be charming, sardonic, and surprisingly well-informed.

Halfway through the conference we had a chance to assay him publicly, for he delivered Cuba's speech. He prepared melodramatically. Everyone else spoke seated at the huge horseshoe table. Che brought his own microphone so he could speak standing; and he had before him a sheaf of papers to which he referred constantly.

From where I sat, behind Secretary Dillon, Che was less than ten feet away. I watched him curiously. This man, born in Argentina, had been by act of the Cuban government made a "native" Cuban. He had been associated with Castro for years; to many, he was Castro's Machiavelli, the power behind the throne. He had plotted with Fidel in Mexico and had fought and lived with him in the mountains of Cuba in the early days of the revolution.

He stood before us in uniform, without a jacket, his shirt open at the neck, tieless—all other delegates were in customary business suits—his major's† insignia gleaming on his shoulders. Behind him,

---

* Guevara, as Cuban Minister of the Treasury, signed Cuban bank notes "Che," an Argentine commonplace nickname, like "Mac" or "Joe" or "Buddy." This was his official signature on Cuban money.

† Cuba's highest rank under Castro, who, along with his brother Raul, is also a "major."

forming a colorful backdrop for him, were the flags of the twenty-one American nations; and as he spoke, it was over the whirring of the movie cameras, recording his words and his performance for all the world. His speech was a masterpiece of modulation, of irony, of half-truths cunningly turned, of rhetorical questions—"Gentlemen" (here addressing himself to Secretary Dillon) "why don't we stop stealing each other's planes? Isn't it time to drop this nonsense?"—and a blanket attack on virtually every opening address made by the other nations. But the United States was his target. At this point we were beginning quietly to canvass delegates for support of economic and diplomatic sanctions against Cuba (the most serious penalty the O.A.S. could impose), which I hoped we would soon achieve; and the fury behind his words—the United States was a "monster"; it sought to devour Cuba—proved that he knew of this move. He ridiculed the Alliance, he assailed Kennedy's promise of economic aid. "These are schemes to give latrines to the poor," he shouted. We were "pulling the legs" of the delegates. The Alliance was a poorly disguised plot by the United States, "that monster of intervention," to isolate Cuba in its own hemisphere.

He was launched on a political diatribe to divert us from the task before us—the grinding out of economic agreements. This was no occasion for a controversy on communism versus democracy. Che obviously hoped to prod us into answering him and turn the conference into a free-for-all, Cuba on one side, the United States on the other.

As he spoke, my eye was caught by a group of men standing silently across the well from Che, staring at him with unconcealed hostility. They were Cuban exiles. I had met one of their leaders, Luis Conte Aguero, a tall, dark-eyed, strikingly handsome man of about thirty-five, formerly a top radio commentator in Havana. He had been one of Castro's most ardent supporters and had broken with him when he became convinced that Castro was a Communist. Now Conte Aguero broadcast from Miami, denouncing Castro bitterly. He headed the "Sentinels of Liberty," a Miami-based Free Cuba organization with representatives in fifteen Latin American countries. Conte Aguero was not staying at a hotel—"I am being watched," he said cryptically—but was hidden away in the Punta del Este lighthouse, where, he said, sympathetic friends gave him a cot in one of the tiny rooms. He told me he had come to tape speeches for rebroadcast in Miami, to present a petition that Cuba be excluded from the Alliance for Progress, and if possible, to obtain recognition as a spokesman for a provisional Cuban government-in-exile. This last was impossible, but I had promised him what help I could, and I enabled him to attend several sessions. But at this moment I did not notice Conte Aguero in the group.

What struck me was the stark hatred shining in the eyes of the exiles as they watched Che Guevara. However they had gotten into this carefully guarded hall—some by means of dubious newspaper credentials—they were present now, bitter, vengeful, obviously holding themselves in hand by great control as Che rose to higher and higher peaks of eloquence, his hands outstretched, pleading, denouncing, cajoling, scorning, defying.

Suddenly he reached forward, snatched a sheet of paper from the table before him, and brandishing it in the best Senator McCarthy tradition, cried: "I have here, in black and white, proof of the true feelings of the United States, proof of how it interferes in Latin America, proof of the two faces it shows the world, one to you, my friends, and one to itself."

What he held was a classified State Department memorandum which, as we were to ascertain, had been stolen two months ago from Teodoro Moscoso, then our ambassador to Venezuela. On June 14, 1961, Moscoso had visited the University of Caracas. Moscoso is a most capable man,* but he committed an error: he carried State Department documents in his briefcase and left the briefcase in his automobile. While he was in the building, Communist students ransacked the car, set it on fire, and seized the documents. Under State Department regulations, classified papers must always be in a place of security under lock and key.

The memorandum, prepared by the staff of the United States embassy in Caracas, was particularly embarrassing. It warned of the danger of more United States aid to Venezuela, and discussed very frankly the shortcomings of the regime of President Romulo Betancourt, a highly respected friend of the United States.

* Moscoso, a Puerto Rican, for two years was United States Coordinator for the Alliance. President Johnson later appointed him a representative on the Inter-American Committee for the Alliance for Progress, from which he resigned May 4, 1964. President Johnson a week later appointed Walt Rostow to assume this post, in addition to being chairman of the Policy Planning Commission of the State Department.

Che read from it dramatically: "All the plans and programs that might be formulated . . . and the economic development of Venezuela, either by the Government or through private capital or by American technicians, would have to be put into operation by the present bureaucracy in Venezuela. But so long as the public administration of the country is marked by ineptitude, indifference, favoritism in Government jobs, thefts, duplication of jobs, establishment of private empires, it would be impossible to have any dynamic projects or efficient follow-up, by the Government. . . ."

Here, Che cried, brandishing the paper again, one saw exactly how insincere, how malevolent, how double-dealing the United States was, outwardly smiling, inwardly despising. . . .

Finally, after two and one half hours, he sat down. His Cuban compatriots were on their feet, applauding. Then, unexpectedly, the place erupted. Things happened so swiftly I could hardly follow them.

A heavy-set man in black shell-rim spectacles leaped to his feet. "Assassin!" he screamed at Che. It was a signal for the little band of Cuban exiles. They charged forward, crying, "Murderer! Pig! Bandit!" almost bowling over the security guards as they rushed at Guevara. The Castro men surrounding him, bearded and watchful, stood there, stony-faced, ready, but making no move. Then, as the guards wrestled with the exiles, a Cuban jumped in front of Guevara, whipped out a Cuban flag and held it protectively in front of Che, as if to say, "If you want to harm this man, you must destroy this flag to reach him."

Now the guards were hauling the anti-Castro men out of the hall. Fists were flying, amid shouts and screams again of "Murderer! Assassin!" Out of the corner of my eye I saw guards hustling the bespectacled man into the lobby, and caught a glimpse of fists swinging as two groups—exiles and guards—poured into each other. Inside, three struggling men were being dragged away, shouting imprecations.

From the lobby the bespectacled man's voice was heard, above the din: "He sold out to the Russians! Assassin, assassin!" as he was carried away.* Inside, Carlos Alberto Clulow, Uruguayan ambassador to the United States and chairman of the meeting, banged his

* He was Dr. Max Azicri-Levy, a Cuban exile leader living in Montevideo, correspondent of *El Avance*, a Havana newspaper published in exile in Miami.

gavel repeatedly: "Gentlemen! Please! Gentlemen!" The place was bedlam.

As the hall quieted down, Dillon turned to me. During much of Guevara's performance he had watched him closely, sometimes with astonishment at this remarkable spectacle of rabble-rousing, name-calling, soaring histrionics. "Chep," he said calmly, "what do you think of answering his speech? Will you take a reading of everybody? What's your own reaction?"

"I can give you mine quickly," I said. "I wouldn't answer it. I'd simply dismiss it as a pack of lies."

This was the consensus of our delegation. It was the usual Castro-Guevara-Lechuga propaganda line. Although I had always advocated replying to Lechuga at the O.A.S., in this instance I thought it best not to dignify Guevara's attack with a reply by a member of President Kennedy's Cabinet. As good a comment as anyone made was that from my friend Carlos Urrutia Aparacio, of Guatemala, who had coined the "red as a beet" phrase about Lechuga. Now, in a fiery address—Guatemala, a Caribbean neighbor of Cuba and therefore directly menaced,* is violently anti-Castro—he ridiculed Che: "If there were not a halo of blood surrounding this flabby Cantinflas, he would actually be amusing."

When Secretary Dillon finally gave his long-awaited address, it lit up fireworks of another nature. The hall was jammed with two thousand people listening with intense interest. He paid no attention to Guevara's speech. He referred, in passing, to the Berlin wall, very much in the news, observing that there were no walls about the free world, that none were needed. Then, quickly, he came to the heart of the matter: the United States commitment. In our private meetings we had concluded that Latin America would need at least twenty billion dollars from outside sources over the next ten years. This, however, was only part of the money involved. We would provide one fifth. The other four-fifths were to come from the countries themselves. Thus, we were talking generally about the sum of eighty billion dollars of commitment of their own resources, and twenty billion of external aid. This meant, eventually, a total expediture of

* In March 1963, Guatemala's army, led by Colonel Enrique Peralta Azurdia, overthrew President Miguel Ydígoras Fuentes, charging that his government was threatened by Castro-inspired leftists.

some $100,000,000,000—$10,000,000,000 a year for ten years. Nothing of this magnitude had ever been dreamed of before.

Dillon spoke for an hour and a half. When he uttered the words "twenty billion dollars," the room echoed with applause. When he finished his address, there was a standing ovation. But as everyone stood, applauding, Che Guevara, who with his entire delegation had remained seated, suddenly rose and started to leave the room, even though there were still other speeches to be heard.

This was the signal for minor bedlam again. Reporters, photographers and newsreel men descended upon him. The shout was heard, "The Cubans are walking out!" When Guevara rose, his men rose with him, and they followed him out of the hall into the lobby, accompanied by popping flashbulbs. But Che, instead of making for the double exit doors in the lobby, led his men directly to the ladies' rest room and, as cameras ground, marched into it. For a moment, time simply stood still. There was a woman's scream from within, and a red-faced Che charged out, snarled at the photographers, and strode into the adjacent men's room. For some reason, though signs in three languages had been printed above each room, he had become confused. "This is no walkout," one spectator managed to say, almost choking with laughter. "It is a call of nature—probably the most publicized in history!"

But neither Che's eloquence nor his public exigency brought him any support. The final document was drafted and approved. On the night of Wednesday, August 16, there was another dramatic session, lasting far into the evening. Che denounced the United States and attacked the Alliance, this time as "an attempt to find a solution to Latin American contradictions within the framework of imperialism." Dillon replied sharply: "This conference has been inundated by lies from Cuba. My government does not recognize the present government of Cuba. We will never recognize it, for to do so would be to betray the thousands of patriotic Cubans still waiting and struggling for freedom in their country." Placing our cards openly on the table, speaking more bluntly than ever before, he declared: "It is obvious the Cuban government has no interest in economic progress under . . . the Alliance for Progress. It sent its delegates here for political reasons. As long as the government of Cuba is under the control of a foreign power—namely, the Soviet Union—

the United States has no intention to make its funds available to that government."

Next morning, one by one, representatives of twenty republics of the Western Hemisphere stepped forward and signed the Charter of the Alliance for Progress*—all but Cuba.

The date was August 17, 1961. The first Punta del Este Conference was closed, the work of the Alliance now began.

---

* The final document—to be known as the Charter of Punta del Este—followed the lines we had sought. High points were: 1) to achieve an economic growth in each Latin American country of at least 2½ per cent per capita per year; 2) to reform tax systems to insure needed revenues and to redistribute the tax burden more fairly; 3) to institute agricultural reforms to increase productivity and a more equitable land distribution; 4) to raise the standard of living in Latin America by creating new job opportunities, improving public health, developing low-cost housing, controlling disease, eliminating illiteracy and assuring each child a minimum of six years' schooling.

5. BEHIND THE CURTAIN— POLITICS, LATIN STYLE

I have written in some detail of the substantive activities of the Conference of Punta del Este, because I did not wish to distract the reader from this great achievement by calling his attention to what was going on behind the scenes. But, with the charter signed, this is as good a place as any to lift the curtain.

Our delegation, some thirty-five strong, was made up of Mr. Dillon; Bob Woodward, Assistant Secretary of State for Inter-American Affairs; Arturo Morales-Carrion, Deputy Assistant Secretary of State for Inter-American Affairs; John M. Leddy, Assistant Secretary of the Treasury; Edwin M. Martin, Assistant Secretary of State for Economic Affairs; Harold F. Linder, President and Chairman, Export-Import Bank; Lincoln Gordon, Consultant to Secretary Rusk and destined shortly after to become United States Ambassador to Brazil; William Turnage, Chief of the Economic Section of the Bureau of Inter-American Affairs; Dixon Donnelley, Public Affairs Assistant to Secretary Dillon; Richard I. Phillips, Public Affairs Officer for the Inter-American Affairs Bureau; Dick Goodwin; James W. Symington, Deputy Director, Food for Peace, and son of Senator Symington; Simon Wilson, of the United States delegation to the O.A.S.; my aide, Winston Lill; and a score of technical experts who had prepared the working papers to guide us in drafting the final documents. I had also asked Mario Bermudez, New Orleans's International Relations Director, to meet us here.* As a Colombian, he not only knew everybody in his country's delegation but had a wide acquaintance among other delegations. Among us, we knew virtually every major Latin American diplomat at Punta del Este. My job was, first, to consult with Dillon, especially on his speech—each country delivered one major address, the order of appearance decided by lot—and second, to act as liaison between our delegation and the twenty Latin American delegations.

This meant—and I shall dispense with the overworked word, "diplomacy"—to persuade them of what we thought best, so as to get their support for measures we wanted passed, and to interpret to our own people the true attitude of the various Latin American delegates toward the issues before us. Since the conference soon broke down into a series of working meetings where technicians hammered out details of the complicated financial agreements, I found myself much of the time involved in the second phase of my duties.

If I have learned one thing in my years in and out of Latin America, it is that the Latins believe there is a time for work and a time for play. There is a protocol here as rigid, if not as specified, as the protocol that requires a delegation to enter and leave a plane in the order of importance, to greet and be greeted in the order of rank, to be seated at dinners and be served according to a well-established hierarchy. The typical workday of the Latin differs sharply from ours. We begin early, finish early, then go on to other matters. Latins start late, enjoy a long lunch period, start late again in the afternoon, and work until mid-evening. Their best working hours are from six to nine at night. After that, the social events take over—cocktail parties, dinner parties, dances—the gathering-up of friends, warm, affectionate socializing. At such events you really learn—if you are a diplomat among Latin Americans in Washington, or Buenos Aires, or Mexico City, or Punta del Este—what is going on. Here you learn how much cooperation you will receive;

* Bermudez had come to Punta del Este as an official of International House to arrange the Power Pack for Peace project, which is described in the next chapter.

here you size up possibilities and plan your diplomatic moves for the next day.

Here Bungalow No. 50, where Mario Bermudez stayed because of lack of hotel accommodations, proved an oasis in a desert. The weather was forbidding; the usual places of entertainment were closed; the hotels—there were two in town—were small, it was almost impossible to receive or entertain in one's room. Bungalow No. 50, with its hi-fi, bar, kitchen complete with cook, and cheerful fireplaces, became a stopping-off place for many Latins between and after formal sessions. Although each night a different delegation gave an enormous party at the Cantegril Country Club, this was attended by a thousand people, and it was almost impossible to do more than greet a friend and go on to another. But at Bermudez' bungalow (which we also used as working headquarters for the Power Pack for Peace project), it was possible to relax and talk. We were fortunate, too, that nearby was the villa of Mr. and Mrs. Max de Bomchil, who were among several prominent Buenos Aires families that had opened their villas for the duration of the meeting. They frequently had us and our friends as guests. Thus in a relaxed atmosphere, I was able to see such friends as Carlos Sanz de Santamaria, finance minister of Colombia, twice Colombian ambassador to Washington;* Costa Rican Ambassador Manuel G. Escalante; Dr. Roberto T. Alemann, Argentine's immensely personable economics minister, later Argentine ambassador to the United States; Guillermo Sevilla-Sacasa, Nicaraguan ambassador to the United States and dean of the diplomatic colony in Washington; and many others.

Frequently friends from the United States dropped in. These included James McCloud, President of Industrias Kaiser Argentina; Bill Doherty, vice-president of the AFL-CIO;† Blair Bolles, vice-president of Fairbanks, Morse and Company; and other business and labor leaders who, because of their interests in Latin America, had come to Punta del Este as observers and were regularly briefed by our delegation.

Here we saw world events much more through the eyes of our Latin American friends. In the first week of the conference, while the Soviet space achievements and the Berlin Wall occupied the

* Señor Sanz de Santamaria is O.A.S. Chief of the Inter-American Committee for the Alliance for Progress.

† Bill Doherty is United States ambassador to Jamaica.

international press, in our little Latin American world of Bungalow No. 50, the most sensational news was the political implications of the latest plane-hijacking incident. A twenty-seven-year-old Castroite named Alberto Charles Cadon, of French-Algerian descent, had broken into the cockpit of a Pan American plane flying from Mexico City to Guatemala, and forced the pilot at gunpoint to change his course to Havana. When the plane landed there, it was discovered that among the seventy-three passengers was Colombian Foreign Minister Julio César Turbay Ayala, one of Castro's most outspoken enemies. When Castro learned whom he had netted, he drove at once to the airport, apologized profusely to Turbay—now almost purple with indignation—and immediately ordered the plane and all passengers released. What delighted us was that we knew that Foreign Minister Turbay was not on a routine journey but on a secret mission, on behalf of Colombia, to round up support among Latin American countries for future O.A.S. action against Castro. Nothing could have been calculated to strengthen Turbay's hand, or to mortify Castro more, than to have this indignity heaped upon the Colombian Foreign Minister.

Most Latin American countries would have liked to move against the Cuban regime, but feared to do so, some because Fidelismo elements at home might be stirred up, others because they might be denounced as lackeys of the United States. It was clear to us that our problem would be: At what point could we persuade the hemisphere to act against Castro; and how could we, the United States, with the abortive Bay of Pigs behind us, help bring this about without being charged with intervention?

How sensitive the issues were, how we could be held up on a mere choice of words because they might be interpreted as aimed at one republic or another, was emphasized in the struggle over the Preamble of the Charter of Punta del Este. The United States delegation wanted to state clearly that the Alliance was established on the principle that "free men working through the democratic institution of free and repeated elections would best satisfy man's aspirations." Brazil took exception. This was an economic conference, they said, and our statement was a political statement. If we would not say "free and repeated elections," but put it in other terms, they would go along. Finally it was suggested: "free men working through the institution of representative democracy," the Brazilians arguing that if one supports the institution of representative democracy, one means free elections repeatedly held.

"Why fear the word 'free'?" we asked.

It led to an all-night debate. In the end, the Brazilian view was supported. Our delegation later was criticized for having "backed down." But we felt the final declaration was substantially the same, and it was better to go ahead with it than risk losing not only Brazil, but Argentina, and perhaps other neutral countries. The debate, even more sharply, underlined these difficulties. John Moore, with the typical impatience of the red-haired Irishman that he is, snapped: "I'm sick to my stomach. Why can't we say what we mean!" I could only reply that this was the kind of frustration one had to learn to live with.

Another matter concerned me personally. As United States delegate, I would take my place as the member of a four-man O.A.S. ambassadorial team to go to the Dominican Republic, shortly after the Punta del Este meeting, to investigate the situation there. In 1960 the O.A.S. had imposed political and economic sanctions against the Trujillo government.* (This was precisely the penalty I wanted imposed, sooner or later, upon Cuba.) Sanctions, in this case, stringently limited trade and diplomatic relations of all the O.A.S. countries with the Dominican Republic. But now Trujillo was dead of an assassin's bullet, and President Joaquin Balaguer was attempting to restore political freedoms that had been crushed for thirty-one years; as a result of sanctions, a series of chain reactions had taken place, the consequence of which was economic distress for the Dominican people; the entire situation there was confused and unclear. At our final briefing at the White House before leaving for Punta del Este, Mr. Kennedy had said to me privately, "The Dominican Republic delegation will undoubtedly sign the Charter at Punta del Este. They will be part of the Alliance for Progress." Since we had no diplomatic relations with the country, protocol required that I was not to talk or fraternize with their delegation.

* The O.A.S. Foreign Ministers Meeting at San José, Costa Rica, on August 20, 1960, had voted sanctions against the Dominican Republic because Trujillo had been involved in a plot to assassinate President Romulo Betancourt of Venezuela. In June 1960, a bomb exploded in Betancourt's car, his chauffeur was killed, but he escaped with slight injuries. Sanctions are voted upon a country when it is deemed a threat to hemisphere security.

But, said Mr. Kennedy, "I'd like you to arrange to maintain some kind of liaison with them within the limits of diplomatic practices. I don't want them to think we are their enemy." Thus, among those I saw was Dominican Finance Minister Ortiz, who assured me that his country would support our views and would sign the Charter of Punta del Este as a good partner of the Alliance. I said I looked forward hopefully to matters being recitfied in his country in the near future if democratization was truly effective. Whether this was in accord with the President's terms—"within the limits of diplomatic practices"—I don't know. But I did it: I was asked to do it.

The informality of our bungalow in those short periods when we could relax delighted the ambassadors. Of all the social gatherings ours were the gayest and most friendly. The ambassadors might stroll in to find young Symington curled up in a chair with his guitar, strumming his favorite folk ballads. Jim, one of the most intellectually curious in the delegation, and genuinely interested in Latin culture, spent much time among the people of the country. He was one of our most attractive ambassadors of good will. One evening, when about a dozen guests were present, Jim entertained for hours, playing most beautiful songs that were pure Americana, out of our early West—folk songs, cowboy songs and ballads—accompanying himself to great effect. The ambassadors were deeply moved. For some, early United States history was all violence and exploitation. "Only now do I believe North Americans have a soul," one colleague told me with great seriousness. Or the ambassadors might wander into the kitchen of the de Bomchil villa to find Dick Goodwin working over a frying pan, trying a new kind of omelette, the recipe for which had been given him by Zarita de Bomchil herself.

If Che Guevara was the center of attention, so, too, was Dick Goodwin. The rumor had already spread through Punta del Este that Dick was Kennedy's intimate. Like Kennedy, he had gone to Harvard; he spoke with almost the same Bostonian accent. A onetime law clerk in Supreme Court Justice Frankfurter's office, he was obviously a brilliant young man. Dick neither confirmed nor denied that he was the personal emissary of the President of the United States. I felt that he was feeling himself out. He sat at our parties, smoking his cigar, his dark, quick eyes alert, nearly always surrounded by people. The ladies, particularly, lionized him. They saw on him the magical Kennedy imprint. He talked with many persons, and interviewed key people, so that others thought he was undoubtedly conveying private information as to what Kennedy wanted, and this added to the aura about him. He was intrigued by Che. In a way, they held similar positions. Both were aggressive, free-wheeling, impatient; and each informally had the ear of his chief.

Once, toward the end of the meeting, as Dick and I entered the lobby of the conference hall, we saw Che, just arrived for session. While the rest of the *barbudos* held back a respectful distance, Che stood in the center of an admiring group of ladies, having his picture taken with them, exuding charm in all directions. Dick said, "I'd like to pick that fellow's brains and find out what makes him tick."

I could understand his curiosity, but I shook my head. For Richard Goodwin, President Kennedy's closest adviser on Latin American affairs, to be seen talking with Major Ernesto Guevara, the Marxist mastermind behind Fidel Castro, would shake most of the chancelleries of Latin America. I wondered whether Dick, yet to mark his thirtieth birthday, knew that in this company of Latin American diplomats, both of the left and right, he was surrounded by, and competing with, some of the shrewdest, most cynical and most experienced politicians in the world. These men, growing up in the pressure cooker of Latin American politics, bilingual and trilingual, knowing intimately the personalities of their political friends and enemies, socially at home with them, aware exactly how family and marital circumstances influenced relations among presidents, foreign ministers and ambassadors, conscious of strengths, weaknesses and *quid-pro-quos* unknown to outsiders, playing the game of international politics like chess masters, were formidable opponents. Pitted against them on their home boards—trying to understand them, to anticipate their moves, to counter their gambits and traps—even the most adroit American intellectual must find himself again and again stalemated and even checkmated.

I said aloud, "Dick, all I can say is, I'm steering clear of him. We just shouldn't have a thing to do with that bunch."

Dick chewed thoughtfully on his cigar. "Well, I don't know—" he said. "I'd still like to know what goes on behind that beard."

The fact was that Dick knew as well as I that no one in the United States delegation was to have anything to do with Guevara.

There had been rumors of secret meetings between Guevara and some of us. These were not true. John Leddy, who briefed the press, said categorically in an off-the-record session that "no member of the United States delegation had or will have any contact, even of a social character, with Guevara." This had been rigidly followed. None of us recognized the existence of the Cubans. When President Haedo gave a state dinner and we found ourselves seated at the same table, we were still completely remote. Only the iciest inclination of the head had indicated that we had ever seen the Cubans before.

Dick and I continued into the meeting, and the subject did not come up again.

I had no idea, that evening of Wednesday, August 16, when the conference went into the night session in which Che angrily denounced us and Dillon retorted that Cuba had "inundated" us with lies, that Dick Goodwin and Che Guevara were scheduled to meet secretly that evening.

From the very first day, Guevara had started a subtle campaign to meet one of us. The most powerful weapon Castro could use to establish his Communist state securely in Latin America, and give his agents free hand on the continent, was to prove, or show, or suggest, that the United States privately was not opposed to such coexistence in the hemisphere—or, at least, was prepared to discuss it. This would make ridiculous all United States strictures against Castro; it would make ridiculous Colombia's attempt to round up anti-Castro support among the other republics; it would completely pull the rug from under every hemisphere attempt to fight Communism. Guevara, to be sure, made no strong effort to contact Dillon. There was little to hope for from that highly sophisticated Wall Street banker, nor was there much hope in Bob Woodward or me. He knew, however, that Dick was intrigued, that Dick was curious. He concentrated on Dick Goodwin.

The rumors of secret meetings were part of his campaign. Two days before the conference ended, Che made an overt move. He sent a box of Havana cigars to Dick with a note in Spanish: "As writing to an enemy is difficult—and I am not good at writing—I hereby extend my hand." Meanwhile, he had approached several Brazilian delegates to act as go-betweens to bring him and Dick together. The Brazilians were in a good position to play this role. Since President Quadros of Brazil admired Castro, they had no compunction about being seen with Guevara. To cover their tracks, however, they, in turn, used Argentine delegates as go-betweens to contact Dick. Three times the Brazilian-Argentine combine arranged a time and place for Goodwin and Guevara to meet, and three times, for one reason or another, the meeting was not held. Dick, it was understood, was reluctant to go over Dillon's head—but he remained curious. The third time was Wednesday night, August 16. The Brazilians arranged a small supper party at the Cantegril Country Club. Che and Dick were invited separately—Che by the Brazilians, Dick by the Argentinians. Had the two men come there, they would have been brought quietly together. But this fell through when the conference went into its long and violent night session.

Next morning, August 17, the Charter was formally signed. That afternoon I hastened to fly back to the States—most of the delegates remained in nearby Montevideo for a day or two of rest—but I had two weeks of military reserve duty to carry out in Louisiana, and I was already four days late.

Toward midnight that night Dick Goodwin was having a snack in a Montevideo bar with Horacio Rodriguez Laretta, a member of the Argentine delegation to Punta, and adviser to Foreign Minister Adolfo Mugica of Argentina. A Brazilian delegate sauntered in. He said he knew of an entertaining party going on in the apartment of Gerson Augusto de Silva, another Brazilian delegate, who was celebrating his birthday with an open house. Everyone was invited. Why not go there?

Goodwin agreed. The three men went to de Silva's apartment on the ground floor of 1103 Avenida de Julio, in downtown Montevideo. There he found among the guests another Brazilian delegate, Edmundo Barboza da Silva, special counselor to Foreign Minister Afonso Arinos of Brazil, a handful of other delegates, and two Brazilian newspapermen.

At about this time Che Guevara was waiting in the lobby of a nearby hotel. Shortly before one o'clock, an Argentine delegate called for him in an automobile and drove him to the apartment.

This is the story of that then-secret conference, as I learned it: Dick and Che shook hands formally. There were now in one room the adviser to the President of the United States; the adviser to the Premier of Cuba; the adviser to the foreign minister of Brazil; the adviser to the foreign minister of Argentina.* Now Dick and Che, with Barboza da Silva and Rodriguez Laretta, adjourned to a back room, closed the door, and began their conversation.

Guevara opened the talk with a smile. "Shall this meeting be conducted as between enemies meeting on neutral territory, or as between two private individuals who wish to discuss a common problem?"

Dick, brusquely: "As between enemies. I must also remind you that I am not authorized to speak in the name of President Kennedy or in the name of the American people."

Still smiling, Guevara said he was pleased with the "North American authorities," because by backing the invasion at the Bay of Pigs, they had given the Castro regime a military victory and the opportunity to enhance its prestige throughout the world.

Goodwin replied, with equal irony, that the same could not be said for Cuba, which failed to attack Guantanamo Base, for had it done so, the United States reprisal would have meant a United States victory.

Guevara, at this, turned serious. Under no circumstances, he said, would Cuba attack the United States base at Guantanamo Bay. Cuba wanted to talk things over with the United States, negotiate all points of difference. "We are ready," he said, "to enter into negotiations with the United States because we want to find a solution to all our common problems, but we will do this under one condition: that there be no prior conditions." What Guevara was demanding was United States recognition of the Castro government, of Cuba's economic and political regime. He added that his country was ready to indemnify the owners of United States sugar plantations, factories and other properties that Castro had expropriated, the indemnification to be in Cuban goods.

Goodwin, who had remained noncommittal throughout the dis-

---

* I tell this story in some detail, not only because I have not seen, even in the most bizarre back-room politicking in red-neck Louisiana campaigns, such Alfred Hitchcock goings-on; but also because repercussions of this meeting were to plague us—and me, particularly—for months, and almost cause us to fail in what I consider a major achievement of the Kennedy administration: the ousting of Cuba by the O.A.S. from the inter-American society.

cussion, said simply, "I will report this to Washington"; now he added that he doubted the United States would be willing to negotiate with Castro.

"But the simple exchange of hijacked planes could open the door to such negotiations," Guevara said. Cuba wanted peace, he went on; it was busy fighting counterrevolutionaries—he suggested that he believed these forces were financed by North American interests—but Cuba wanted the United States and all the American republics to realize that the Cuban revolution was here to stay. "It is not reversible at this late hour," he declared. And he added, "I hope you realize that we are no longer in the United States sphere of influence."

Was Cuba today in anybody else's sphere of influence, Goodwin asked.

Guevara replied, "We do not have, nor do we intend to have, any political or military alliance with anyone unless we are pressed toward it." He made an offer: if the United States would promise not to attack Cuba again, Cuba would make no military or political alliances. In the course of his talk, he described the Castro regime as "socialist."

Shortly after 2 A.M. the four men emerged from the room. The conference had lasted a little over an hour. Goodwin left; Guevara remained. The newspapermen were sworn not to reveal that the advisers to Kennedy and Castro had met.

Che, with this under his belt, hurried from Montevideo to nearby Buenos Aires. There he met secretly again, this time with President Frondizi of Argentina; and on the same mission—coexistence in the hemisphere. Here, as well, everyone was sworn to secrecy.

Despite these pledges, word of Frondizi's meeting with Guevara leaked out. It caused a sensation. The Argentine military—vehemently anti-Castro and particularly bitter toward Guevara, who once wrote a manual explaining how citizens can take over the military—exploded in anger. The uproar was so intense that President Frondizi was forced to make a fireside TV chat to his people and reiterate that Argentina was pro-Western and democratic. But, significantly, when the question was repeatedly flung at him, "How could you possibly meet with Guevara?" he finally retorted, "If the United States could meet with Major Guevara, how could I refuse to see him?" With this news, Foreign Minister Adolfo Mugica—

whose adviser, Rodriguez Laretta, had brought Goodwin to Che Guevara—was attacked so bitterly that he was forced to resign.

Meanwhile, sowing disorder in his wake, Che Guevara had gone from Argentina to Brazil, where President Quadros not only greeted him enthusiastically, but decorated him with Brazil's highest order, the Cruzeiro do Sul. The reaction compared only to what had taken place in Argentina. Newspapers wrote furious editorials. The Cruzeiro do Sul was given only to foreigners who rendered distinctive service to Brazil. What distinctive service had Che Guevara—"this false Cuban and authentic Communist"—rendered to Brazil? Among the most violent attacks on Quadros was that of Carlos Lacerda, a former newspaper publisher, Governor of Guanabara State (in which Rio is located) and a powerful force. Lacerda had been chief among those who helped to drive President Getulio Vargas, seven years before, to commit suicide. (I had seen Vargas and talked with him only a few hours before his death.)* To many, Lacerda was Brazil's conscience.

Quadros's reply was to send an abrupt letter of resignation to Congress. He drove to a military airport, saying he was going into exile; but he remained in the plane for some five hours, waiting, it was said, for Brazilian leaders to plead with him to reconsider. When nothing happened, Quadros had no alternative but to fly off to exile. He was succeeded by leftist Vice-President João "Jango" Goulart, forty-three—the same Goulart who nearly three years later, in April 1964, was ousted in a sensational military coup after bringing Brazil to the brink of Communism.†

One understands this chess game only if one understands the following:

1. Castro's strategy—and Che Guevara's—was to win approval for, and to soften, strong policy against Castro wherever it existed.

2. Rodriguez Laretta, who brought Goodwin to Guevara, was a close associate of Rogelio Frigerio, the pro-Castro adviser of President Frondizi of Argentina. Frondizi, at heart, was pro–United States. But many believed that Frigerio, an enigmatic figure who represented the Peronista party in Argentina, was Frondizi's "gray

---

* See Chapter XIV.

† Goulart had been a protégé of Vargas and was Secretary of Labor in his Cabinet.

eminence" and had enormous power over him. Thus, although Frondizi was anti-Castro and pro-West, he was constantly pushed in the other direction by Frigerio, who had a considerable following in Argentina.

3. By making it possible for Guevara to see Goodwin and make capital of it (despite all United States strategy to prevent such a contact) Laretta and his fellow Frigerioistas were able to exert pressure on President Frondizi to see Che Guevara too.

4. The pro-Castro Brazilians, for their part, then casually leaked the news to the continent that both Goodwin and Frondizi had discussed matters with Che—giving Che (and Castro) increased prestige among the Latin Americans—indeed, to such a point that President Quadros, when Che came there, felt justified in decorating him.

5. In the cold war on the Latin American continent, these three triumphs in swift succession, the first making possible the second and third, represented victory for Castro, Che and Company. It suggested to Latin Americans that accommodation *was* possible with Castro, and disheartened those, north and south of the border, who wanted a hard, not soft, line taken toward Cuba.

Was there a stalemate here? Or even, checkmate?

And there was more to come.

We had not heard the last of Messrs. Quadros, Frondizi, Frigerio, the undercover Argentine and Brazilian agents, their doubletalk, the debate over the hard and soft lines on Castro.

6. PRESIDENT KENNEDY TOWN

To financial experts and the diplomats at Punta del Este, the Alliance for Progress was a historic achievement. But what did it mean to the average farmer or peasant or illiterate citizen in any one of the republics in whose names we had met?

Before we left Punta del Este, thanks to an idea by then Vice-President Johnson, I was able with the cooperation of President Haedo and a number of industrialists to dramatize the Alliance—not only to the people of Punta del Este, but to millions who saw the event over television, here and abroad. It was a project known as Power Pack for Peace—to provide, through the Alliance, a portable power package to backward towns, to give them what they badly needed: water, electricity and transportation.

In its simplest terms, it meant a pack made up of three items: a lighting system operated on a diesel engine, which is inexpensive; a water purification plant with pipe and drilling equipment; and a Jeep with a power take-off that could be used to drill a well, cut wood, and also serve as transportation for town authorities.

The story properly begins the fortnight before I left for Punta del Este, when I spent a July weekend as guest at the Westhampton home of William H. Weintraub, a big, hearty man who had been advertising agency counsel to Henry J. Kaiser. Among other guests were Stephen A. Girard, president of the Kaiser Jeep Corporation, James McCloud, president of Industrias Kaiser Argentina, which makes Jeeps and Kaisers in Argentina; Representative Eugene J. Keough, Democrat, of New York, member of the House Ways and Means Committee; and the late Ted Patrick, editor of *Holiday* Magazine.

Bill Weintraub, speaking casually, remarked that Vice-President Johnson, who had just returned from his trip to India (during which he had invited the much-publicized camel driver to the United States) had told friends about the many backward towns and villages without electricity he had seen there. As a Texas rancher, Johnson knew how expensive it was to establish rural electrification; yet he felt how desperately the Indian villages and towns needed current. Johnson had asked: Did Fairbanks Morse still manufacture those little electrical plants we used to have in Texas? His father had one on their farm, he said, and as a boy his chore was to kick it up at 5 A.M. each morning to furnish electricity for the day. "A little generator like that would be a godsend to some Indian town," the Vice-President added. Whereupon, a month ago, Fairbanks Morse had sent one, as a gift, to a town that Johnson had chosen.

"My gosh," I said to Bill, "There are more than three thousand towns in Latin America without water or electricity." I would be in Uruguay for the conference—why could we not choose such a town near Punta del Este, and make a gift, a "Power Pack for Peace" to dramatize how Alliance money, correctly channeled, could meet basic needs? And why limit it to an electrical unit? Why not water? And transportation? "Besides," I said, becoming fired up by the thought, "the place, the time, the circumstance will be ideal. We shall have the top people of Latin America there—the economists, the opinion makers, the press."

We agreed. Girard arranged for McCloud to provide a Jeep; Bill Weintraub said he would see if Fairbanks Morse would supply the water-purification plant and generators, with technicians to install them. I would enlist the cooperation of President Haedo of Uruguay, to assure that it was carried out under the highest auspices. I realized there was not only a social objective here—to help a community—but a chance to propagandize both the Alliance, and American private enterprise. That was fine with me. We needed private enterprise in Latin America. That was one of the tenets of the Alliance. Because I believed we needed it, I had persuaded Henry Kaiser to come to Latin America seven years before—a trip which resulted in the establishment in Brazil and Argentina of Kaiser enterprises which today are valued at many millions of dollars, are owned 70 per cent by the local people, and are giving employment to more than 30,000 persons.*

From Bill Weintraub's house that afternoon I telephoned our New Orleans representative in Montevideo, Paco Tourreilles, owner of Radio Clarin, Uruguay's principal radio station, and asked him to expedite matters with our mutual friend, President Haedo.

Later, in Punta del Este, Mario Bermudez, Governor Gustavo Salazar of Maldonado department (in which Punta del Este is located) and I drove about one afternoon, after conference sessions, to find a suitable village. We found it—a settlement of some three hundred people that had not even a name, whose inhabitants lived mainly in log huts with thatched roofs. It had no water, no electricity, no transportation. The housewives trudged half a mile to the nearest village each morning for water to fill their buckets, then trudged back, carrying the buckets on their heads.

Next day I brought President Haedo there. He was enthusiastic. The press became excited, too. Stories began to flow back to the States. Presently word came that NBC's *Today* show had requested permission to film the presentation of the Power Pack for Peace for showing in the United States. The presentation, we planned, would take place on a Saturday when there were no meetings of the conference.

To save the village the cost of the customs duties, we arranged for International House, New Orleans, as a nonprofit organization, to be recipient of the gift, and in turn to present it to the village.

The machinery and technicians had been flown down a week before my arrival. Where to dig the town well? Paco Tourreilles recommended that it should be dug in front of the house of Doña Carmen Gutierrez, a warm, motherly woman in her fifties, and the village's leading citizen. Water was found, and the well was dug.

A few evenings after my arrival, as I was sitting with President

---

* The story of the trip with Henry Kaiser which led to the founding of the Kaiser automobile empire in Latin America, is told in Chapter XIV.

Haedo in his lodge, he said, "What shall we call this village, this town?"

"It's up to you, Mr. President," I said.

"It's known now simply as Barrio Bosque—roughly, a 'section in the woods.'"

"That's no name for it," I said.

"Let's call it Pueblo Washington," he suggested—"Washington Town."

"Mr. President, George Washington was a great President, but he is dead. President Kennedy is living."

"Ah, Chepito!" he cried. "Of course, we shall call it Pueblo Kennedy—no, Pueblo Obrero President Kennedy—'President Kennedy Workers' Town.'" He immediately ordered a sign to be painted.

Now much excitement. Two boys were given a scholarship by Fairbanks Morse to enable them to go to the Kaiser plant in Cordova, Argentina, and learn how to operate and maintain the equipment. We erected a platform with bunting—the American and Uruguayan and O.A.S. banners side by side—I arranged that not only all delegates were invited to the presentation ceremonies Saturday at 6 P.M., but also that buses should bring people to the scene from various parts of the country. His Eminence the Archbishop of Montevideo agreed to partake in the ceremonies and give his blessing to the town and its equipment.

Saturday came. As dusk fell we began. President Haedo made a speech; Governor Salazar made a speech; and I spoke. As I reached my last line, "I hope this light will illuminate—" I threw a switch. The town lit up for the first time in its history.

People cheered and wept. The floodlights played on the modest wooden door, trimmed with Coca-Cola bottle caps, of Doña Carmen's house. It opened to show Doña Carmen herself, dressed in her Sunday best, carrying a tray before her with an empty pitcher on it. Majestically she moved forward into the bright lights, approached the well and, while the people waited breathlessly, turned the spigot.

Water—clear, fresh, clean—flowed. Again, cheers. Doña Carmen filled the pitcher, replaced it on the tray, put the tray on her head, and with the bright lights and television cameras on her, approached President Haedo, waiting for her, on the platform.

He leaned over, took the pitcher of water and drank from it. He held it aloft. "I drink this water to show you that it is not only good for you and your children, but it is good also for your President."

Again, cheers and applause.

Then Doña Carmen spoke, very simply. "Today life begins for us. For forty years, every day of my life, I have walked these many kilometers to the next village to bring water. And now the North Americans have brought all this to us in the days of one week."

The Archbishop blessed the Pueblo Obrero President Kennedy, he blessed the equipment, he blessed all of us there. The deed to the bright-blue Jeep, which had an admiring crowd around it, among them Governor Salazar, who seemed hypnotized by it, was ceremoniously presented to Doña Carmen, as head of the town committee. President Haedo announced: "We are a proud people, Ambassador Morrison; we cannot accept gifts," and formally gave me one Uruguayan peso, worth three cents. We concluded the evening's ceremonies with rousing entertainment by Gaucho dancers, and a gigantic *asado,* or outdoor barbecue, at which more than a thousand persons were guests of President Haedo.

Next evening, after being told the gratifying news that through the *Today* show in the United States, and coverage by Brazilian and Argentinian television, an estimated fifty million people saw the presentation, I could not help making a sneak visit back to my little town, to see how it was getting along without the crowds. The lights were on, the pump was working, all was well—but the bright-blue Jeep, which had been parked next to the well in front of Doña Carmen's house, was missing. Doña Carmen herself only shook her head. "It is the Governor," she said. "He has taken it."

I telephoned him. Governor Salazar was most pleasant. "Ah, Mr. Ambassador. Alas, there is no one capable of driving the Jeep in Pueblo Kennedy, and to keep it from harm I myself drove it home last night. It is with me now. Yes, I will see that it is back in the town tomorrow."

Next day I passed President Kennedy town. The Jeep was gone.

Another telephone call. "Mr. Governor, the Jeep belongs to the town. It was given to the town for its needs."

"Yes, yes," said the Governor. "To be sure it will be there tomorrow."

Tomorrow, unfortunately, we left for the United States.

I had no idea that I would be back in Punta del Este again, but five months later, when the O.A.S. foreign-ministers conference was held, I found myself once more there. I drove to President Kennedy town. It had grown almost double in size. There stood Doña Carmen's house. An addition had been built to it, decorated not only with Coca-Cola tops, but shining beer covers. The Jeep was missing.

"It is the Governor," Doña Carmen said resignedly. "I have called him again and again to ask for it, to take some villagers to the hospital, but he keeps it."

I appealed to President Haedo this time. There was an interchange of telephone calls. "He will return it now," said the President. "I have his assurance." He chuckled. "Who is to know what a man's weakness is?"

A third time I came to Uruguay—in October 1962—to address the Inter-American Municipal Organization Conference. A beaming Governor Salazar met me at the airport in his car. The Jeep was not in evidence. En route to Punta del Este, we passed by President Kennedy town. I glimpsed the Jeep, standing where it belonged.

When our conference was over, I paid a courtesy call on Doña Carmen. No Jeep. "Mr. Ambassador," said Doña Carmen, arms akimbo, "the Jeep was here the day you drove by with Governor Salazar, and that is the only time I have seen it since the night it was presented to us." She was no longer chairman of the town committee. Governor Salazar had removed her because of the complaints about the Jeep.

I called the Governor. Apologetically he explained he had been using it "for urgent matters of state." I exploded. "It was not given to the state, sir! It was given to Pueblo Obrero President Kennedy. You are guilty of misappropriating property. In my country that is punishable by a prison sentence. I advise you, sir, to return that Jeep at once!"

He returned it.

A few weeks after that, in the Uruguayan elections, he was roundly defeated. There is no doubt in my mind that his uncontrollable passion for the bright-blue Jeep was his undoing.

7. THE PRESIDENT, THE STATE DEPARTMENT— AND TROUBLE IN THE CARIBBEAN

Not until some time after Punta del Este did I know about the Goodwin-Guevara meeting, and then whatever anger and frustration I felt as the whole story, with its overtones and undertones became known to me, I had to swallow. What had been done in the field in which I had to operate ran counter to everything I felt was good political strategy. I would have to meet it by my own devices.

I was learning certain facts of life with respect to the Kennedy administration. A certain theory had come in with Mr. Kennedy. Traditionally, policy is set by the President and is carried out by the State Department. The Kennedy administration, I began to realize, had altered this sharply. Now it was set by the White House but carried out by Mr. Kennedy's executive assistants, often without the State Department or Congress being involved.

Kennedy, because of his admiration for ideas, his intellectual approach to government, his determination to get things done, attacked long-seated problems with the strategy of an impatient, vigorous young man. He surrounded himself with like minds, men who like him slashed impatiently, even highhandedly, through red tape to get to first causes.

He believed that State Department career men were not necessarily the persons to solve the problems before him. He wanted young intellectuals who were also activists—men who blended thought and action—who could take a quick survey course in the field to which they were assigned, master it, then act, allowing subordinates to deal with such picayune matters as protocol, hurt feelings, and even national outrage. In some cases, the people Kennedy surrounded himself with simply moved into existing vacuums.

I was certain that Dick Goodwin had moved into the Latin American vacuum in the White House. It was in abeyance; no one was dealing with it; so Goodwin ended up with it. The result was that Assistant Secretary Bob Woodward, who had spent thirty years learning the intricacies of Latin America, found himself cast in the role of a technician, feeding information to the White House, where Goodwin made many of the actual decisions.

I don't know that John F. Kennedy ever stated his theory in so many words. I do know that he cared little for tables of organization. I believe he believed that power seeks its own level; that the stronger personality wins out; that policy can be best set by a strong personality, by the man who comes to the top in the power struggle. You are appointed to a position, and you are either made or broken by that position. If you grasp power, all to the good. The only mistake is to make a mistake.

However, even here the situation was complicated by subtle factors that had little to do with politics. For example, if you are a presidential aide and your office—as was the case with Goodwin, Schlesinger, Rostow—is in the White House, a few feet away from the President's, you can drop in, present a proposal concerning a course of action—or explain why a course of action wasn't successful—and emerge whole.

But if you are not on the White House staff but in the State Department, to get an idea to the President, you must go through an assistant secretary, who must sell it to an undersecretary and/or the Secretary, before it ever reaches the White House, where it probably must start out again on the level of a presidential aide. Then it is a long way, indeed, to the President's ear. And this can cause many frustrations.

President Kennedy spoke briskly. "Gentlemen, if we can get through the first year of this administration without losing the

Dominican Republic or the Congo to the Iron Curtain countries, I shall consider it a good year in the foreign field."

It was early September, three weeks after Punta del Este, and we were meeting in the Cabinet Room, perhaps a score in all—Secretary of State Rusk; Attorney General Bobby Kennedy; Assistant Secretary of State Bob Woodward; General Richard Bissell, of the Central Intelligence Agency; Steve Smith, the President's brother-in-law, working in a special section of the State Department called "Operations"; Sargent Shriver; my alternate Ed Jamison, who also headed the Regional Political Section of the Bureau of Inter-American Affairs; and several others.

In a few days I was to leave with three other ambassadors—those of Panama, Ecuador and Colombia—to carry on an O.A.S. investigation of the Dominican Republic, to determine whether President Joaquin Balaguer's "democratization" measures were sufficiently effective to warrant removal of the diplomatic and economic sanctions. This meeting with President Kennedy was to brief us all, and specifically to give me my terms of reference as the United States member of the O.A.S. team.

Bobby Kennedy had arrived late, and he took a seat next to the President. I had concluded, some time before, that if the matter was one in which the President took a deep interest, one would find The Family—the first team—on hand. This was the case now.

The meeting began with only State Department officials present. Then, one by one the family began to arrive. I knew then that it was top level, and a certain machinery was being set in motion. Steve Smith's designation—"Operations"—was a cryptic term for private liaison work. Bobby was always at his brother's side in these matters. The President would make a decision; and in the days that followed, the family branched out and checked up to see that things were moving as the President wished.

The President opened the meeting by stating that the Dominican Republic was crucial to us. The way we handled this situation would affect the entire hemisphere. Over the years Trujillo had forged the country into a monolithic organization so well put together, authority so perfectly centralized, that the entire nation could be seized overnight by a powerful hand and become its instrument. Were this to be a Communist hand, the country would become Communist. Were it the military right, the country would become a military dictatorship of the right. At this moment, it was extremely vulnerable.

The Dominican Republic was, in many ways, a small carbon copy of Cuba. It lay close to our shores; it was an island republic; it was a sugar economy; it had a large Negro population, a large Spanish population; it had suffered from a long, cruel dictatorship. The parallels—geographical, political, historical—were startling. Another Cuba in the Caribbean would be an utter disaster for us.

Matters were in crisis now, because under President Balaguer's liberalization process, political groupings of every coloration were springing up. This was desirable. We encouraged it. But the consequent confusion, the people's long removal—more than three decades—from democratic liberties, the unemployment and mass economic distress flowing from the sanctions—all these made for a critical situation. In June an O.A.S. investigating team had been sent to probe charges on the spot of police terror following Trujillo's assassination. It had returned after ten days to report that there were hopeful signs the country might move toward democracy, but it was too early to reach any firm conclusion. But for thirty years, one had to remember, every important figure in the government, the judiciary, the army, the police, the newspapers, had been put in by the Trujillos. The people wanted to wipe the slate clean and were ripe for demagoguery.

This erupted early in July. Nearly 10,000 persons, mainly students, met in a rally in the capital city, Ciudad Trujillo. The meeting began peacefully enough. The National Civic Union, which called it, was the largest opposition political group—pro-United States, anti-Communist, antimilitarist. Its final speaker, however, was Maximo Lopez Molina, a Castro follower, who had just returned from exile in Cuba—one of the twelve known Communists allowed to return as part of the restoration of all political freedoms. Lopez Molina according to spectators incited the crowd to such antigovernment fury that it marched upon Radio Caribe, the government-owned station, poured gasoline over the premises and burned it down. A dozen students were injured. A few hours later a pro-government mob raced through the streets seeking Lopez Molina, broke into his apartment and, when they did not find him there, reduced it to a shambles. At last reports, he was in hiding.

The situation had simmered dangerously on into September. Our new four-nation O.A.S. team was to go to the Dominican Republic, take testimony, judge the temper of the people and the stability of its government, decide whether the country was still a menace to the security of the hemisphere, and recommend continuation or removal of sanctions.

For the meeting with Mr. Kennedy, our Bureau of Inter-American Affairs had prepared a memorandum, copies of which were distributed to us. It listed ten items, among them: ought we to elevate the rank of our military attaché in the Dominican Republic; ought we to increase the size of our military contingent there; ought the C.I.A. add to its intelligence personnel on the scene; what should be our attitude toward President Balaguer and toward Rafael "Ramfis" Trujillo, Jr., eldest son of the late dictator, and chief of the armed forces? Item by item, we went down the list, the President reading each aloud, then looking up to hear our opinion. It was decided that we should encourage Balaguer to continue his democratization process. We realized antagonism existed toward him and young Trujillo, since both were identified with the late dictatorship. But if they could maintain law and order, keep the military in line—here Ramfis* could be most effective, for his father had always treated the military as an elite—and so carry the troubled nation through to the elections scheduled for May 16, 1962, all would be well. A team of O.A.S. technicians was already recommending election procedures. Under Dictator Trujillo these had been a farce. All workers in the country belonged to one party, the Partido Dominicano. Party dues—10 per cent of one's salary—were automatically deducted from one's wages. The P.D. controlled newspapers, radio stations, employers' organizations, shopkeepers, trade unions; there was no competition. Balaguer had invited the O.A.S. election analysts—one from the United States, one from Colombia and one from Panama—to come to the Dominican Republic and set up the machinery for the first free elections in thirty years.

High on our memo in the White House meeting was an all-important question, what to do about Communist activity in the country. General Bissell gave us a list of twelve Moscow-trained Communists whom the C.I.A. felt strongly the Dominican Govern-

* Young Trujillo, thirty-two, dark-eyed, dark-skinned, somber, was nicknamed "Ramfis" because friends thought he was the image of the glowering Egyptian prince in *Aida*.

ment should deport. All were active there on the political scene. We discussed this delicate question at some length. Political freedom was the very essence of Balaguer's democratization. Yet the threat of a Communist take-over . . . President Kennedy turned to me, his mind made up. "Chep, please talk privately to President Balaguer. Tell him it's a message from me. You'll be there, of course, as an O.A.S. member, but arrange to see him on a U.S. mission. Tell him that I would very much like to see him expel *at once* the twelve men on this list."

When I left the Cabinet Room, I thought I had a clear picture of my duties in the Dominican Republic. Next morning, at a State Department staff meeting, I found some of those present still debating the issues.

"Wait a minute," I said, "I thought the President made a decision on this—why debate it now?" Whereupon one man, who must remain nameless, spoke up. "Yes, but we have to protect the President."

"You have to *protect* the President?" I must have sounded as astonished as I really was. "Against what?"

"Against his mistakes," was the reply.

"Oh, no," I said. "I can't buy that. If we say we're going to protect the President and then overrule him on the ground that we're protecting him—" I shook my head. "I'm going down to the Dominican Republic to represent the United States. I have my answers. Don't confuse me, please."

The aftermath of this particular phase of my story may be told here. I broke up my two-week visit to the Dominican Republic to return, on the first weekend, to Washington, for the state reception for President Manuel Prado of Peru. I attended a White House dinner in honor of the Peruvian chief executive. After dinner we were in the smoking room with the men when President Kennedy came up to me and, with a characteristic punch on my shoulder, pulled me aside. "Chep, who is this fellow who said he had to protect me against my mistakes?"

I tried to pass it off. "He didn't exactly put it that way, Mr. President. He was trying to say that maybe there would be something you wouldn't know."

The President, quite serious, said, "That's the trouble with some of these people. I read a book the other day that talked about how little influence the President has. Chep, I'd like to know who it was."

I felt myself turning red. I did not want to tell him. "Please, Mr. President, don't ask me, because I can't tell you. I don't think he meant any harm—he was merely trying to reason with these decisions and perhaps that's part of the system." I knew the President understood what I had in mind. Presidents and presidential appointees come and go, but the personnel of the State Department remains, and they think about the system and how things, in their opinion, should be done, and what channels should be used, and by whom.

The President would not be put off. He continued to prod, and I continued to resist: "I just can't do it." And presently other persons were about him and I was released from my special torture.

Next day we had a luncheon at the Pan American Union for President Prado. This is customary. First, the White House dinner, then a luncheon given by the O.A.S. In the middle of the luncheon, Sargent Shriver brushed against me. "Chep, I was talking to the Chief at breakfast this morning. He wanted to know who it was."

"Sarge, don't ask me, please," I said, almost pleadingly. "I have to live in the system. If you force me to squeal on someone, I'll simply destroy my future working arrangements, and I need these people, I need their technical brains—"

Sarge said, "I'm going to be telling the President, and he's going to be calling you on this." And he was off, with a grin.

I knew I would escape that inquisition because I had to leave early next morning to return to the Dominican Republic, where I still had a week more to examine the complex and tragic situation there with my colleagues.

At four o'clock that afternoon, when I returned to my office, Steve Smith was waiting for me. "Chep, this fellow who said—"

I laughed. "Oh, no," I said, and I shook my head. "You're not getting it out of me."

Whether Mr. Kennedy called next day I do not know, for by dawn I was on a plane returning to my assignment.

I can only look back on our committee's arrival in the Dominican Republic, the week before, as memorable. We landed at 1 P.M., Tuesday, September 12: four ambassadors—Augusto Guillermo ("Bill") Arango, of Panama; Gonzalo Escudero, of Ecuador; Alberto

Zuleta Angel, of Colombia; and myself—plus four alternates, aides and staff, on a special plane from Washington.

The reception that was given us here was quite different from the one I had witnessed at Montevideo a few weeks before. Here, at the airport outside of Ciudad Trujillo, we were welcomed with wild enthusiasm. An excited, cheering crowd of some two thousand people was waving little O.A.S. flags and carrying banners that read "Welcome O.A.S." "Democracy, yes! Fidelismo, no!" "Viva the P.D." "Balaguer guarantees us freedom and work!" But as we came in for our landing, there, in a little street outside the airport, I saw the telltale row of parked buses. This effusive, unified support of the government and of us had been engineered. For, as we soon learned, nine miles distant, where the road from the airport to Ciudad Trujillo traversed the Rhadames Bridge, an angry crowd of nearly four thousand was being held back by police. They had demonstrated all morning in the city; then, waving antigovernment banners, they began a march on the airport to meet us. The police halted them at the bridge, under orders from President Balaguer; there they now waited, milling about, addressed by one leader, then another.

Meanwhile, at the airport we were formally greeted by Dr. Carlos Federico Perez y Perez, Undersecretary of State for Foreign Affairs, and other government officials, and we entered limousines to take us to the city. Bill Arango and I got into the first car, Escudero and Zuleta Angel in the second, my alternate, Bill Bowdler, an extremely brilliant political expert, and another alternate in the third, and our cavalcade was about to set off, when a government car, a sub-machine gun protruding from a window, roared by. About ten o'clock that morning the car had passed through the waiting crowd —there were conflicting reports of what happened, some said the people, recognizing it as belonging to the Trujillo family, attacked the car with a barrage of stones and bricks, others that they halted it and shouted insults at the occupants. In any case, one of the men inside leaped out and began to shoot, and a bullet struck and killed a well-known Dominican physician. The entire city was tense.

There was nothing to do but go ahead. We started off and sped toward Ciudad Trujillo at sixty miles an hour. From our dashboard radio a breathless voice in Spanish was describing our arrival: the P.D. crowd at the airport, the elaborate speeches, our departure from the airport, the huge crowd awaiting us at the Rhadames Bridge. "They are waving banners reading: 'Down with the Trujillos!' and 'Down with Balaguer'" came the announcer's voice. Then, after a pause: "They are waving another banner: 'Morrison con los Trujillos!' ('Morrison is with the Trujillos')."

I looked at Bill Arango wryly. I was not too astonished. The Trujillo decoration, no matter how long ago, no matter how explained, was hard to live down, especially in this tragic country today. I said, "Bill, we're going to have a time of it. They've put on a real production for us—both sides."

Arango smiled grimly. "They gathered up the people, stuck them in buses, put flags in their hands. But when we reach that bridge, we'll just have to take what happens."

Save for a motorcycle escort on either side of us, our lead car was unprotected as we drove swiftly toward Ciudad Trujillo. The announcer's voice came—violent fighting now at the bridge. Weeks ago, to protect human life, President Balaguer had disarmed the police and equipped them instead with sticks, and the police were fighting the crowd with these, struggling to restrain them.

I thought about Nixon being stoned in Caracas, and for a moment I had to fight off a chill of fear. It was a curious experience. I thought, simultaneously, of Nixon, and of the afternoon, so long ago in this same country, when I sat with Trujillo and described a World War II action to him. Sitting now in the limousine bearing down on the city, the same icy fear struck at my stomach, a queasy feeling I had not known since the days when I was under fire in Normandy.

I had little time to think about it. We roared around a turn and the Rhadames Bridge—the entire scene—was spread before us. The mob had broken through police lines; a mass of humanity was pouring down on the road, which paralleled the sea, blocking it completely.

Then we were in the midst of it. The banners waved madly: "We are starving!" "Give us Liberty!" Our car came to a sharp halt before the press of bodies. Shouting, screaming, fighting to get at us, to talk and scream and wave their banners at us, the mob completely engulfed our car. They began rocking it from side to side. Fortunately, it was a heavy Cadillac and not easy to overturn. Suddenly, at my window, inches from my face, appeared the hideous, bloody face of a dead man. The body, draped in a Dominican flag, was held aloft by a dozen raised hands, and on its chest was pinned a scrawled sign in huge letters: "MUERTO POR DE TRUJILLOS! (MURDERED BY THE TRUJILLOS!)." It was the body of the physician who had been shot that morning. The crowd had refused to give it up to the police; for three hours they had been carrying it about, waiting until they could exhibit it to us. For a nightmare space of minutes we were held there, the car rocking, the dead man, his nose almost mashed against my window, the staring eyes open, and the crowd screaming and cursing, the dead face staring at me.

Slowly we began to move. Fists were pounding on the hood, the sides of our car. "Brutality!" the voices cried. "Liberty!" "Down with the Trujillos!" We began to gather speed. The two motorcycle policemen alongside our front wheels literally forced their way—and us—through the crowd. It must have taken us ten minutes to move a hundred feet. But once we got beyond the crowd, we moved rapidly again.

At that moment, as I was about to turn to Ambassador Arango, I felt a sharp blow on my shoulder. A rock hurled at us had smashed my window—still smeared with the dead man's blood—and struck me. I had hardly heard the crash of glass. If a rock could hit me on the shoulder, it could hit me on the head. I ducked forward, to protect myself as best I could, and shouted, "Driver, don't stop, keep moving! *Adelante,* forward, forward!"

We raced on and without further incident arrived at our Hotel, the Embajador. Save for a few reporters, it was all but deserted. I was concerned about Bill Bowdler; our full committee was here, we were exchanging notes, but Bill's car, two places behind mine, had not yet arrived. We called the American embassy, and then the police, who assured us that he was safe; his car was being escorted to the hotel. And presently Bill, a tall, lean six-foot-four career man with four years of service in Cuba, unbent his long frame and emerged from his car in the circular driveway of the hotel. "Some ride," he said. He had not been harmed. "They shook us up a little—" He shrugged his shoulders.

Presently, after we had had a drink or two and had settled down, Consul John Calvin Hill, Jr., our top man in the Dominican Republic (because of sanctions we had no ambassador stationed here), called on us. He briefed us on the situation. The army had rushed tanks and troops into the city to restore order. They were patrolling the streets even as we spoke, armed with rifles, clubs and fire-engine hoses. "This has been a bloody day," he said. "Do you know that all shops have closed? They'll be closed tomorrow; they're holding the funeral of that poor fellow who was shot. That means demonstrations tomorrow, too." He had word that in Santiago, the second largest city, storekeepers were to strike tomorrow as well.

Later, I was in my room, toying with the rock that had struck me. It was about half the size of a baseball. Someone knocked on the door; I opened it to find Robert Berrellez, the Associated Press correspondent in the Dominican Republic, a stocky, gray-haired veteran of Latin American intrigue and violence. He had something he wanted to tell me.

I had great respect for Bob's skill and integrity as a newspaperman. His dispatches, which appeared in the New Orleans *Times-Picayune*, had always seemed to me sane and objective. What he had to tell me, in substance, was this:

At the very moment our cavalcade was approaching Rhadames Bridge, he had been atop a hill overlooking the road, setting up his camera to photograph what happened. He turned to find a few yards away, standing atop the hill with a portable loudspeaker, Pedro Barinas, chief of a Communist front that had just come into existence in the country, and a man whose name I recognized as that of one of the twelve Moscow-trained Communists listed by General Bissell of the C.I.A. "I saw the whole thing, saw and heard this fellow," Bob said to me. Barinas directed the entire demonstration. It was he who made the decision to send the crowd against the police as soon as our motorcade came into sight, it was he who urged the mob to break through the police lines and blockade the road. He shouted through his loudspeaker, "Let's go down and beat them up!" Then the crowd surged out onto the road. As the struggle continued, as our cars were trapped, here was Bob with his camera on the hill, using a telescopic lens to capture the scene, and here was Barinas, the Communist, by his side urging on the crowd.

At one point Bob turned to him. "What kind of man are you?" he demanded. "You're sending the people on, and you're safe here on top."

Barinas looked at him and retorted sardonically, "I just start the fights. I never get into them."

I thanked Bob for his information. I made up my mind. Our committee was to pay a formal call on President Balaguer at 10 A.M. tomorrow in the Presidential Palace. I decided to see him tonight, at his home, while we were both upset over the day's events. I would constitute myself a United States committee of one —as President Kennedy had asked me—and carry out my mission. The C.I.A. had cited Communists. Here was eyewitness evidence of Communist direction of Dominican rioting—a rioting, we were to learn later, that before the day was over had resulted in four persons killed, thirty-seven wounded, and enormous damage done to property. It had been the worst outbreak since the terror that immediately followed Trujillo's assassination on May 30.*

It was nearly ten o'clock of a typical rainy, tropical night when Bill Bowdler and I drove to the home of President Joaquin Balaguer in the center of the city. Before we reached the rather modest brick house in which he lived, we had to proceed through three cordons of troops that were placed in concentric circles around the area. We approached the house, to see the porch; there was the President, sitting on the porch, rocking in a rocking chair, his father on one side, his mother on the other, the three rocking peacefully, with hardly a sound save the rain hissing on the luxurious foliage of the trees. The contrast between this scene and what we had both been through—the knowledge that the entire country was like a volcano and here the President rocked quietly like a peaceable burgher on his porch of a late summer night. . . .

The house was set back about thirty feet from a fence, with flowers planted in front of it. President Balaguer greeted us cordially, introduced us to the two old folks, who nodded pleasantly without halting their rocking, and we walked to the other side of the veranda, facing the ocean, and sat in rocking chairs, drinking coffee and talking.

* The evening of May 30, 1961, Trujillo's chauffeur was driving the dictator, age sixty-seven, to visit one of his mistresses outside Ciudad Trujillo. On the road to San Cristóbal, some miles from the capital, the car was suddenly blocked by two cars in front, two behind. In the exchange of gunfire, El Jefe was fatally shot. The reprisals literally bathed the capital in blood.

It had been a tragic, a frightful, a macabre day, we agreed. "Yes, a sad, sad way to advertise our country all over the world," Balaguer said. I had known him for many years. Not only had he visited New Orleans, but I had seen him on my several trips to the Dominican Republic. A small, curly-haired, bespectacled man, perhaps only five feet three, gentle in mien, a soft-voiced bachelor in his early forties, one who might be dismissed as mousy, save that when he stood before an audience, he seemed to grow a foot in height, his voice powerful, his language moving and poetic. A lawyer and a historian, in his wildest dreams he had never anticipated that he would be President of the Dominican Republic. Yet he had been elected President in May 1960—with Trujillo's blessing, to be sure—and now that Trujillo was gone, he and Trujillo's son were the rulers of the country. On their shoulders depended the future of this island republic.

"Mr. President," I said, almost formally, "I come to you now not only as an O.A.S. representative, but more truly, as a representative of my country, and I bring you a message from President Kennedy."

While he listened soberly I told him our hope. We knew there were twelve active Communist leaders in the country. We felt that though much of the turmoil came from well-intentioned citizens of the Dominican Republic—indeed, the entire country was like a drunken sailor, released at last from the tyranny of "El Jefe"—it was our belief in Washington, based on our C.I.A. sources, that the Communists were inspiring the riots.

I said, "I know you're concerned whether these men are Communists. I have a story to tell you." I repeated what Bob Berrellez had told me. "This is eyewitness evidence. What further proof must you have to deport this man Barinas?"

Balaguer knew, of course, that the twelve were in the country. "I allowed them to return as part of my pledge to permit complete political freedom," he explained. He added that his police had already eliminated the headquarters of the Frente—this was Barinas's organization. (Later that night, driving back to the Hotel Embajador, we passed Frente headquarters and saw police ripping down loudspeakers which had been set up to blast Frente propaganda into the central square of the city.)

I said that we felt that if he and Ramfis could keep law and order, democratize the country, rid it of the oppressive methods of the past, the people would be convinced of his sincerity. "But how can you keep law and order, Mr. President, and still allow these twelve men, whose only desire is to upset law and order, to remain?"

Balaguer shook his head. "If I deport them, the people will say I am acting as a dictator and confirm all their fears—" He threw up his hands.

Bill Bowdler spoke up, in his quiet, unassuming way. "You know, Mr. President, I was one of the last Americans in Cuba." (He had been a United States political officer at our Havana embassy until the very end.) "I know from sad experience that you can't do business with the Castro crowd. They will use the very liberties you give them to destroy you."

It was a curious conversation, rocking gently on the porch, in the warm, wet darkness, hearing the rain, aware of the troops invisibly about us, the restless, bitter people in the cities, my three colleagues back at the hotel probably sound asleep after a tense, wearing day.

Balaguer nodded slowly. He had no need to prove his anti-Communism. I had heard him speak on the subject, and had read a magnificent speech he had delivered at the United Nations, a masterful job in which point by point he brilliantly described Communism and destroyed it.

We returned to the twelve names. I would like to be able to report to President Kennedy that these troublemakers had been sent out of the country. Balaguer sighed and finally nodded. Yes, he would take action against them. It would be his first move, since Trujillo's death, that in any way limited democratization. Not only had half a dozen political parties sprung up where for decades there had been only one, but opposition newspapers were publishing, the 10 per cent deduction from every worker's wages for the P.D. had been reduced to 5 per cent—the money went for social welfare now —and he hoped in a few weeks to eliminate it altogether. He revealed that he was going to invite the leaders of the three principal opposition groups to take posts in his Cabinet; surely with a coalition government he could manage until the elections. He would ask Dr. Viriato Fiallo, a veteran foe of the late dictator, head of the large National Civic Union (U.C.N.), and recognized as the island's most popular political leader: Dr. Manuel Tavarez Justo, chief of the Fourteenth of June Party,* more radical than the U.C.N.; and Angel Miolan, secretary general of the Dominican Revolutionary Party (P.R.D.), which had been founded in exile two decades ago and whose president was Dr. Juan Bosch, one of the great figures of the democratic-left movement in Latin America.

"As you see," President Balaguer said, almost wistfully, "I am trying to do what I believe is correct, to do everything in my power for the good." On that note we said good night. His parents, who did not speak English, had already quietly retired. Bill and I drove back to the hotel, discussing the wording of the cable I would send to Washington. We believed that Balaguer, though he suffered from having been President under Trujillo, genuinely wanted to restore democracy. Could he do it? And keep the country safe?

I was walking through the lobby minutes later, bound for my room, when a soft voice sounded. "Mr. Ambassador!"

I turned. "Eduardo," I said, in some surprise.

It was Eduardo Morales, Dominican Consul General in New Orleans. He wrung my hand more cordially than I shook his. When I had first been appointed ambassador, he was one of the first to congratulate me; and when he learned I was to be a member of the O.A.S. investigating team, he had said, "Mr. Ambassador, don't be astonished if I greet you in Ciudad Trujillo."

He invited me to have a nightcap with him. I pleaded weariness and went up to bed. Morales was a man created by Dictator Trujillo. He was dark, ingratiating to the point of irritation, with an excellent memory for names, a great respect for the power structure, and an almost slavish devotion to influential people. I had always known, when dealing with him in New Orleans—as dean of the consular corps in the city, he was involved in virtually every consular activity in New Orleans—that his entire career hung on a thin

* In what must certainly have been proportionately one of the most costly and bloodiest attempts at invasion, on June 14, 1959, a group of a few hundred Dominican exiles and Cuban revolutionaries landed at Constanza, on the Dominican coast. Trujillo was waiting for them. He had laced the airfield with cables that caused their planes to crash; scores of men were killed; and Trujillo, according to reports, rounded up the remainder, took them to Ciudad Trujillo and slaughtered them.

thread, on the whims of his dictator. With Trujillo's death, his loyalty was not so much to President Balaguer, as to Trujillo's son, Ramfis. Morales told me he had left New Orleans at the request of his government, "who wished me to be here at the same time you are here so I can render you any services you need."

I would have preferred that Morales had remained in New Orleans, rather than play the role of liaison between me and the government. He was identified with Trujillo, he would be watched, I would be watched—the placard attacking me was very much on my mind; I had been charged by my President to encourage Balaguer and Balaguer's program; my position was most delicate—I could only be embarrassed and our investigation would be complicated by this gentleman breathing down my neck. As it turned out, during our two weeks in the country Eduardo Morales seemed to pop up from behind every pillar in the Hotel Embajador lobby each time I entered and left.

Next morning at breakfast Bill Bowdler was reading the local newspaper, *El Caribe*. On the front page were photographs of Pedro Barinas and another leading Communist. The government had announced their deportation.

"Two down—ten to go," said Bill dryly.

By week's end eleven had been expelled. One, Lopez Molina, who had incited the burning of Radio Caribe, could not be found.*

If the day of our arrival was chaotic, our second day was one of the most melancholy. Our program was to remain at the Hotel Embajador for several days, receiving delegations of political leaders, newspapermen, students, farmers, trade-unionists, businessmen, doctors, lawyers, and other professional people—all segments of the population—and taking their testimony. We had first, however, to make our courtesy calls on President Balaguer and Ramfis Trujillo, the latter at his military headquarters, San Isidro Air Base, about twelve miles from town. These were routine. We took statements from both and promised to discuss matters after we had completed our two-week investigation.

Returning from San Isidro we came upon the funeral of Dr. Victor

* There were rumors that Molina had been Dictator Trujillo's "pet Communist." He had been in and out of the country before Trujillo's death; many argued that he could never have entered had the dictator not permitted it to prove that he did allow opposition.

Rafael Estrella Liz, the physician who had been killed the day before. The government had refused—probably fearing violence—a service in Colon Cathedral. The result was a mass demonstration, nonviolent, silent, subdued, and so all the more impressive in its dignity. We came upon Calle El Conde, the great avenue of Ciudad Trujillo; thousands of men and women moved slowly down its center in an enormous funeral procession. Shops were closed, shutters down; along the sidewalks, at intervals, stood steel-helmeted troops in combat uniform with rifles at the ready; between them the procession slowly wound, led by four priests and their acolytes bearing crucifixes, while behind the coffin came hundreds of sorrowing women dressed in black, black scarves over their heads, intoning prayers for the dead as they walked. It was not an easily forgotten sight.

We began our investigations.

8. THE LEGACY OF TRUJILLO

In the Hotel Embajador, in Ciudad Trujillo, we set up shop, and the delegations called on us, each eager to present its interpretation of the Dominican scene. The Dominican Party, representing the government, and the three opposition parties: the National Civic Union, the Dominican Revolutionary Party, the Fourteenth of June Party. Widows, weeping; intense university students; a furious opposition spokesman with a list of 134 names of persons who allegedly had disappeared *since* Trujillo's death. In the first two days we heard testimony of every kind, pro and contra the government. But clearest of all was the fact that economic sanctions were strangling the country.

Not a single house had been built in Ciudad Trujillo in the last year. Business was at a standstill. People feared to invest—if they had money to invest. Among small-town inhabitants, there was actual starvation. President Balaguer's P.D. had opened soup kitchens in eighteen of the country's twenty-five provinces. Emergency appeals for food had been cabled to United States relief agencies. Half of the nation's 600,000 workers were unemployed. No roads were being built, no goods were being shipped, scarcely any traffic was on the highways. The greatest blow, growing out of sanctions, had been the cutting-off of sugar trade with the United States. Before sanctions, the Dominican Republic sold sugar to us at the United States price of 5.8 cents a pound, against a world market price of 2.5 cents.* The lost sugar revenues alone amounted to $30,000,000. Although this was a smiling, fertile land, able to produce coffee, cocoa, bananas, rice, corn, it was sugar that kept the holds of its ships full, its ports busy; it was sugar cane cultivation, harvesting and processing, that kept its workers employed. Here was an object lesson—and my colleagues were as impressed as I—of the danger inherent in one-crop economies, precisely the sort of imbalance the Alliance hoped to correct by helping nations diversify their agriculture.

I considered the Dominican Republic a special case on the world's political agenda. When the O.A.S. foreign ministers meeting in San José in 1960 had voted sanctions against the Dominican Republic because of Trujillo's assassination attempt against President Betancourt of Venezuela, yet took no real action against Cuba, I had been distressed. Cuba had not even been mentioned in the resolutions at San José, though we all knew Castro was exporting his revolution to Guatemala, Nicaragua, Haiti and Panama—simply as a beginning. To me this was a far greater threat to *hemisphere* security than an attack, however reprehensible, on the person of Betancourt. I had hoped the foreign ministers would invoke Articles 6 and 8 of the Rio Treaty to brand Cuba as an aggressor, authorizing other countries to take any measures "including the use of arms" to deal with her. But too many of the American republics feared repercussions at home, and so the vast punishment machinery of the O.A.S. had been turned only against the Trujillo regime.

I had always thought the potential of this small nation on our doorstep had been underrated. It had the same terrain as Puerto Rico, but was blessed with deep rivers that ran north and south, about twenty miles apart, irrigating thousands of acres. Its farm lands were among the most fertile in the world; on its central plateau grew some of the finest coffee in the world. It was a rich land which for so many years had been exploited as a private plantation. The money siphoned off by Trujillo—estimates rose as

* We could not buy sugar abroad at the lower rate because our own Louisiana sugar industry would have been unable to compete. We paid our growers the higher rate.

high as a billion dollars—had never been put back into the economy. Much of it now was believed lying in numbered accounts in Swiss banks, or in dummy accounts in France.

To me the Dominican Republic had far greater promise than Puerto Rico or Haiti; its tourist possibilities equaled those of any other Caribbean country. It had lovely beaches at Boca Chica, ten miles from its ancient, beautiful capital, Columbus's first landing place in the New World. In the West was Barahona, as dreamily lovely as Hawaii. In the center was Constanza, at an altitude of nearly 5,000 feet, with perfect climate, breath-taking waterfalls—a tiny Switzerland even to frost on cool mornings. In my visits I had fallen in love with this beautiful country which had so much to offer, whose people were so warm, hospitable and unaffected. If only it had the opportunity to fulfill its promise!

Now sanctions, imposed because of a man who was no longer alive, were suffocating the country. Because of a dead man, a nation of 3,600,000 people was paying an enormous price. With 50 per cent unemployment, how long can a country remain free? And when it collapsed completely, who would take it over?

I believe that I was, far more than my three colleagues, emotionally involved in this mission to the Dominican Republic, more concerned with its fate, both personally and as the United States representative on the committee.

Repeatedly I asked our witnesses: If sanctions weigh so heavily, what is your will? Do you ask us to remove them? Shall we recommend this relief to the O.A.S. if we conclude that the Dominican Republic is no longer a threat to hemispheric security?

The government spokesmen were emphatically affirmative. Sanctions had to go, said Luis R. Mercado, chairman of the P.D. We have started a far-reaching progressive democratization program, we are correcting abuses, we are moving ahead, we are struggling to repair, overnight, evils rooted in the country for more than a quarter of a century—but help us! Your sanctions paralyze us.

We were told—this was Ramfis Trujillo's warning—that if sanctions remained he could not guarantee to keep the military in line. To insure its own safety it might strike against the government, take over the country in a military dictatorship.

Business and professional interests—landlords, merchants, doctors, lawyers, architects—pleaded, too, that we remove sanctions. To our astonishment, the replies from other groups were in the negative. The opposition parties too wanted sanctions to remain. However divided among themselves, they were unanimous in one wish: "Get rid of the Trujillos." Removal now of sanctions would only strengthen the regime, making it impossible to dislodge it. Dr. Viriato Fiallo, chairman of the U.C.N., said that if sanctions remained the situation will worsen until the people revolt and the government will be forced to leave.

I thought, How can we gamble on the direction a revolt will take?

Few of our sophisticated witnesses believed that Ramfis Trujillo wished to become a dictator. He had categorically stated he would not be a candidate for the presidency. I could not believe that he would give up his playboy life to devote himself to the arduous job of running a country, as president or as dictator. Even granting the best of motives, however, to both Balaguer and young Trujillo, most witnesses were convinced they must be removed—together with Ramfis's two uncles, Generals Hector and Arismendi Trujillo.

"You read it on our banners, gentlemen," one witness said stiffly. "Get rid of the Trujillos—uncles, cousins, aunts, all of them."

Secretary General Angel Miolan of the Dominican Revolutionary Party summed up the situation—the nation could move in one of three directions: toward a "rightist tyranny"; toward a "popular explosion" that the Communists would attempt to exploit to set up a "Cuban-type tyranny"; or toward a "regime of representative democracy," which was the only hope to save the country.

I seized on this. What of Dr. Balaguer's offer to the three opposition parties to join him in a coalition Cabinet until free elections were held next May?* A firm refusal. The three would join no government in which Balaguer and his P.D. played a role. If, however, he stepped aside and allowed the three to form a government . . .

"Impossible," Balaguer replied. How could a government be deemed representative and democratic if a major party was excluded?

* The confusing political interplay was emphasized when police raided headquarters of the Dominican Revolutionary Party and arrested Miolan and fourteen of his associates, charging they found nineteen homemade incendiary bombs, iron bars, pipes and a stiletto on the premises. The very next day Balaguer called Miolan to the National Palace and formally invited him to join the coalition government!

Sitting in our hotel, taking testimony from disputing spokesmen, we found it extremely difficult to gauge the feelings of the people themselves. The political picture was muddled by the proliferation of new organizations, the publication of new manifestos, the demands and accusations of new newspapers springing up almost overnight—each party seemed surprisingly able to afford offices in the principal cities to print and distribute propaganda, even to publish its own newspaper.*

The wangling before us intensified. In the morning we heard that the government was insincere, little better than when under Trujillo; in the afternoon, in accents just as emphatic, we heard that the government genuinely concerned itself with the people's interests . . .

On the second night I turned impulsively to my colleagues. "Gentlemen, we've been in this hotel two days. We can stay here a month, seeing these people, but I don't think we'll learn much more. We'll only hear speeches. I'm restless. There's something going on in this country outside this hotel, and I want to find out." Cities and towns, I knew, were isolated from each other, not pulled together by a network of communications. "Let's go out—without press or police or government officials—and talk to the people, the farmers, the small-town folk."

This raised difficulties. Our hotel was air-conditioned, and the country was unbearably hot at this time of year. By the time I had telephoned Miami and requested a United States Air Force DC-3† so we could use Ciudad Trujillo as a base and fly to various areas between dawn and midnight, all three of my colleagues had begged off. Arango, chairman of our committee, had to return to Panama, leaving his deputy, Miguel Corro; Escudero, a rather frail man, and frequently ill, felt it best not to go; and Zuleta Angel, whom we elected chairman after Arango left, wished to remain and continue hearing witnesses.

As a result, when I took off at eight o'clock the following morning for Santiago, the second largest city, I was the only committee mem-

* I suspected, but could not prove, that our own C.I.A., interested in furthering Balaguer's "progressive democratization," subsidized these parties. Two weeks before we arrived, the State Department had invited Dr. Fiallo, head of the U.C.N., to visit Washington.

† From Ramfis, at his headquarters at the San Isidro Air Base, came the offer of a Dominican Air Force plane, but this would have identified us in the people's eyes with the government. The offer was refused.

ber. The rest were alternates: Bill Bowdler; Santiago Salazar, of Colombia; Corro; and Dr. Antonio José Paredes, of Ecuador.

It was a grueling but memorable tour, broken by my swift flight back to Washington for the weekend of Peruvian President Prado's visit. Our trips into the interior showed us a country blighted far beyond what we had seen in the capital. Port towns were especially hard hit by the reduction in shipping, warehousing, and other tangential industries. Farming areas were better off; farmers at least could grow some food and escape starvation. In Santiago, called the Dominican Texas because of its independent attitude toward the capital, we expected to find strong antigovernment feeling, and did, particularly since it was also national headquarters of the U.C.N. We paid our respects to the governor of the province. He turned out to be the father of the Dominican consul-general in Washington; he was an elderly, old-school gentleman, who walked painfully with the aid of a cane, and was obviously dazed by recent events. He was typical of the governors we found through the country. Most of them had been appointed by Trujillo as young civil servants; they had lived secure, protected, knowing only the values of their society, loyal to El Jefe, who always provided them with the money they needed for roads, schools, hospitals, factories—and prisons. Now, in their seventies and eighties, they were lost. "It is terrible, terrible," he lamented. "What has happened to us?" Still living in the feudal era of Trujillo, they were unable to understand the situation.

We emerged from his palace to find the town square full of people. Word had spread that the O.A.S. had arrived. At U.C.N. headquarters, we sat in a circle of fifteen local leaders—professional people, most of them, physicians, attorneys, schoolteachers. The party secretary, an impassioned young man, leaped to the attack at once.

"The Balaguer government is not establishing reforms; it is a mockery," he declared. "Balaguer himself, though of admirable character and intellect, is a prisoner of the same elements that governed during the Trujillo regime. There is Ramfis, and waiting behind Ramfis are his two uncles. And look about you. The Poleros [Balaguer's police] are everywhere. They may not have guns, but they are still police, they still imprison civilians, they still represent the old regime, and they still beat us, if not with rifles, then with clubs." He charged that prominent businessmen in Santiago who closed their shops in sympathy for those killed on the day of our arrival in the Dominican Republic had been thrown into prison. Others gave us names of people allegedly tortured and murdered.

What did the secretary want the O.A.S. to do?

"Oust the Balaguer-Trujillo government. No sanctions removed until they get out!"

I played devil's advocate. The Dominican Republic had signed the Charter of Punta del Este. I had seen its minister of finance affix his signature. The Dominican Republic was now our partner in the Alliance for Progress. As long as sanctions remained, however, the Alliance was powerless to give his country the millions of dollars in loans, grants and subsidies it so desperately needed.

The secretary shot a long glance from his dark, burning eyes. "Of course we must build our economy," he said, impatiently. "But if sanctions are removed it will be a victory for the Trujillos. It will only make them richer. They own the country now—airlines, shipping lines, automobiles, iron, steel, sugar, coffee, cocoa, tobacco, beer, insurance—name it and they own it. Trujillo is gone, Mr. Ambassador, but Trujilloism remains!"

Near Santiago lived Ramfis's uncle General Arismendi Trujillo, older brother of the late dictator. It was a question which of the two uncles—General Arismendi or General Hector Trujillo (who for eight years had been President before Balaguer)—was more feared and disliked. Each had his private army, each lived like a feudal lord. I called briefly on General Arismendi. He greeted me at his hacienda, wearing khaki uniform and leather boots, a Sam Browne belt, and a pearl-handled pistol on each hip. His private militia (his *Cuculous*) was said to number three thousand. It was the talk of the country, arousing tremendous bitterness. At least two thousand of them, it seemed to me, were lined up for my inspection, a rough company in khaki trousers, armed with rifles as well as the wicked-looking knives used for cutting sugar cane. The general and I had little to say to each other; it was a courtesy call, because I was in the vicinity; when I left and went on, it was only to find more anti-Trujillo sentiment.

It was everywhere the same. In the port town of Puerto Plata in the north, in San Cristóbal, San Pedro, La Vega, Moca, Constanza, even in La Romana, in the heart of the depressed sugar-cane area.

"We'll go without food, we'll starve, if it means we can get rid of the Trujillos." In Constanza the local secretary received us in his home, little more than a hut, where we drank warm lemonade and fought off myriads of tiny, stinging flies. Whether the party was N.C.U., P.R.D. or Fourteenth of June, it did not matter. They disagreed over personalities, their political demands differed, but "Out with the Trujillos"—the entire Trujillo family—was common to all.

Each time we emerged from a meeting the town population seemed waiting outside, chanting "*Li-ber-tad! Li-ber-tad!*" and blowing horns as a signal to tell others it was safe. At the beginning, people feared to speak to us. Radio Havana endlessly attacked us on the air as "imperialistic lackeys who had come under orders to whitewash the government."* As the days passed, as newspapers reported our trips into the interior showing us engulfed by people —I was in an open-necked sports shirt and white slacks; anything but the top-hatted, striped-pants emissary they expected—they began to trust us. Each welcome was more emotional. I felt we truly got the temper of the people. In these surging, excited crowds, the words were a refrain: "Don't listen to the government. The moment you go they'll be on our backs again. The Poleros are still out, maintaining the system. Help us! Help us!"

Dusk fell one evening as we were in Puerto Plata. We were walking down a dark street in a poor area toward the field in which our plane awaited us. Now a strange thing occurred. It seemed to me I heard babies crying distantly. Then I realized that for some time I had been hearing the sound. Everywhere this sad accompaniment, now weak, now wailing. I turned to one of our guides.

"They cry for hunger," he said. "They have been put to bed, these little children, without any food."

I could not get the sound out of my ears. We had seen children begging, three-, four-, five-year-old children, one hand rubbing their stomachs, the other outstretched for pennies, their thin faces piteously screwed up. We had walked through wretched slums—and the slums in Latin America are unforgettable. We had seen a people that had suffered years of mistreatment. And yet, knowing that

* Later Radio Havana found a new reason. In return for the lifting of O.A.S. sanctions, Balaguer, they charged, had made a deal to give the United States air bases for another invasion of Cuba.

much of this could be changed by one recommendation in our power to make, they still hated the Trujillos so bitterly that they preferred to continue this Calvary rather than risk keeping the regime.

Even among the clergy, the priests and nuns, those most charitable of people, I found few to speak well of the government. At the Episcopal School in Puerto Plata, a minister who once had a pastorate in Louisiana told me:

"I believe Mr. Balaguer to be a decent man, with decent instincts. Oh, you will hear that he cannot be trusted because he was Trujillo's puppet, but he is an honest man. He means well. I doubt if he can really change conditions. He was under the finger of the old Trujillo. Now he is under the finger of the young Trujillo, who is the real power here because he controls the military. And Trujillo is his father's son. When you leave, my friend, I suspect that unless something drastic happens, we shall be pretty much back where we were before."

It was different from what I had expected. I had expected the Trujillos to be highly unpopular in many quarters, but I was unprepared for the almost universal wave of hatred. As mayor of New Orleans I had met El Jefe; I had met his son, Ramfis. Although I knew Trujillo for the dictator that he was, he and his son had not seemed ogres. I knew of their rigid hold upon the country, the building of their fantastic private fortune, their ruthlessness, their almost medieval cruelty toward their political enemies. But when you meet a man as your guest, or your host, when you eat and drink with him in the course of social and diplomatic intercourse, smile at the same witticisms, see your wives exchanging snapshots of their children—it is difficult to perceive this man as the monster he is to his people. It is difficult to grasp the truth. One fights it. Is this, perhaps, the fatal weakness in men's relationships with each other? In the jungle, the wildcat, the hyena, or the poisonous reptile is recognized on sight; but its human counterpart disarms you because, looking upon him, you see simply another man?

Toward the end of our stay in the Dominican Republic, Salazar and I went to midday Mass one Sunday in Colon Cathedral. A large U.C.N. rally was to be held at sunset. People from the provinces poured into the city. On our way we passed within a block of Plaza Independencia, and hearing a voice booming from the loudspeaker, we strolled to the edge of the crowd, which already seemed several thousand strong, and stood there listening.

If we had thought we would be undetected, we were mistaken. At once we were surrounded by passionate, gesticulating Dominicans. From the loudspeaker presently came the words in Spanish: "We are proud to present the United States ambassador, Mr. Morrison . . ."

For a moment I waited, almost tense. The universal hatred for the Trujillos to which I had been exposed these last few days, the memory of the banner, "Morrison is with the Trujillos!" . . . But all I heard was applause. The crowd broke into a sea of waving white handkerchiefs. At last I've made it, I thought, relieved, they've accepted me. Salazar and I waved back, and indicated we were bound for the cathedral, some blocks ahead. When we resumed our walk, hundreds broke away from the crowd and joined us, shouting, "Don't leave us. Innocent people are being jailed!" We almost had to fight our way forward, the people clinging to us, shaking our hands, eagerly talking, questioning. Meanwhile, I became aware of the sound of planes. I looked up. It was a squadron of Dominican Air Force fighters. They came lower; they swooped down dangerously close to our heads; they were buzzing the crowd! People began to scream and run in all directions. Salazar exploded: "But it is so stupid! Don't they know they only antagonize!" After the single pass, the planes flew on, however, the rally continued, and the crowd accompanied us to the very door of the cathedral before turning away, waving their handkerchiefs at us.

Twenty-four hours later I called on General Rafael "Ramfis" Trujillo, Jr., Chief of the Armed Forces, at his seashore chalet in Boca Chica, not far from San Isidro, his military headquarters. I was driven there by Marco Gomez, his aide, a former mayor of Ciudad Trujillo, whom I had met before. When we arrived, Ramfis was entertaining a breathtakingly beautiful blond German girl, about twenty. He presented me to her; she nodded sweetly and vanished.

With our committee I had paid a formal call on Ramfis on our very first morning in the country. He had received us in his general's uniform, a young edition of his father as I had remembered him fifteen years before. Our meeting had followed diplomatic protocol, and we had simply exchanged amenities. Now my visit was private and informal, and I spoke to him as one who had been his host at the Mardi Gras in New Orleans, and I felt free to be completely frank.

The room in which he received me might have been a drawing room in a palace, sumptuously furnished, looking out on his private beach. When we spoke, there were only the three of us: Ramfis, Gomez and myself.

I began bluntly. "Ramfis, I've just come back from a tour of your country. If you could have put on a mask and gone incognito with me through the provinces and seen what I saw, heard what I heard, you would be shocked and astounded."

Ramfis, who despite his youth has immense dignity, matched only by his pride, poured me a bourbon-and-water, poured himself one and took a seat. "I do not understand what you mean, Chep," he said.

"I began my tour thinking this regime could be spared," I went on. "I thought it could serve as a caretaker government until the elections. I cannot make that statement now. I don't think it will last that long. It is like putting your finger into a dike to stop a flood. The resentment, the bitterness, the accumulated hatred against your family . . ." I said it was almost impossible to describe. And I had not found it among Communists, or wild-eyed anarchists, or plotters and madmen; I had found it among the rank and file, the people themselves, in towns and villages from one end of the country to the other. "The moral force alone, I am afraid, is bound to sweep you and Balaguer aside."

"But why?" he asked. "I have tried to do so many worthwhile things. I have agreed to set up a hundred-million-dollar foundation and place all our sugar properties in trust for the people. I have backed Balaguer in his changes. The military have been very correct; they have interfered in nothing."

I said, "The people have no faith in you or in Balaguer. They concede that he is making reforms, but they say that the moment we leave, these reforms will be forgotten. They refuse to separate you from your father. They fear that you plan to be a dictator and will take over, if not as soon as we leave, then at some time later."

Ramfis said, in a tired voice, "I did not think the people were so much against me. I really didn't think they disliked me as much as you say."

If he was telling the truth, I could only be amazed at his isolation in his own country. Yet he was kept as much as possible from his people. He was surrounded by aides, as had been his father, reared in the almost oriental tradition of telling the monarch only what he wished to hear. He rarely went into Ciudad Trujillo, and then only over roads swept clear by his soldiers. He spent virtually all his time here, at Boca Chica, where he lived like a potentate, or at San Isidro, where he ruled like a Roman consul. He was, of course, not ignorant of the demonstrations—these could not be kept from him—but he regally dismissed these as Communist productions, artificially inspired, not reflecting his people.

He asked, had I heard any threats against him? Did I think his life was in danger?

There could be no answer to his question, although had I been in his shoes I would have feared for my safety. I turned the question: "Do you fear for your life? Do you think that what happened to your father can happen to you?"

He shrugged his shoulders and replied with a Dominican proverb to the effect that one never knows today what will happen tomorrow. Then he added, "My mother and children are in Paris. She calls me every night. She is very concerned over me . . ."

He rose and began wandering about the room, thinking aloud. He could fly off to Paris at any time he wished, but he did not want to leave in such a situation. Enough had been written in the press abroad against the Trujillos. The family name was now in his keeping. He would not have anyone add to all the other epithets hurled at them that he, Ramfis, was a coward and fled the country to save his skin.

He had no wish to rule the Dominican Republic. He had no desire to be a dictator. He asked, almost rhetorically, "What is there I can do to convince the people of this?"

Marco Gomez, a heavy-set, dark-eyed man, sat in a big easy chair, smoking and thoughtful, but saying nothing. If asked, he would reply. Otherwise, he was silent.

I had been turning something over in my mind. I had come hoping that we could lift sanctions, thus stabilizing the country so it would not fall to Castro, or be taken over in a rightist coup. I could not recommend this now. To lift sanctions while the Trujillos remained would make it appear that the United States supported them and wanted a return to dictatorial rule. Furthermore, so long as the government was a Balaguer government, backed by the Trujillos, the opposition parties would refuse to join in a coalition.

The stumbling block was Ramfis Trujillo.

If Ramfis could be removed and taken out of a position of power, Balaguer, relieved of this albatross about his neck, might succeed in his democratization. If Ramfis were out of the picture, no longer head of the Dominican Army, the door might be opened to getting rid of his two uncles, Generals Hector and Arismendi Trujillo.

Yes, the stumbling block, the keystone, the log that held this menacing jam-up locked together was the young man in yellow slacks and silk dining jacket who now stood near the window, drawing slowly on his cigarette as he looked out on the Caribbean surf.

I heard myself say aloud: "Ramfis, would you leave the Dominican Republic permanently if sanctions were removed?"

Ramfis turned abruptly from the window. Before he could say anything, I added quickly, "You could give your people no better proof that you have no intention of becoming a dictator, that you are not counting, as they think you are, on the lifting of sanctions to put yourself more strongly in power."

He looked at Gomez, whose face was inscrutable, and then pondered for several minutes. Finally he said, slowly, "If sanctions are removed, I will resign as Chief of the Armed Forces and leave the country."

"Very well," I said. I wanted to shout hurray, but held back. "Why not write a letter to that effect to the chairman of our committee, Ambassador Zuleta Angel of Colombia? The committee will certainly publish your letter. Then the people—and the world—must believe you."

Ramfis crushed his cigarette. "All right. I'll do it. Right now."

The three of us sat down at a table and, together, prepared the note Ramfis signed. Between us we phrased the letter, and particularly its key sentences:

"Conscious of the necessity that the Dominican Republic return to the inter-American family of nations . . . I am fully disposed to contribute, without omitting any sacrifice, to a decent solution . . . I have the firm intention to renounce irrevocably my position as Chief of the Joint Staff of the Armed Forces as soon as sanctions imposed on my country are lifted. . . ."

We talked for a few more minutes. Emboldened, I brought up his two uncles, and the intense feeling I had found against them. If they were to leave the country, this alone might do much toward satisfying the people, and might make it possible for the Balaguer government to continue until elections.

Ramfis nodded. He would talk to his uncles. I gathered that he thought that if he was prepared to renounce power, there was no reason why he should not persuade them to leave at once and facilitate matters.

As I left with Gomez, to be driven back to the city, Ramfis said something to me that was to prove significant. "Remember, Chep, if they leave at my request and you don't remove sanctions, then they will return. Judge for yourself whether that will be good or bad."

Ramfis's letter was received and published. It marked the first break in the Dominican stalemate.

Before our committee departed for Washington, and while I was still in a euphoric state over my success, I spent an afternoon with my colleague Salazar indulging in my favorite sport, water-skiing. It was a restful Saturday afternoon, our last in the country. We skied from a beach not far from Boca Chica, where Ramfis had his chalet, in a quiet bay about half a mile from San Isidro Air Base.

Each time Salazar and I skied out, we passed the famous Trujillo yacht, the *Angelita,* moored in the bay. There were people aboard. Each time they waved gaily and made signs indicating that we should join them. We hesitated. As we skied along, side by side, listening to the Latin rhythms from the yacht, I said to Salazar: "Perhaps Ramfis is aboard. That would be bad. We cannot be in a position of accepting courtesies from him."

Salazar, a skilled tennis player, a first-rate athlete, and an attractive and prepossessing man, smiled. "I don't see him. I see only pretty girls."

We skied; they continued to wave; finally as the day wore on, we went aboard. We found a gay, companionable crowd. Ramfis was not among them. We were offered drinks; there was an orchestra; we danced and were graciously entertained. Later, a launch took us back to shore.

Weeks later, in Washington, my secretary Pat Mahony was reading the cables when she came across one that brought her up short. Pat, one of those remarkably efficient and resourceful Girls Friday who knows more about what you do and why you do it than you do yourself, walked into my office.

"Mr. Ambassador, didn't you tell me that you had an uneasy feeling when you went aboard the *Angelita* that afternoon?" I had told her the story in strictest confidence—how Salazar and I had gone aboard and danced.

"Yes," I said, a little puzzled.

"Well, it's no wonder you felt so uneasy—and you also felt a little chilly," she said.

I stared at her. I hadn't the least idea what she was talking about. She handed me the cable.

It stated that the body of Generalissimo Rafael Leonidas Trujillo, Sr., had been found aboard the yacht *Angelita*—hidden in the refrigerator.

I was shocked, confused. "But Pat," I said, "he was buried with great honors, he had an enormous funeral, thousands of people in Ciudad Trujillo . . ."

Yes, it was true. There had been a magnificent state funeral, all pomp and ceremony, but it was not El Jefe who was buried there amid the tears and lamentation. As I was to learn later, the family, fearing that the grave would be violated, the body removed, mutilated, perhaps even hung up publicly by the heels as had been done years before to Mussolini, had substituted another body. They had taken Trujillo's body and hidden it in the *Angelita*'s refrigerator.

"Oh, my," I exclaimed aloud, as I realized it. "The refrigerator is immediately below the deck we were dancing on!"

Evidently, it had been the hope that El Benefactor's body would remain hidden there until the Trujillos could manage to transport it elsewhere—probably to Paris—for secret interment. But charges that the Trujillos had hidden millions in gold aboard their yacht had led authorities to seize it and search it.

I thought, Incredible, this ghastly, ghoulish story. Yet it pointed a moral. This man was so hated that he was not safe living or dead. This could be said of few other men in history.

9. PRIVATE NOTES FROM AN AMBASSADOR'S NOTEBOOK

The kaleidoscopic nature of what was going on between the United States and the various Latin American countries, on such matters as the O.A.S., the Alliance, the Dominican Republic and Cuba, is perhaps best reflected by entries jotted into my journal during the next crowded eight weeks. If there is no pattern discernible, it is because none existed. Diplomacy has been defined as the art of the plausible. I found it an art of improvisation—doing one's best, by whatever means at hand, to move the plausible from the realm of theory to the realm of action. I had no idea, when I came to my office in the State Department in the morning, what I would find. The cable board with its endlessly proliferating messages from our ambassadors throughout the world, could change the firmest plans at a moment's notice. The world was only as stable as those teletyped messages permitted it to be.

To be sure, I knew—perhaps more than most—what had been talked about at Washington cocktail and dinner parties, which themselves mirror international events. As an eligible widower, living away from my family, I attended so many of them!—especially because Latin American diplomacy partakes more deeply of social relationships than any other. Latin diplomats almost invariably go out to celebrate. Time and again I joined with one or another of my O.A.S. colleagues to take two pretty ladies out. Not having a wife, I was not restricted. I could break certain protocol, which made it possible for me to know my colleagues better and to deal more closely with them.

Sometimes my calendar—especially on Friday night, busiest of the week in Washington—showed four or five parties. Any party given by the Latin American colony was a must for me. For the United States ambassador to the O.A.S. when in Washington not to make an appearance at an affair given by a Latin diplomat would be noticeable. There were parties given by the Latin American diplomatic colony; by the European; by the Cabinet; by the Congress; by the news media; by the military—there were more generals, admirals and the like, of various nations in Washington than in any other capital of the world, and as a member of the Army Policy Board I was invited to most of them. As it had been at Punta del Este, so it was, on a far more enormous scale, in Washington. The guests I met at social affairs included the very men I dealt with during the day. Often a debate that had stopped at 6 P.M. at the Pan American Union was taken up even more vigorously at midnight in a drawing room.

Thus, a distillation of my journal entries, from which I have excluded all social events:

October 1, 1961. Began working on our Dominican report as soon as we got aboard plane returning to Washington. Agreed we won't recommend lifting sanctions now: instead "watch and wait." Zuleta Angel hopeful, Escudero doubtful, Corro depressed. Walked into office this morning to have Toby Hartwick give me latest cable from John Hill in Ciudad Trujillo. U.N.C. just presented ultimatum to Balaguer: they'll join coalition only if some thirteen Trujillos leave the country immediately, including Ramfis, Generals Hector, Arismendi and Pedro [I had forgotten Ramfis had a third uncle, also a general], and two other Trujillos, respectively Air Force Chief and Admiral of the Navy. Ramfis retorted with what I think is misplaced humor: "I will not leave. The Trujillo family has more members than the opposition group that demands our departure." This, of course, is Ramfis talking for public consumption. Privately, I understand he's seen Uncles Hector and Arismendi, but they're not enthusiastic about leaving.

October 6. Bewildering number of hats I wear. Not only attend meetings of O.A.S. Council, but also of Subcommittee on Dominican Question, General O.A.S. Committee, Inter-American Peace Committee, and today I became Chairman, O.A.S. Committee on Cultural Affairs and Public Information. State Department's Speakers Division has also lined up speeches I'm to make around the country on the Alliance, sometimes three a week. Means flying in and out of Washington. I seem to be living on planes.

October 7. Met with representatives of Ed Murrow's U.S. Information Agency, and press sections of State, Treasury, U.S. Chamber of Commerce, World Bank, *et al.*, on how best to put over Alliance story to people of Latin America. Must map over-all program. I'm against high-powered Madison Avenue type news releases sent below border. They'll resent them, not use them. Better idea, suggested by Dick Phillips, Public Information Officer, State Dept., and Grady Upton, Exec. V.P. Inter-American Development Bank: each country to set up its own National Commission for the Alliance; we send them the facts, they'll tailor the material for their press, radio. Use *their* Huntleys-Brinkleys to tell Alliance story.*

October 8–10. Quick trip to Lima, Peru, for Chiefs of Mission meeting—regional gathering of our ambassadors to discuss problems.

October 11. At White House meeting Kennedy says he's asking M.† to fly to Dominican Republic and try to induce the two uncles to leave. This very confidential.

October 12. I could spit bullets! M. just dropped into my office, puzzled, unhappy. His D.R. trip is off. Someone leaked to press that he was going there on a mysterious mission and he had to deny it. Result: George McGhee, third ranking in State Department, will fly down, do what he can. Question: Who leaked the story? Why? Is

---

* One charming anecdote I especially like. In Ecuador, where it's most difficult to win the confidence of illiterate, distrustful Indians, the Alliance sponsors puppet shows. In each village one puppet is made up to resemble the most respected farmer in the village. Puppets during the performance discuss new methods of farming; the audience soon finds itself questioning them, debating with them as if they were actual persons. By the show's end, the Alliance's principles have been advanced beautifully on this very special level.

† This was Bob Murphy, top troubleshooter for Truman and Eisenhower before being chosen by Kennedy.

someone afraid that M. is too capitalistic for the task?* Are they "protecting" the President again?

October 13. Balaguer says he must have Ramfis on hand to keep military control. Army respects Trujillo name—probably only ones who do. (You can't say Ramfis hasn't had a long career in the Army. His father commissioned him a colonel at the age of nine.)

October 13. (*Later.*) Problem: How do we launch definitive action against Cuba? For U.S. to lead a movement to penalize Castro in the O.A.S. only to have Latin nations reject this in a showdown would be a tremendous blow, a diplomatic Bay of Pigs for us. If it is done, it must be the wish of two thirds of the Latin countries.

A double-barreled problem: to call a foreign ministers' meeting simply to discuss the matter required fourteen votes. To take specific action against Cuba, then, also required fourteen votes. Would fourteen countries vote to censure him—to punish him? Perhaps even impose the same heavy sanctions we imposed on the Dominican Republic?

Understand Colombia plans to move for meeting of foreign ministers—when the time comes—on the question of hemispheric security. President Lleras Camargo has been leader in this for a long time, as witness sending his foreign minister, César Turbay, around Latin America to canvass attitudes toward Castro (the trip interrupted when Turbay's plane was hijacked).

October 15–18. Quick trip to Chiefs of Mission meetings, Costa Rica.

October 16. Riots at Santo Domingo University in Ciudad Trujillo, the cables report. Balaguer insists on keeping as rector Dr. José Machado, a Trujillo appointee. Students ran wild, tore down photographs of El Jefe, began attacking his statue on campus. Interesting thought: so many revolutions below the border begin with college students. Are they the true conscience of the people?

October 19. Great excitement at O.A.S. Council. Ambassador Juan de Lavalle of Peru accuses Cuba of using "its diplomatic officers, official missions and secret agents" to infiltrate other American republics, "instituting subversion and revolt." Charges that every Cuban embassy in Latin America is distribution center for Communist propaganda. (What really happened, I learned, was that exile

* Murphy was chairman of the board of Corning Glass Corporation.

Cuban Student Directorate agents raided the Cuban embassy in Lima and uncovered reams of such material. Embassies have diplomatic immunity, are traditionally safe from examination by local authorities.) This anticipates Colombia's action—but can't hurt. Why is it the anti-Castro Cubans who have to disclose this? Lechuga's at no loss for an answer: denies everything, charges that Peru is acting under U.S. orders.

October 19, 20. Seems all hell's broken loose in D.R. Student rioting has spread to principal cities. Poleros everywhere with hoses, rifles, tear gas; students throwing rocks, scrap metal, racing through streets shouting, "Out with the Trujillos!"

October 23. Urgent cable from John Hill: Generals Hector and Arismendi and 15 other Trujillos (but not Ramfis) departed country secretly reported bound for U.S. en route to Bermuda where yacht *Angelita* awaits them. Understand Hector and Arismendi were escorted to a plane and told bluntly that they had to get out. This could be best news so far.

October 24. Near riot in Idlewild Airport, New York, when Dominican exiles attack passengers coming off a Dominican plane thinking them members of fleeing Trujillo family. Mistaken identity. Somehow the Trujillos did leave the D.R. Bermuda reports they arrived and immediately boarded *Angelita.* (Grotesque thought: is El Jefe still on ice?)

October 25. Bitter session in O.A.S. Lechuga makes formal denunciation of Peru's accusation. I support Peru, pointing out that 1,000 Cuban refugees a day are pouring into U.S. alone—"eloquent testimony to conditions in Cuba under the Castro regime." Thanks to excellent staff work, I am able to quote statements made only day before in Moscow by Blas Roca, high official of the Communist Party in Cuba, and one of Castro's top advisers, now attending 22nd Congress of the Communist Party of the Soviet Union. Roca boasted before his fellow Communists that Cuba was the "example," the "springboard for revolution" for the rest of the Americas, and publicly advocated guerrilla warfare "as a means of wresting political power from constitutionally established governments."

My overriding purpose in sticking my oar in was to make clear that while Castro in Havana, Che Guevara at Punta del Este, and Lechuga here were insisting their revolution was a non-Communist revolt in the best Freedom Fighter tradition, it was in truth a

Communist-Marxist revolt; that Cuba had established "such intimate political, military, economic and cultural ties" with the Soviet Union, Communist China, and other countries associated with them," as to make Cuba "an appendage of the Communist system."

In the end, Council referred Peru's charges to the Inter-American Peace Committee. Since I'm one of its five members, I can keep my oar in.

Latter part October, early November. Two-week interlude. Make half-dozen speeches. Finish Dominican report. Our Inter-American Peace Committee—Ambassadors Lima of El Salvador, Zuleta Angel of Colombia (who had been in D.R. with me), Clulow of Uruguay, Mayobre of Venezuela and myself—decide to send a form letter to all American republics asking them to submit any evidence they have that would support Peru's charges.

November 9. Colombia drops bombshell we've been waiting for, demands convocation of O.A.S. on highest level—that of foreign ministers—to consider threats to the peace and independence of the American states. O.A.S. Council will hold extraordinary session December 4 to vote on resolution.*

November 14. Things moving so well in D.R. we propose partial lifting of sanctions. More than a dozen assorted Trujillos gone, Maximo Lopez Molina, the long-sought pro-Castro demagogue, seized, everything beginning to look rosy. All of us much relieved. If we finally see end of D.R. mess, we can really concentrate on Cuba. Everywhere I speak on the Alliance, audiences invariably want to know: Why should we support the Alliance and pass out our good American dollars to Latin American countries who won't do anything about Castro's infiltration, and for all we know, increasingly become sitting ducks for him?

November 15. Disaster written on everybody's face when I walk into office this morning. Generals Hector and Arismendi are back in D.R.! They only went away "on vacation," they explain. But they've installed themselves at Ramfis's headquarters at San Isidro. Does this mean a military coup, and everything up to now goes down the drain?

November 17. (Friday.) Ramfis has resigned, left the country. No

* Although neither the Soviet Union nor Cuba are mentioned in Colombia's resolution, everyone in the O.A.S. knew its purpose was to bring Cuba's role out into the open and then decide what to do about it.

one controlling the Army. It's Generals Hector and Arismendi versus Balaguer—and I can't forget those troops Bill Bowdler and I had to walk through to get to Balaguer's house. The very guards protecting him are Trujillo men! Ramfis did call this. He had told me, "If my uncles leave and sanctions aren't removed, they'll come back." This will be a bad weekend here.

November 17. (Later.) We withhold proposal re partial lifting of sanctions. O.A.S. Committee on Dominican Question in almost continuous session. Rusk, everybody else, staying in town over weekend. Rusk repeatedly on telephone to Kennedy, in Los Angeles on political fence-mending trip.

November 18. (Saturday—early A.M.*)* Action! Twelve U.S. warships, led by Aircraft Carrier *Franklin D. Roosevelt,* with 1,800 Marines from Guantanamo, and including Cruiser *Little Rock,* three destroyers, on way toward Dominican Republic. Do we go in?

November 18. (Saturday—about noon.) Rusk announces that U.S. military forces will land in the Dominican Republic if President Balaguer asks for them!

November 20. (Sunday—before dawn.) Just learned a jubilant John Hill has telephoned from Ciudad Trujillo. The people are dancing in the streets—they're shouting "Viva Yankees!" and "Hurray for the gringos! and the U.S. fleet!" Great emotion on the island. Balaguer has won out, the two generals have capitulated, they flew into exile two hours ago!

As reports come in, it's easy to put the pieces together. Our fleet remained outside the three-mile line. It never went into Dominican waters although it would have, had Balaguer asked. This was not necessary, because of the peculiar physical formation of the southern coast of the country. It rises like an amphitheater from the sea so that from shore one sees the ocean spread out below like a vast stage; one can see four or five miles out to sea. Our fleet was clearly visible to the two generals at San Isidro. They saw the jets landing and taking off, the Marines waiting, the warships at the ready. Meanwhile, Balaguer, ten miles away in the capital, speaking to the people by radio with all his great eloquence, rallies them; he's abolished Ramfis's position; he, the President, has taken command of the Army. The Dominican Air Force, under young General Rodriguez Echevarria, based in Santiago, is loyal to Balaguer. The government is in control.

The two generals had to give up; they were immediately sent under police escort to a commercial plane, put aboard, and flew off. The Dominican Republic has avoided civil war; the military coup and its backlash—which might have led to a Communist take-over by pro-Castro elements—was averted.*

We begin to catch up on sleep in Washington.

November 20. Obviously, a hard pill for Castro to swallow. Even as Dominicans were celebrating in the streets, Radio Havana was beaming them incitement to revolt: "All power in the hands of the people! All weapons in the hands of the people! The weapons are in the barracks. Nothing can stop it. Take the weapons necessary to destroy the repressive elements!"

November 22. Lechuga, bitter, vituperative, formally accuses the United States of intervention in the Dominican Republic. (Simultaneously, Soviet and Cuban delegates at UN in New York attack U.S. on identical charge.) I answer Lechuga the moment he finishes his diatribe in the O.A.S. Council:

"The United States rejects the charge that the stationing of these units of the United States fleet on the high seas outside of the territorial waters of any sovereign government was an act of intervention. They were there with full knowledge of the constitutional authorities of the Dominican Republic. They were entitled to be where they were, in international waters. And, Mr. Lechuga, had we moved in and intercepted the air or sea space of the Dominican Republic, I would still reject your charge, for we would have done it at the request of President Balaguer. . . .

"What hollow mockery, this protest from a dictatorship which has made itself subservient to the foremost dictatorial system of modern times! . . . Mr. Chairman, I submit that in this instance the Cuban attack has reached a new low of irrelevance, hypocrisy and slander. . . ."

Lechuga, breathing fire, denounced the United States and charged that we were an aggressor under the Rio Treaty. When he had

---

* It has been charged that Ramfis was not entirely innocent in the sudden attempt at a military *coup d'état.* Some say he grew tired of the situation, decided to fly to Paris with his blond girl friend, and in a drunken moment telephoned his two uncles to return and take over the country. I don't believe this. Not that he would be incapable of this, but I think he was sincere in his wish not to bring disaster to his country.

finished his bitter statement there was a silence. Then the chairman said, "We shall proceed to other business." At the UN the Moscow protest was disposed of in similar manner.

November 27. Our Inter-American Peace Committee form letter goes out to all American republics asking for evidence to back up Peru's charge, so that we can consider it.

November 28. Trouble again in the D.R. Opposition leaders have called general strike to force Balaguer to step down in favor of a provisional government. I can only think, wearily, that the situation is, in State Department lingo, "fluid."

November 29. Lechuga's reply to our form letter burns the morning mail. Cuba rejects each of us—El Salvador, Venezuela, Colombia, Uruguay, and U.S.—as "unqualified" to consider Peru's charge, because we're "both judges and parties to" the case. Attacks each nation for "anti-Cuban" attitudes, saves us for the last: "The position of the United States is so obvious that we do not wish to tire the attention of the members . . ." The U.S. "is the director and inspirer of the diplomatic maneuvers against Cuba in the Inter-American system . . . accusations, breaking of relationships, et cetera . . . and is the party most responsible for the military aggressions against my country."

December 1. Our Inter-American Peace Committee categorically rejects Lechuga's statement that our countries are "unqualified" to consider the Peruvian matter. We formally ask Cuba: Will she allow us five to come to Cuba and make an investigation on the scene?

There is no reply. But none is needed, now. The showdown is on its way.

It is necessary at this point, before picking up my journal again, to sketch a little background for the reader. One of the most important documents in the hemisphere is the Inter-American Treaty for Reciprocal Assistance of 1947, called the Rio Treaty, because it was drafted there—a nonaggression pact inspired by President Roosevelt as the very essence of his Good Neighbor policy. Roosevelt recognized that certain episodes in our history were not likely to give too much confidence to small Latin American nations living in our shadow. Our Marines occupied the Dominican Republic for eighteen years, from 1916 to 1934. They occupied Haiti from 1915 to 1934. They occupied Nicaragua for twenty years, from 1912 to 1925, and again from 1926 to 1933. Roosevelt's promise, sealed after his death in the Rio Treaty, was that the United States would never do this again.

Since then our motives, vis-à-vis Latin America, had to be chaster than the queen. Hence the enormous achievement of the Alliance for Progress, which made it possible for us, despite these long-rooted suspicions and easily awakened fears, to work for improvement below the border in concert with other American republics.

Each American state jealously guarded its sovereignty, knowing that it had the Rio Treaty as a protection. By the same token, the treaty was rarely invoked, for the American republics were reluctant to accuse any of their neighbors of aggression. Under the Rio Treaty, any aggression by one nation against another is considered aggression against all of the members of the Inter-American system, so that all, therefore, take collective action against the state hapless enough to be branded an aggressor. That action can even include use of arms; it is a most powerful clause. Furthermore, at the tenth Inter-American Conference that produced the Declaration of Caracas of 1954 it became clear that there was a growing acceptance of the principle that the Rio Treaty should cover not only armed aggression, but indirect aggression, such as subversion. Therefore, in my opinion, Cuba was guilty of aggression.

Several countries had always challenged the interpretation that subversion was indirect aggression and could be treated in the same manner as armed aggression. Mexico and Brazil had both taken legal exception to this.

Whatever the case, I was of the school that sought precisely this move—to invoke the Rio Treaty against Castro, to bring about a situation in which the Latin American countries would join the "Colossus of the North" against whom they had guarded themselves for so long, in a move to punish one of their own. Natural fears existed here, aside from legal niceties. Not the least of these was the fear of precedent. If the powerful United States could "maneuver the O.A.S." to punish *this* country, then why could it not move the O.A.S. to punish *that* country? Had not Raul Roa, Foreign Minister of Cuba, already sardonically called the O.A.S. the "Organization of American Colonies"? Who, then, would be safe from us?

These were the problems behind those which appeared to face us. Psychological, emotional, racial, historical—complex, indeed, would be the influences playing upon the yes or no vote on what to do about Cuba.

December 2. (*Saturday, early* A.M.) Fidel Castro is reported to be making a major policy address. He has been talking steadily, in Havana, over radio and television, for five hours, from midnight until dawn. Toby Hartwick, adviser on our O.A.S. delegation, rings me at 7 A.M. He's excited—and he's a calm man. "Chep, I don't know how true this is—all we have are press reports and he could have been misquoted—but Castro is said to have declared, "I'm a Marxist-Leninist and will be one until the day I die!"

December 2 (*Saturday, later* A.M.). Yes, Fidel said it. Even more: he declared that he was influenced by Marxist-Leninist theory as a university student and that if his radical views had been known at the beginning of his revolution, those opposed to him today would have been fighting him from the first! He's pulled the rug from under so many who refused to believe it. Gone, now, all protests that he was not a Communist, but only an agrarian reformer correcting abuses, that Castroism was not Communism, that Cuba is not ruled by a Communist regime. Question: Why did Castro make this announcement, knowing we were going to vote in the O.A.S. on the Colombian resolution in seventy-two hours? Obviously, because he was convinced that the fourteen votes could not be gotten, and our failure to do so after he had publicly proclaimed himself a Communist would mean a sensational triumph for him and a public repudiation for us from the Latin American world.

I was convinced that we could gather the fourteen votes, and so call the foreign ministers meeting to consider strong action. We could call the meeting under one of two umbrellas. One was Article 49 of the Act of Bogotá, which specifies "for reasons of urgent concern." But this could mean a riot, or the price of coffee. The other is Articles 6 and 8 of the Rio Treaty, which would put the entire discussion on the basis of aggression, smoke Cuba out and at the same time have hanging over her the possibility of taking the strongest possible action against her. Some countries would, of course, be reluctant to invoke the Rio Treaty; Argentina, Brazil, Mexico, Bolivia, Chile and Ecuador would abstain or vote No. These included the largest countries on the continent, representing more than one half of its population. But I was convinced we could get the other fourteen.

December 2. (*Saturday, still* A.M.) We have a State Department session this morning. Just before going in, I talk to Adlai Stevenson, who's just come in from New York for it. "Adlai, you know I'm going to have to do a selling job in the O.A.S. Monday. I'm positive that we should go all out and call the meeting under the Rio Treaty. I certainly hope you are with me on it."

Adlai frowns. He disagrees. "I'm sorry, Chep. If we insist on the Rio Treaty, we're going to divide the hemisphere. I don't think we should show a division either to the hemisphere or to the world. We have to keep these people on our side, and we'll lose them if we insist on what you want."

Adlai sincerely believes this, of course, but the temper of the American people as I know it is for strong action. They'll be outraged if what emerges from a major foreign ministers meeting is a milk-toast resolution—especially after Castro's defiant statement. We go into our session. Nothing is achieved. We will not fight for the Rio Treaty. I come out, discouraged. I shall have to make that U.S. speech in the O.A.S. Monday. After breathing fire and thunder for so long, now, with the chips down, must I—my country—to put it bluntly, chicken out?

December 2. (*Saturday afternoon.*) I confide in my colleague Ambassador Zuleta Angel of Colombia, who presented the Colombian resolution to the O.A.S. He has sat beside me on many committees, the Subcommittee on the Dominican Question, the Inter-American Peace Committee, and others. Like his President, he is a scholar; former dean of the School of Law and Political Science at the National University of Colombia. We see alike on this issue.

"There's one ace in the hole," I say. "If *your* government insists on the invoking of the Rio Treaty, we must go along with you regardless of how some of my colleagues may feel. It's your resolution and if you only stand by your guns, we'll be successful."

I learn a little later that Foreign Minister Julio César Turbay will telephone President Lleras in Bogotá tonight for a final decision as to how they will proceed.

December 2. (*Saturday afternoon.*) A talk with Ambassador Carlos Clulow of Uruguay. A highly capable man, a onetime professor of mathematics and lecturer on the quantum theory at the University of Lausanne, a sociologist, economist, writer. He has been very disturbed by Castro's speech. For nearly ten years Fidel had hid his true political orientation. It was a betrayal. "I represent a democratic country—one of the most democratic in the world.* How can we not vote to name Castro? How can we be neutral on this issue?"

December 3. (*Sunday, early* A.M.) Word has come from the Colombian Embassy: "The President said, 'We must invoke the Rio Treaty; we must take our stand and sink or swim with it.'" Perfect, perfect!

December 4. The O.A.S. Council meeting. An explosive, emotional, bitter session, hour after hour of debate. I demand of my colleagues: "After Castro's speech, how can anyone have any further doubt of where he stands? The basic issue before us is clear; it has come into much sharper focus in these last three weeks. It is the intervention of an extracontinental totalitarian system in this hemisphere, using Castro's Cuba as a base. Dr. Castro has at last personally and publicly aligned himself, as well as his regime, with the Sino-Soviet bloc, prescribing his formula for extending Castro-Communism throughout the hemisphere. . . .

"My delegation firmly believes that the independent governments of the Organization of American States have a responsibility to act collectively to protect the sovereign and political independence of the peoples of this hemisphere from any extension of the treachery of Fidelismo, and to let the Cuban people know they are *not* alone, that they are *not* abandoned in their struggle to regain their freedom."

Four times Ambassador Vicente Sanchez Gavito, of Mexico, tried to delay the vote. Costa Rica, Guatemala and others said it was clear that Castro was a threat. Carlos Urrutia Aparacio, who had coined the "red as a beet" phrase about Lechuga, said, "Many of us did not wish to believe Castro was a Communist, nor that his regime

* Uruguay has been described as the country with too much democracy. It has a nine-man executive authority, then headed by President Haedo as chairman, made up of six of one party, three of the opposing party. The same ratio goes through all levels—state government, county, city. This "committee rule" often makes it difficult to get quick decisions, and the coalition of opposite parties—Blancos and Colorados—frequently results in compromise solutions.

seeks to establish a satellite of the Soviet Union on this continent. But his speech does away with any slight doubts and underlines the urgent need for action."

Lechuga assailed everyone who attacked him. What was taking place, he declared in a long, vituperative speech, was "part of a general plan of aggression against the Cuban people," a preface to an armed invasion of his country. He turned to Urrutia Aparacio: "Even now planes and arms are being gathered in Guatemala for another attempted invasion of Cuba!"

The Guatemalan ambassador retorted, "I flatly deny that. It is ridiculous. And it is evident that Castro is a pawn in the international chess game of Communism."

The bitterest attack on Lechuga came from my friend Dr. Guillermo Sevilla-Sacasa, of Nicaragua. All but rising out of his seat, shaking his finger at the Cuban ambassador, almost choking with emotion, he managed to say, "Lechuga should not sit in that chair. It belongs to the thousands of innocents slaughtered by Castro!" A most powerful denunciation none of us is likely to forget.

The vote came; it could not be stalled off. As the roll was called, an urgent telephone message came for Carlos Clulow, of Uruguay; he had to leave the room to take it. He returned a few minutes later, his face pale, sat down, and sent me a note: "Instructions just received. I am to abstain. But do not worry."

A cryptic note, not too clear. I could not understand. *Abstain?* Abstain meant the loss of a positive vote. I had counted and recounted the yes votes we could depend upon. We had thirteen. No more. Clulow's abstention meant we would lose. But his yes would give us our two thirds.

The roll call came to Uruguay, toward the very end. Carlos's voice sounded: "Sí!" He had defied his orders, to save us at the very last moment. I could have dashed over and kissed him.

The Council of the Organization of American States had voted to hold a Consultative Meeting of Foreign Ministers to deal specifically with the Communist threat in this hemisphere. Not with matters of urgent concern, not with the price of coffee, but with the Communist threat. The meeting will be held in January.

Monday, December 4. (*Later.*) I am with Carlos: he has been called to the telephone. On the other end of the wire is Foreign

Minister Homero Martinez Montero. I hear Montero's voice, icy and restrained: "I want you to answer two simple questions, sir. First, at what time did you receive my instructions? Second, at what time was the vote taken?"

Clulow replies in a voice equally cold. "I will answer neither question. You may have my resignation as of this moment," and he hangs up. He turns to me. "I could not dispute my conscience," he says. "I feel that if we are not counted now, then nothing matters."

The showdown had just begun.

10. INTERLUDE: TWO MYSTERIES

In the curious world of diplomacy, now and then events occur that are never cleared up. They remain enigmas. In late 1961 and early 1962, I was faced by two of these.

The first came with a message that George Ball, Undersecretary of State, was anxious to see me. I made an appointment to see him that afternoon. When I arrived at his office, waiting with him was Abram Chayes, Legal Adviser to the State Department. Both men greeted me almost somberly.

"Chep," said George, in a heavy voice, "I called you over and had Abe on hand because we have a report here that while you were in the Dominican Republic you were given a bribe to be favorable to the Trujillo family."

I looked at him, thunderstruck. It was no joke. Neither he nor Abe were smiling.

George added, in obvious embarrassment, "Now, don't get me wrong. We have to check into these matters. You can pour your heart out to Abe here and tell him all you know."

I tried to control my temper. "First of all, I don't know anything about it. It's a complete fabrication. It's fantastic. A bribe? What kind of a bribe? Who is supposed to have given me what?"

I must have spoken with more vehemence than I realized, for George gestured, as if to say, "Gently, gently." Then he said, in effect, that it had been alleged that Eduardo Morales, Dominican consul general in New Orleans, had given me, in Ciudad Trujillo, the sum of $250,000—a quarter of a million dollars. Mr. Ball did not say so, but presumably this would be money given Morales by the Trujillos to give to me, to persuade me to use my influence to lift sanctions on the Dominican Republic and presumably, to do what I could, at the same time, to keep the Trujillos in power so they would benefit from the lifting of sanctions.

I sat for a moment, feeling numb. Then I said slowly, "George, Abe, let me tell you this. All my financial dealings are handled through my bank, The Bank of New Orleans. I don't carry a great deal of money on me. I am not a wealthy man. I give you carte blanche to check any accounts, any deposits, I have, anywhere. But you will find that all my banking is done in New Orleans. I live here, but I still bank in New Orleans, because I am a director of that bank. Any salary, any income I receive, I put in that bank. I would be happy to call Larry Merrigan, the bank's president, right now, and you can talk directly to him about this."

I turned to George Ball. "How does a report of this type come out? Even though it's untrue, think of the damage it does!"

George said, "Chep, that is why I asked you to come here and told you about this myself. I know about it; Secretary Rusk knows about it; Abe knows about it; and you know about it; and that's the way it will stay, because obviously the mere fact that we're investigating—and we must investigate, like it or not—could be damaging to you."

I left Ball's office. I simply could not understand it. Morales, though ever-present in Ciudad Trujillo, had been most correct.

In the next two weeks I had two conferences with Abe Chayes. I answered all his questions. I thought, This is a hot, thankless job, with so many pitfalls, so few satisfactions. Each time I saw George Ball thereafter, I asked him if he had learned anything. He had not.

Nothing ever came of it. I never learned who started it. Cudgeling my brain later, the only possible clue I could dredge up was a television interview on Friday, November 3, in Bradenton, Florida, when a panel of newsmen asked me whether sanctions would be lifted from the Dominican Republic. I could not predict, I replied carefully. But now that Generals Hector and Arismendi had left (this was before they returned to precipitate the crisis of November 18–20), and since Ramfis had promised to resign when sanctions were removed, *if* a coalition government could be achieved, it would be possible to remove sanctions, and we could start the Alliance for Progress in one more country.

When I returned to Washington Monday, copies of two astonishing cables lay on my desk, one from our embassy in Venezuela, the other from John Hill in Ciudad Trujillo, both expressing consternation that I had predicted removal of sanctions! Agence France Presse had so quoted me. In Venezuela there were demands for my dismissal; in the Dominican Republic, there were angry repercussions among the people. I was staring at the cables when my secretary said Steve Smith was on his way down. "Chep," he was saying a moment later, "the President's upset about your statement and these cables. We've got to work out an answer to cool off our embassies."

"But it's not true," I protested. "Steve, I never said it."

Was there a tape of the interview? There was; we ordered it sent up from Florida at once. When it arrived it bore me out. We issued a public denial. But denials rarely catch up with charges. Some amount of damage had been done to me in an area in which I was particularly vulnerable.

Could this have led to the bribery charge? Or did the smear originate in the Dominican Republic after our subcommittee issued our report recommending that sanctions should *not* be lifted now?

Nor was I ever able to get to the bottom of a less serious, yet considerably disturbing episode. It falls into three parts. The first occurred on December 6, when Hal Hendrix, Latin American editor of the *Miami News*, wrote that "reports are increasing in and out of Washington that President Kennedy has decided Ambassador deLesseps Morrison was not the wisest choice for the O.A.S. post." I could not understand this story, appearing as it did two days after our triumph in the O.A.S. Council. Hal did not indicate what "reports" he had heard, seen or been told about. Then, the last week of December, I went to Miami to participate in ceremonies in the New Year's Day Orange Bowl game, in which my alma mater, Louisiana State University, played the University of Colorado. While there I took out to dinner Mrs. Diana Maneen, a lovely widow, and very knowledgeable. She had just been with a group of Boston friends who had come to Miami from Palm Beach, where the Kennedys were also spending their holidays. Her friends had told her, she said, that the rumor in Palm Beach was, "Chep Morrison is on the way out," that I was to be "removed." She knew no more than that.

I tried to forget what I had read and been told. Each time I saw Mr. Kennedy on later occasions, there was nothing I could discern in his behavior toward me that suggested he found fault in my work.

Then, one morning, weeks later, I opened my *New York Times* to read, with dismay, that I was planning to resign. The story had been written by Tad Szulc, veteran Latin American writer for the *Times*. According to him, I planned to give up my job as ambassador in the spring or summer to return to politics. I knew Tad Szulc. I had first met him in Dick Goodwin's office the day I had seen President Kennedy and accepted my appointment—June 9. I had met Dick Goodwin for the first time that day, too. The President had called Dick in to tell him the general tenor of the press release he wanted sent out about my appointment. Then Dick and I had gone into Dick's office, where he dictated a rough draft of the statement to his secretary. When it was typed, he asked me if I would go over it for any errors in fact. I had taken it to a desk at one side, and while I was reading it, two men strolled into the office and began chatting with Dick. He introduced them to me. One was Tad Szulc; the other was Philip Geyelin of the *Wall Street Journal*.

Now, at breakfast, I was reading this story predicting my resignation, and even speculating as to my successor. This, wrote Tad, might be Arturo Morales-Carrion, Deputy Assistant Secretary of State, who had been interim United States delegate to the O.A.S. before I came aboard; or it might be James Loeb, currently ambassador to Peru.

I had long ago concluded that Tad believed Dick Goodwin's point of view more valid than mine in those instances where we differed. I could only assume that Tad, or *The New York Times*, thought these men preferable because they agreed with Goodwin's philosophy. It distressed me to read the article. I immediately denied it publicly; I had no intention of resigning; I had promised Mr. Kennedy I would serve until I ran for governor again, which meant late 1963. I had no reason to go back on my word. I thought, How would this make me appear in the eyes of my Latin

American colleagues? If they thought me a lame duck, what value would I have from now on? They would not be inclined to work with me; they would be preparing to make contact with my successor; certainly my words, my opinions, my arguments, would lack permanent authority. And this, as I was really getting into the machinery of my job!

I never learned Tad's source for his story; nor did I feel it proper to ask him, since he had not checked his story with me. Was it tied up in some way with the Palm Springs rumor? With the misquoted interview? Was it planted? Was it a trial balloon?

BOOK TWO

11. SHOWDOWN

In the President's office, where four months ago we had met to discuss how to keep the Dominican Republic safe for the West, we were gathering again. This time the problem was even more far-reaching: How could we succeed in imposing on Cuba sanctions that would throttle her economically and isolate her diplomatically from the rest of the hemisphere? And how wise was this to attempt?

A few days from now, Secretary of State Rusk was to lead our delegation to an O.A.S. meeting, again at Punta del Este—this time a gathering of the foreign ministers of the American republics.

This Tuesday morning, January 16, 1962, a wintry sun came through the long windows as Mr. Kennedy, rocking gently, shot a quizzical glance at Dean Rusk, beside him, then unexpectedly turned to me and said, "Well, Chep, you kick it off. What do you think we ought to do at Punta del Este?"

I had counted on sitting back and listening to the others—McGeorge Bundy, Goodwin, Schlesinger, Woodward, Rostow—especially since I felt particularly conspicuous. A few days before, William S. White, the political columnist, had written in the Washington *Evening Star* a column entitled, "Separating the Boys from the Men." He discussed the problems facing us at the forthcoming meeting, and added, "The men are at last being separated from the boys as we confront Castro, Soviet satellite in Cuba. . . ." Among the men, he listed Mr. Kennedy, Senator Smathers of Florida, and deLesseps Morrison. Among the boys he included Chester Bowles, Adlai Stevenson, and others of what he called the "don't-be-beastly-to-Castro" school. In that second category he named Goodwin and Schlesinger, both of whom now sat a few feet from me. Washington is really a small town; there was no doubt they had seen the piece, too.

Because this difference of opinion in our delegation was so pronounced, the President had called us together to reach some kind of meeting of minds. There was a definite fear that a tough approach would break the unity we had achieved at the first Punta del Este meeting. After all, Brazil and Mexico opposed sanctions against Cuba; it was doubtful whether Argentina, Ecuador and Bolivia would support them. If we *demanded* sanctions and rode roughshod over Brazil and Mexico and other countries who favored a soft line toward Cuba, we might bring on an irreparable split in the O.A.S. This was a serious point of view—and a legitimate one. But I happened to believe that it was dead wrong. Any compromise, I felt, would be very unwise in view of what we knew and what we had seen.

Between the time of Peru's charge that Cuban embassies were distributing Communist propaganda and today's White House meeting, my colleagues and I on the Inter-American Peace Committee had made three quick trips for on-the-scene investigations. We had divided into two subcommittees, one headed by Ambassador José Antonio Mayobre, of Venezuela, and the other by me. Between us we had visited Ecuador, Peru, Costa Rica, Nicaragua, Honduras, El Salvador, Guatemala and Haiti. In every country except Haiti—where a foreigner, even another Latin American, is immediately conspicuous among the French-speaking Negro Haitians—we had found hard examples of Communist intervention. Perhaps the most bizarre example was in Costa Rica. A Cuban baseball team had arrived a few months before, to tour the country, some seventy members strong—thirty is the usual size of a visiting baseball group—and when Ray Telles, our ambassador in San José and his

C.I.A. associates briefed me on it, I was able to put a few pointed questions to government officials.*

Suspicious of the large number of Cuban players, Costa Rican security had made a thorough check of their baggage. Intermingled with bats, balls and gloves were sixty-three packages of Cuban Communist propaganda, and $10,000 in cash. This was impounded at once. Further investigation disclosed that most of the visitors were not ballplayers at all, but Communist agents who planned to infiltrate the various communities the team visited and form political groups in each town to subvert the regime of President Mario Echandi. The Communists had employed similar Trojan Horse techniques in British Guiana, making use of the Cuban soccer team.

Almost as dramatic was Ecuador. Here a member of the Senate, disguised as a laborer, had attended a closed workers' meeting at which, he charged, a member of the staff of the Cuban embassy took the platform to accuse the President and Cabinet of Ecuador of high crimes against the Ecuadorian people.

These and other cases had been part of our documentation presented to the O.A.S. Council. I believed that one reason the O.A.S. had failed to name Cuba at the 1960 San José meeting, at which it imposed sanctions on the Dominican Republic, was the weak report presented by the Peace Committee at that time. Our report was strong, well documented.

Among other matters to be taken up at today's White House meeting was a State Department recommendation that no Congressman should be included in our delegation to Punta del Este. Here again I disagreed; I had written a memo arguing that since the conference was to be a political conference, we should have in our delegation elected representatives—not only appointed officials—answerable to the people. We should take with us the ranking Democrat and Republican in each congressional subcommittee on Latin American affairs: Senators Wayne Morse, Democrat, of Oregon, and Bourke B. Hickenlooper, Republican, of Iowa; Representatives Armistead I. Selden, Jr., Democrat, of Alabama, and Chester E. Merrow, Republican, of New Hampshire.

* Not infrequently government officials, fearful of stirring up trouble, were reluctant to tell us of these cases, and we learned about them from other sources.

Now, with the battle lines drawn, the President had asked me to speak up, and I did.

"Mr. President, it may sound like I'm beating the same old drum, but I say let's work for sanctions against Cuba. Our Peace Committee reports are well documented with hard examples of Communist intervention. We know where Castro stands. I think it would be a tragic error to go into the conference and not ask for the most stringent action."

There was a silence. Goodwin, who came into this meeting with a new title, Deputy Assistant Secretary of State for Inter-American Affairs,* pulled on his cigar. Rusk looked thoughtful. Bob Woodward tapped his fingers. We were seated as though in two opposing camps—in the center, the President and Rusk; to the left, Goodwin, Schlesinger and Walt Rostow; to the right, Bob Woodward, Bundy, Ed Jamison and myself.

Goodwin said, "I've just come back from two weeks in Brazil and a few days in Argentina. I talked to a lot of people. I believe Brazil is our next big danger point. If you think a Communist Cuba is bad, just think of a Communist Brazil. Then we really lose Latin America."

He was concerned about ex-President Janio Quadros of Brazil. The irrepressible Quadros, after his melodramatic exit from office, had gone with his wife on a leisurely trip around the world. His supporters at home, banded together in "The Popular Movement for Janio Quadros," were already maneuvering to bring him back to power, this time as prime minister under the new parliamentary government established to limit the authority of President João "Jango" Goulart, who as Quadros's vice-president had moved into office when Quadros resigned. Goodwin believed that Quadros sooner or later would make a typically dramatic—and triumphant—reentry into Brazil and take over. "I don't think we should do

* About a month before this meeting, President Kennedy, in the face of growing press criticism of Dick's role in the White House, had announced his transfer to the State Department. This was seen by many as a demotion (as deputy assistant secretary, Dick was now ostensibly under Assistant Secretary Bob Woodward). It was not. He now simply wore two hats. Actually, the appointment was an additional move to clear Mr. Kennedy's lines of communication, to have a trusted colleague at State. For Bob Woodward, it added a new dimension to his dilemma. Whom did Dick Goodwin work for—President Kennedy or Woodward? What was the chain of command?

anything that might antagonize the Quadros group," he concluded. "I see no point in alienating the future leader of the biggest country in Latin America."

"Dick, I disagree one hundred per cent," I said. "I don't believe a coward ever becomes a hero. I know Quadros was elected by a landslide vote, but we're dealing with a very strange character. And he fell apart in his first real crisis. He ran away. He made a fool of himself by sitting out in that airport for five hours waiting to be begged to come back. How can the Brazilian public ever again believe that he's stable enough to govern the country? And with all its problems?"

I cited a poll just taken in the State of Guanabara, in which Rio is located. It showed that Quadros came in third or fourth in a contest among prospective candidates to lead Brazil. Ex-President Kubitschek, the man who built Brasilia, had taken 33 per cent of the poll. Quadros, the great vote-getter, had received only 17 per cent—even less than the man he had defeated for the presidency in 1960. In my opinion, Quadros was no longer a force in Brazil. The strength of this eccentric man had been his popularity among the people. Without it, he was finished.

President Kennedy commented: "Brazil is a big question mark. We can't take lightly any chance that she might turn Communist. . . ."

Schlesinger observed, in his clipped manner, that his fears were similar to Dick's. Quadros, with his extreme leftist leanings—this man who had decorated Che Guevara; this man who had publicly called on Castro on the eve of his own election—might capture public sentiment again.

Goodwin said he had talked with Brazilian Foreign Minister Francisco San Tiago Dantas, and San Tiago Dantas and his aides made clear to him they hoped the United States would not press for strong action against Cuba,* since this would harm the Cuban people, and the people of Brazil had no wish to do this. Brazil also held inter-American unity a prime objective and desired not to jeopardize it.

* I was quite upset. Among my Latin colleagues, San Tiago Dantas was known as "San Tiago de Cuba" because of his pro-Castro bias. [Santiago, Cuba, is the city in which Castro began his revolution.] Obviously he would try to promote a soft line toward Cuba.

Walt Rostow spoke. It was clear that all three—Rostow, Schlesinger and Goodwin—were of the opinion that we had to accommodate ourselves to Brazil, and try to move her as far as possible, but not part company.

I said, "It's obvious Brazil doesn't even have a consistent domestic policy, so how much less an international policy? How are we going to follow Brazil if they don't know where they're going themselves?" Why should our policy be dictated by a country suffering from internal confusion, and whose foreign minister was pro-Castro? This was dangerous.

President Kennedy rubbed his ear and turned to Dick. "What do you think we ought to do, Dick?"

"We ought to work with the Brazilians at Punta del Este and come up with a resolution that they and we can both support," he replied.

I interrupted. "Then you'll come up with a very weak action, indeed. Brazil isn't willing to go very far except to condemn Communism. Any compromise we make with Brazil will be on Brazil's terms. If the people I've spoken to, the audiences I've addressed, are any indication, the American people want something a lot stronger than that. Frankly, I think the American public will spit on us if we come home with a namby-pamby resolution."

I felt very strongly, and I wanted to say what I felt. I believed it was especially imperative that we press for a resolution blaming Cuba as an aggressor, and then for the imposition of sanctions. I had seen what sanctions did to the Dominican Republic. I wanted the same penalty put on Castro's shoulders.

President Kennedy asked, "Do you think we have the votes for it?"

I said we had fourteen votes. Exactly two thirds.

President Kennedy said, "I'd certainly like to go with more than just fourteen, Chep."

We began to analyze the votes, and it came to me that it was comparable to analyzing a stock's future on the New York Stock Exchange. We had thirteen sure votes without Uruguay. The voting on December 4 had made that clear. Uruguayan Ambassador Clulow's last-minute yes had given us our fourteenth vote. Could we count on Uruguay again? Clulow in the end had emerged victorious. When his yes vote was made known in Uruguay, people cheered him.* Labor, industry, the press, supported him and the nine-man Council of State that rules Uruguay voted 7 to 2 to refuse his resignation. Uruguay was in a difficult position, sandwiched between the two largest powers on the continent, Brazil and Argentina, both of whom opposed strong action on Cuba. The Council, of which President Haedo was chairman, was divided into six members of the Blanco party, three of the Colorado party. Though Haedo was my friend, I knew that he veered toward his powerful neighbors. The three Colorado members, I assumed, were with us, because they had publicly criticized Haedo's views. We knew, too, that one Pedro Nardonia, leader of the rural faction in the majority Blanco party, also was for us.

But even if we assumed that the Council of State by a 7–2 majority favored strong action on Cuba, what about Foreign Minister Martinez Montero, the man who would cast the vote at Punta del Este? He owed his position to President Haedo. They were the two who had voted to accept Clulow's resignation. Did this mean that although the majority of the Council of State supported us, Foreign Minister Martinez Montero, reflecting Haedo, would vote against us?

Fascinating, I thought: the knowledge of what strategy to use at the forthcoming conference—indeed, the determination of issues important to the very future of the United States—hinged on the most elaborate analysis of the viewpoints, political and psychological, of persons completely unknown to ninety-nine per cent of United States citizens.

To determine whether we could count on Uruguay's critical vote meant knowing not only the character, personality and politics of the man casting the vote, but also those of the key figure behind him—sometimes, even, knowing their family involvements—and from all these, as a tea reader might from tea leaves, attempting to predict their actions.

We moved on to Argentina. We had hoped to win Argentina's vote. Two emissaries of Argentina's foreign minister were in Wash-

---

* One vigorous dissent came from Dr. Jorge Batlle Ibanez, editor of the Montevideo newspaper *Acción*, who charged that Clulow had "sold the Uruguayan vote. Carlos promptly challenged him to a duel—which is legal in Uruguay—but a three-man honor court finally ruled there were no grounds for a duel between an editor and a diplomat who disagree on foreign policy.

ington now;* anything was possible. Dick Goodwin spoke about Rogelio Frigerio, President Frondizi's political adviser. He described this man, a wealthy banker with onetime Communist leanings, a kind of unofficial spokesman for the Peronista party, as the most important man in Argentina. It had been Frigerio's man, Rodriguez Laretta, who had brought Goodwin together with Che Guevara in Montevideo in the now-famous "secret meeting"—to my mind, all part of the attempt by pro-Castro elements in Argentina and Brazil to maneuver us into taking a soft line toward Cuba.

"I doubt that Frigerio is so important," I said. At the risk of being rude, I added, "Dick, you go over there once or twice in your life—you meet Frigerio and the others—these are the sort of persons that take you over and try to sell you a bill of goods—the kind of persons who are really against our interests."

The President said nothing, but listened.

Goodwin's dark face flushed. "I do know, Chep, that Frigerio would tell me something one night and next morning when I spoke to Frondizi, he echoed Frigerio's words."

"But Dick," I said, "you don't even speak Spanish. How can you tell? Neither Frondizi nor Frigerio speak English. It's all through an interpreter. How do you know what really is being said?"

Dick shrugged his shoulders, as if he had said what he wanted to say. Bob Woodward and Jamison were saying little; Rusk was listening patiently. I thought how much of the world he must be concerned with—Laos, Algeria, Indonesia, nuclear disputes—and here we were spending hours on one aspect of one phase of our work. I felt very much alone. No one seemed willing to take up the cudgels.

After Bob Woodward gave his analysis, careful, well thought out, and several others made their points, the President spoke. "I don't feel that we can go ahead with an action that will yield us only fourteen votes representing small nations, while the three largest—Brazil, Argentina, and Mexico—abstain. I don't think that's a good picture to project to the world. If we could get Argentina—"

"Even if we don't get Argentina," I said, "I'm convinced that we'd be better off with fourteen votes for a strong action, than with twenty votes for a weak action."

There was silence. I plunged in once more. "I'll make a very

* Deputy Foreign Minister Oscar Camilion and Señor Carlos Ortiz de Rozas.

simple statement. We'll succeed at Punta del Este, or we'll be defeated there, based on the decision of one man."

"Who is that?" the President asked.

I said, "You, sir. If you tell us you want us to go all-out to get every vote we can for strong action, we'll get the votes. I don't know how many more than fourteen, but we'll have fourteen and we'll try for more. I know some countries simply can't afford to oppose us if we are determined to ask for their vote."

Mr. Kennedy said, with a sad smile, "I'm afraid I can't come to that conclusion yet, Chep."

"You're the key figure, Mr. President," I argued. "If you are determined in a strong stand, we will succeed."

He said, in the same tone of voice, "I wish it were that simple."

We had settled nothing in our two-hour discussion. Again and again it was, "We'll think it over some more . . . We'll consider it. . . ." Again and again, expression of the fear that if we put Brazil on the other side, not only would this divide the hemisphere, but Brazil might become another Cuba.

As we rose to go, finally, Mr. Kennedy said, "Wait a minute, gentlemen. We have something else to discuss. The question of the two Senators and the two Congressmen."

Schlesinger, who had been rather silent, suggested that we should not have them as members of the delegation. We had a difficult job as it was. Hickenlooper, a Republican, might issue a statement at Punta del Este contrary to what the Secretary would say. It could only complicate matters.

When it was my turn to comment, I disagreed again. "Senator Hickenlooper can make the same statement in Washington, and it will be read in Punta del Este and have the same effect. I'd like to have the four men along. They'll reflect a broader viewpoint of United States thinking. I'd like to believe that if we decided to do something, and Senator Hickenlooper understood the reasons for it because he was there, he might support it. If he remained home in Washington, unaware of the complexities behind what we were doing and why we were doing it, he might say he was against it. Furthermore, Mr. President, I strongly feel that the more you keep the Congress a part of what you're doing in Cuba, the better off you'll be."

At this point Mr. Kennedy, with a grin, put up his hand. "I've heard enough. The Congressmen will go."

As we were waiting to be ushered out I said—it seemed to me then that, talkative as I have been in public life, I was more talkative in these two and a half hours than in a long time—"Mr. President, I'm glad I got through to you." He grinned, we shook hands, and presently we all filed out. I knew that I was to be involved in the next months in a tug of war, with Goodwin, Schlesinger, and those who believed as they did on one side, I and those who believed as I did on the other, and the President in the middle.

Their over-all strategy, as I summed it up to myself, was: Don't deliver an ultimatum to Cuba; don't insist on demanding sanctions. You risk a rebuff from the large Latin American nations, which would be intolerable, and you risk splitting the hemisphere. Not only may you force Cuba further into the arms of the Soviet, but you may push vulnerable countries such as Brazil further in that direction; and as Brazil goes, so may her neighbor Argentina. Instead, work for a resolution simply calling upon Castro to break his ties with the Communist bloc. Brazil and Argentina would support this. Then, if Castro refuses—if he thus publicly isolates himself—there will be time to call another foreign ministers meeting prepared to vote the severest possible penalties.

Goodwin's argument was that more than two thirds of the people of Latin America—the inhabitants of Brazil and Argentina—were against imposing sanctions on Cuba. But here he talked not of people, but of governments. How could one accept his rationalization when the majority of the people of these countries could not read or write, when one half of them had never even heard of Fidel Castro?* Goodwin was not talking about the Brazilian or the Argentine people; he was talking about the three per cent or less at the top.

How much proof did we need of Castro's stand, anyway? We would not get far slapping his wrist. And we *had* imposed sanctions on the Dominican Republic. We could not have a double standard. We had publicly condemned such a policy in the United Nations.

* When President Kennedy visited Mexico City a few months later, the United States Information Service polled inhabitants of the suburbs of the Mexican capital. One third of them had never heard of Mr. Kennedy; thirty per cent had never heard of Castro. Even more had never heard of Khrushchev. If this was true in a country bordering the United States, what must have been the case in the hinterlands of Brazil and Argentina?

The next night, as I was packing—we were to leave the following morning for Punta del Este—Steve Smith came by. He had nothing special to say. He wished me well, we shook hands, and he went on. Ten minutes later my telephone rang. I picked it up, annoyed, and almost shouted, "Hello!"

The voice said, "Chep, this is Jack Kennedy."

I said, "Wait a minute, let me stand at attention, Mr. President."

I heard him chuckle. Then: "Chep, you've got to be a little more tolerant. You were pretty hard in your arguments yesterday. I appreciate your wanting strong action—after all, everybody's against Communism; you don't have to sell that."

"Mr. President," I said, "if you haven't made a decision as to what we should do, I'm going to argue as vigorously as I can to make you believe that my way is the way we ought to go. I think my view is the view of all the members of the Congress, Republicans and Democrats alike, as far as I see and hear them, and I'm with them all the time. I'm going to try to convince you, and if you don't want me to do that, just let me go home to Louisiana." I was surprised at my own vehemence.

"Oh, no, no, no," came back his voice, soothingly. "I like that. I want you to know your own mind. But I think you were just a little rough on those fellows, disagreeing with them so vehemently."

I said, "Once you make a decision, Mr. President, then I'm on the ball team; I go along one hundred per cent. Or else, if I don't agree, I know I can get out. But until you make that decision, I'm going to keep on trying to make everyone buy my point of view."

"That's all right, Chep—I just want to ask you to be a little tolerant." He paused for a moment. "I had a long talk with Secretary Rusk. He'll tell you on the plane tomorrow how I feel we should proceed. You understand, of course, that having the Congressmen along will make it a little more difficult for him. You're a politician. So I'd like to ask you, if you don't mind, that you maintain liaison, that you try to see to it that they don't make any statement that will conflict with what the Secretary says."

I said, almost facetiously, "In other words, Mr. President, you're asking me to keep them in line?"

"That's right," he said.

"I'll do my best," I promised. "But it's a big assignment."

"They have confidence in you, Chep," he said.

"Thank you," I said; and I felt considerably encouraged when I hung up. I had been depressed after the White House conference. Now it was obvious the President had wanted to talk to me about it; he had sent Steve Smith over to see if I was home, and Steve must have given him my telephone number. The President must have detected that I was down in the mouth, that I felt like a voice in the wilderness; and with his sensitivity, his gift for human relations, he made sure to get in touch with me before I left, and set me up to work as hard as possible, with as much buoyancy as possible, on the job before me.

I recalled that when I left the White House meeting, Bob Woodward had said to me, "Chep, I agree with you and I hope that will be our policy at Punta del Este." This from Bob, one of the soundest, most experienced men in the field, was immensely cheering at that moment. I wished he had supported me more strongly in the meeting, but I realized that protocol made it difficult for a State Department career official to argue in the White House. His place to do so was the halls of State.

12. CUBA SÍ OR CUBA NO

From the first it was a tug of war—a hemispheric tug of war.

The delegations poured into Punta del Este, appearing strangely subdued in comparison to the bustling life everywhere in the resort, now in the full stride of the Uruguayan summer. In August we had met in an economic conference, vast horizons before us; we had been hopeful, forging a new world; there had been optimism in the air. Now there was a battle before us; the newspapers knew it, the delegates knew it; the clash of swords was in the air.

Five months ago, with sirens screaming, the Cuban delegation, led by a swashbuckling Che Guevara, had roared into town; they were unkempt, boisterous and, with their unpressed army twill and uncut hair, almost disreputable in appearance. This time, although they arrived in the same dramatic fashion—motorcade racing through town, with sirens screaming, to their hotel—when they emerged later, they were attired in business suits, conservative, dignified diplomats, led impressively by President Osvaldo Dorticos, Carlos Rafael Rodriguez (top Communist theorist in Cuba), and my perennial opponent, Carlos Lechuga. This time they played a different role. They were the idealists, the socially conscious protectors of the exploited, who were oppressed on all sides by ruling cliques, the oligarchies of the hemisphere led by imperialist United States. They immediately won sympathy, it seemed to me, in the Latin press. Now they were the victims, brought to trial—and they appeared the part. When my father prosecuted a man in our home parish of Pointe Coupee, Louisiana, the accused invariably showed up in court dressed like a school principal. There was no question about it: the *barbudos* were on their good behavior.

As our own delegation arrived with the others, we felt the carefree holiday mood of the resort. Teen-agers walked on the streets in bathing suits, the beaches were crowded with people sunning themselves. They did not look up as we came through. They lay on the beach, plucking at their guitars, drinking, eating. It was as though we were to hold a major political conference in Fort Lauderdale or at Cannes. There was no reason to stare at us; they would read about it in their newspapers the next day. Yet here were the Secretary of State of the United States, the foreign ministers of a score of other countries—the atmosphere of inertia and apathy seemed to epitomize the problems confronting the Alliance for Progress in Latin America.

This theme seemed to be borne out by nearly everything that took place the first days. The United States press appeared pessimistic. We saw such headlines as "U.S. FORTUNES SLIPPING, CUBA CONFIDENT," over a story by Tad Szulc in *The New York Times,* and "HOPE FADES FOR UNIFIED CUBA ACTION," over a report by William L. F. Horsey, of United Press International; Associated Press writer William Ryan observed that a majority of our delegation favored agreement at the cost of a strong resolution. That we ourselves were divided into opposing camps was remarked upon repeatedly. Some correspondents questioned whether the conference should have been held at all, in the face of our dissension and the obvious division in Latin America itself.

Opening day, Monday, January 22, only intensified this dark picture. Pro-Castro demonstrations protesting our conference erupted throughout the hemisphere. In Havana, Fidel himself proclaimed that Cuban "tanks, guns, and armed divisions" would "defend us" from any action taken at Punta del Este. In El Salvador, speakers shouted that United States Marines were about to invade Cuba. In

Venezuela, police had to curb anti–United States riots, in which some thirty persons were killed. In Bolivia, pro- and anti-Castro groups fought in the streets. It was the same story in Brazil, Peru, Mexico. In New York, Castro supporters picketed the United Nations. In Montevideo, the Cuban delegation's arrival had been greeted by some two thousand cheering teen-agers. The delegation went off in limousines to Punta del Este, followed on foot by some three hundred students, singing pro-Castro songs, and prepared to march the sixty-five miles to our conference. Police halted them at a village on the way, bundled them into buses and sent them back. Only five miles away, in Maldonado, capital of the department in which Punta del Este is located, another group of several hundred students rallied under a huge hammer-and-sickle banner, chanting, "*Cuba, sí! Yanqui, no!*" Disturbances broke out in half the republics of Latin America because of our meeting. To add to all this—riots, gloomy press predictions, our own sharp division of opinion—almost in the opening hours Haiti, one of the fourteen votes we had counted upon, suddenly announced she was opposed to sanctions.*

This presaged nothing less than disaster. With Uruguay uncertain, and Haiti out, we had only twelve votes; twelve votes would mean we had to work for compromise, the weakest possible resolution; a weak resolution meant we would have difficulty persuading Congress to vote the millions necessary for the Alliance for Progress; for the Alliance for Progress to fail, for us not to be able to shore up the American republics against Communism—the chain of events was frightening.

I found myself at once assigned to a team to work on Haiti. Other teams began laboring through the day, and far into the night in caucuses, to win over as many as possible of the "soft six"—Brazil, Argentina, Mexico, Chile, Ecuador, Bolivia—as well as doubtful Uruguay. Working with us were the smaller, strongly anti-Castro countries: Colombia, Venezuela, Guatemala, Nicaragua, Costa Rica. Brazil did not wish to punish Cuba, according to her foreign minister; Argentina was in a dilemma, her President Arturo

* Perhaps we should have anticipated this. Days before, Haitian President François Duvalier complained that United States aid was "inadequate." This may have been precipitated by President Kennedy's presenting a $25,000,000 credit to Haiti's neighbor, the Dominican Republic, where matters were at long last resolving themselves.

Frondizi* being pushed against Cuba by his military (who had reacted so violently to his meeting with Guevara) and pushed toward her by Frigerio and other advisers; Mexico hid her reluctance under a cloud of legalities; Chile's President Jorge Alessandri Rodriguez said frankly, "I can't lose sight of repercussions that might flow from any position I took on delicate matters"; Ecuador had abstained in the December 4 vote, but her foreign minister was, I thought, favorable to a strong position and some hope might exist there; Bolivia feared Fidel's influence on her university students, seeking desperately to overcome the tragic poverty of that country; Uruguay, with her unwieldy nine-man Council of State, was an enigma, on the soft side.

Every day we met with the Brazilian delegation—a full-scale gathering with Dean Rusk, Goodwin and Schlesinger (who had worked with the Brazilians and the Argentinians in Washington), Brazilian Foreign Minister San Tiago Dantas and his aides. The Brazilians began by talking "coexistence." Why did we not consider Cuba to us, as Finland is to the Soviet? The Brazilian ambassador to the O.A.S. had suggested this earlier in Washington. It had been indignantly rejected by the Finnish Embassy, which made a formal protest: Don't liken us to Cuba; we are a free, democratic nation, whereas Cuba is a Soviet satellite; how dare you place us in the same category!

Nonetheless, San Tiago Dantas reiterated this at our meetings. We rejected it too. We were to find ourselves caucusing at one point with twelve countries, while the Brazilians were meeting with seven and sometimes eight countries, each of us trying to persuade the others of the validity of our views—and each of us, like captains of opposing teams, meeting the other in hope of converting him.

Here the four Congressmen were enormously helpful. On the second morning, as Senator Morse and I were being driven to the conference, I recalled that Galo Plaza, of Ecuador, had once remarked that his country in reality was ruled by its Cabinet,† and

* Frondizi's blowing hot and cold constantly plagued us. At the December 4 vote Argentina abstained on the question of calling the Punta del Este conference on Cuba. But when he met President Kennedy at Palm Beach twenty days later—December 24—Frondizi implied that he had changed his mind and now supported the idea.

† President Carlos Julio Arosemena Monroy, a brilliant political leader, was unfortunately frequently incapacitated by alcohol, so that his Cabinet found

therefore its foreign minister had authority to swing their vote to us. He, however, depended on the opinion of his adviser, Ambassador Gonzalo Escudero—the same Escudero who had been a fellow member of our Subcommittee on the Dominican Question. I knew from experience that Escudero, a former professor of logic at the University of Quito, was a meticulous lawyer, who prolonged our sessions by arguing the finest points of the law. He was not the enemy of the United States, but he was not particularly our friend. A rather frail man, suffering from various allergies, he had been ill a great deal in the Dominican Republic, slept long in the morning, usually appeared at noon for our complicated sessions, and then found his evening's relaxation at the gaming tables of Ciudad Trujillo. He followed much the same pattern here, staying up late at the Casino in downtown Punta del Este. "Wayne," I said, "if you and I could get to the foreign minister by ourselves—without Escudero at his side—we might be able to convince him. This may be our chance to crack the soft six."

Morse, a direct man, said, "Let's move on it."

I made an appointment with the Ecuadorian foreign minister for 10 A.M. the next morning—as early as diplomatic protocol allowed. It was early enough, I hoped, to avoid any chance of finding Escudero at his side.

We called upon the minister at the hour scheduled. Morse put it to him without equivocation. (Secretary Rusk, interviewed on our arrival, had tied together the success of the Alliance for Progress with the security of the hemisphere. Representative Selden, speaking as chairman of the House Subcommittee on Inter-American Affairs, had also said in an interview that Congress would be unhappy with a weak resolution.) Morse said, in effect: The United States Senate cannot but take a dim view of your country if you fail to take a strong stand on Communism. We ask your support on this vital issue. We believe such support is right and sound for you and for the entire free world.

The foreign minister listened attentively. It was a small room—

---

itself carrying on for him. The necessity for this was underlined some years before, when Arosemena, then vice-president, rose to toast the guest of honor at a banquet in Quito celebrating Bolivian-Ecuadorian friendship: "I drink to my distinguished friend, the Bolivian ambassador. He has always cut our throats in the past and I am sure he will continue to do so in the future." In July 1963 the Army forced Arosemena to resign; he then went into exile in Panama.

the hotels in Punta del Este, as I have said, are not lavish—and the three of us occupied the only chairs available. We went on with our arguments. For nearly an hour we presented the case. We appealed to Ecuador's self-interest: Castro was an enemy of the entire hemisphere; we faced this menace together and the mutual action pending before us was dictated by both wisdom and practicality.

At this moment a knock sounded. The door was opened—to reveal Ambassador Escudero, wide-eyed, alert and ready for action at the unearthly hour of 11 A.M.

The foreign minister brought his colleague up to date. We sat, silent. Ambassador Escudero, perched on the edge of the bed, shook his head. "I do not see, my friends, how we can vote as you say. It will not be legal. It presents juridical questions. The Rio Treaty speaks of armed intervention." Ecuador had never recognized the Caracas interpretation that equated subversion with armed intervention. He was very sorry. . . .

Morse and I fussed with him. He was adamant. If fourteen countries found it legal, why did he find it illegal? And assuming the legality issue could be resolved, was it not true that Ecuador was one of the few countries that could vote with a clear conscience, unafraid of pro-Castro riots? For had not their last elections shown the conservatives in power? If Ecuador voted with the majority, it would insure that other countries could move freely, in accord with the dictates of their conscience.

Nothing availed. The minister would not act without Escudero's approval, he could not go counter to the legal advice proffered to him.

We left with the promise that we would talk more about it.

Although we had not been successful, my experience with Morse heartened me. This man, who at the very first had challenged my appointment, had since then become a warm friend. He was direct, forthright and clear-thinking. He had proved himself often a redoubtable enemy; it was good to have him on the side of those of us who wanted strong action.

Senator Hickenlooper was ultraconservative, a man with a dry wit and a surprisingly fine-focused mind. In his sixties, he had been governor of Iowa years before. He appeared almost forbiddingly austere at first glance; but he turned out to be, on better acquaintance, a warm human being with a magnificent sense of humor. His sharp, concise mind and his ability to cut through extraneous matters to the heart of an issue delighted me.

On the plane to Montevideo, I had sat briefly with Dean Rusk, who told me how President Kennedy felt: The President believed that we should not go forward with only fourteen votes; we must try to get at least one more. If we failed getting a fifteenth, then he would leave it to our best judgment whether to try, anyway. . . . I had then returned to my seat, next to Senator Hickenlooper, who had said, "Chep, give me a rundown." I had told him how I saw it. He knew where he stood: "I'll go for a bad two-thirds vote on a strong action rather than a hundred per cent vote on a pussyfoot resolution."

We had checked into the San Rafael Hotel, a French-châteaulike structure of some two hundred modest rooms adjoining a large gambling casino—one of the two in town—which had been prepared for our conference. Its roulette wheels and chemin de fer and dice tables had been replaced by a huge horseshoe table, hundreds of seats with four-language earphones for instantaneous translation, and all the paraphernalia of an international congress. When we arrived I discovered that, though Rusk, Schlesinger, Goodwin, Woodward and I were to stay at the San Rafael, our four Congressmen had been booked into the Vanguardia Hotel, some twenty minutes away, as if to emphasize their separateness. I thought this isolation unwise, so I transferred to their hotel, where I shared a suite with Senator Hickenlooper and Representative Selden—"Armie," an old friend of mine—while Senator and Mrs. Morse and Representative and Mrs. Merrow were on another floor. Consequently, I was with the Congressmen most of the time—dined with them, attended social events with them, arrived together at staff meetings with them, learned how they thought and felt, and did my best, in accordance with Mr. Kennedy's directive, to keep pace with them.

The two Senators were a study in opposites. Morse was talkative, outspoken, opinionated, controversial; Hickenlooper was quiet, unassuming, taciturn. Morse did his thinking aloud. Hickenlooper played his thoughts, like cards, close to his chest. Morse was impulsive, Hickenlooper, controlled; but both were highly astute observers of everything that went on.

Armistead Selden was a fine man with a first-rate mind, important because he was chairman of the House Subcommittee on Inter-American Affairs. He knew Latin America and felt strongly about Cuba. In Washington, Armie had been a great aid. He would drop in at O.A.S. meetings to observe, and once issued a press statement charging the O.A.S. with failure to hit hard enough. The papers announced: "Blast by Congressman Selden." He phoned me. "Chep, I hope that helped you out a little. I think your Latin friends should know just how strongly the Congress feels about Cuba." Here he was concerned with reaction in his home state of Alabama, where he was soon to run for re-election, and whose people he knew wanted stiff action on Castro.

Representative Merrow, a quiet, stout, deliberative man without too much Latin American background, was a listener. But when he spoke, it was to prod us. Later he was to state in Congress that our delegation "was determined to obtain as strong a resolution as we possibly could." An authority on legislation, he was constructive in his comments. Selden and I spent considerable time together, in and out of conferences, attending dinner meetings, visiting my friend President Haedo, even dropping in at Pueblo Kennedy to see how it was growing.

My "riding herd" on the Congressmen had repercussions. I was accused in our morning delegation conferences, which preceded each day's sessions, of "rolling pills" for the two Senators. When our staff submitted a resolution which the Senators characterized as too weak, sooner or later I was accused of egging them on. The fact was that all four Congressmen were oriented to what they felt was the public will, and to the need to win Congress behind the Alliance if we were to have funds voted for it; and they wanted strong action.

Hickenlooper, I discovered, was slowly coming to a conclusion. It was that Dick Goodwin gave too much weight to those he had spoken with in Brazil and Argentina, on his trip there during the Christmas holidays a month before. I had no idea how strongly Hickenlooper felt until I walked in on him and Armie Selden one evening in our suite at the Vanguardia, accompanied by Charlie Keely, Copley News Service correspondent. Charlie excused himself and went into a bedroom to type out his report while I talked to Armie and Bourke. Beside them on the coffee table was the English-language *Buenos Aires Herald*, summarizing the conference so far. Bourke turned to me. Armie, he said, had picked up information at the conference which indicated that the Argentinians had gained the impression from Goodwin that President Kennedy would be satisfied with a simple condemnation resolution. This could explain why the Argentinians were holding out so adamantly.

"Chep," said Bourke testily, "I'm sick and tired of it. I'm going to tell Rusk just how I feel. Either we're going to take a hard approach —say point-blank what we want to say—or I quit and go home."

I was dismayed. It seemed such a waste for Bourke to have come if he was going now—and so unwise of him to go. I had learned to admire his clarity and precision. At meetings he said little; then he would casually utter a few words that gave the crux of the matter. I could understand his distress at the picture given the world of the United States delegation's fumbling and indecision. Each morning we were supplied with a mimeographed summary, prepared by the United States Information Service, of press stories printed back home, how they were handled, what page they appeared on, as well as editorial comment, even cartoons. Much of it made gloomy reading. We felt no better, either, when Latin colleagues would approach us and cite these very editorials—texts of which had been cabled to them by their Washington offices—and say, "You people don't want anything stronger; look at these." The editorials, naturally, were based on the stories sent home.

Hickenlooper, growing more angry by the minute, said now, "I'm just not going to put up with this. As a member of the Congress, I can't support the situation we're in. We're doomed to failure this way. I'm going to ask for my reservation to go back tomorrow night."

Armie spoke up. "Chep, I think I ought to tell you—I told Bourke that if this is the true situation, I'm packing my bags and going back with him."

"Oh, no!" I exclaimed. Bourke, Armie and the others had come because I had insisted. They could not go now. "Bourke, we've come this way together—we've had a solid front—I think Rusk feels we're correct in our view but like any tolerant man he's trying to do justice to everybody's opinion at this point." We needed Bourke—he was the leading Senator on the Republican side; he spoke with authority; he was essential. And we needed Armie too. They simply could not go back.

Hickenlooper said, "No, we're too divided in the delegation. I'm unhappy. I want to go home."

I was driven to use an argument I would not otherwise have used. "I'll tell you, Bourke, that at the White House meeting, when we talked about you and Morse and Armie and Merrow coming along, I was strong for it, but some of the others objected that you might be making statements to the press contrary to Rusk. So I'm pretty unhappy myself, right now."

"Now, now, Chep," said Hickenlooper, soothingly. "I'm not going to do anything like that. I'm convinced the Secretary is honest and forthright, and naturally he has to listen to a lot of advice. I understand that."

I said, "Bourke, you and I and Armie and Morse can sell him. But we've got to stick around to do it."

Hickenlooper thought this over. "All right," he said, finally. "I'm going to discuss this matter with Dean Rusk, but if we get nothing better than a simple resolution condemning Castro, I'm leaving tomorrow night."

So it was left: Hickenlooper would see the Secretary; Armie would talk to Dick Goodwin.*

I walked into the bedroom, which I had "loaned" to Charlie—he was working on a portable typewriter—and I said, "Charlie, this meeting in the other room—whether you heard anything or not—is off the record. Okay?" Keely looked up, nodded good-naturedly, and later joined the three of us on the balcony overlooking the bay, where we talked of other matters.

Later Armie spoke to Goodwin. He said, "Dick, the word we're getting is that you came down here and gave these people the idea that all you wanted was a resolution condemning Castro. If that's

---

* When an unnamed "United States spokesman" was quoted at Punta del Este, it was often Dick Goodwin. He had a generally sympathetic press. He had close friends on *The New York Times, New York Post* and *Washington Post,* and these defended him often. His chief critics were Keely, whose articles appeared in the *Washington Daily News;* Hal Hendrix of the *Miami News;* Dom Bonafede of the *Miami Herald,* and the *Chicago Daily News* veteran Latin American expert, Gerry Robichaud. The press controversy over Goodwin was about equally divided, though later he was transferred to the International Peace Corps when Congress got into the debate about his qualifications for the State Department job.

all, what are we batting our heads against the wall for, trying to get a stronger one?"

Dick denied it vehemently.

"All right," said Armie. "I'll take your word for it, but you did leave some people with that impression. Now, the monkey's on your back, and you better get it off."

Next morning Hickenlooper saw Rusk briefly before our delegation met. I do not know what they said to each other. Nor do I know what Rusk may have said to Dick. In our meeting Hickenlooper minced no words. Our delegation was speaking with two voices. There was considerable discussion. Then Rusk said firmly: "I must have complete knowledge of what every member of the delegation is doing. From now on we work as a team, everyone on the same course." That course, he made clear, was for strong action: we would go all out to obtain a two-thirds vote, at the least, on a strong series of resolutions.

When it was over, Senator Hickenlooper and I walked out to have breakfast. I asked him if he felt satisfied. He nodded. "All right, I'm convinced the Secretary has this moving in the right way. We've just got to get behind him and give him all the help we can and pull in every vote we can."

During this period I saw little of Schlesinger. He was busy writing speeches and helping draft basic material. Walt Rostow was working on a special, most important project—the resolution we hoped to put through providing for the Inter-American Security Organization, which would set up a Special Consultative Committee on Security—an O.A.S. watchdog committee to guard against Communist subversion. I myself had the feeling that matters were finally coming our way, forced by Hickenlooper's demand that we clearly indicate our course.

He did not leave that day. We all entered the next delegation meeting as friends. From then on we worked as Secretary Rusk had asked—as a team.

That night, perhaps in celebration of having kept our delegation intact, we went out to the Cantegril Country Club, Armie, I and Charlie Keely, whom I dressed up in a spare tuxedo I had brought. It was a little big, but Charlie's note pads must have filled it out, because it looked like it was tailored to fit. No international conference is all work, and that night we enjoyed ourselves.

Later in the evening President Haedo sent a message to me: Would I come to his lodge? "We've had enough of these high officials," he said. "Let's go out and see the common people." He took me to Maldonado, the department capital. We arrived at about midnight; an enormous dance was in progress. He introduced me. I danced; about 3 A.M. he announced, "Ambassador Morrison will be judge of the beauty contest."

I demurred. "I'm a politician, Mr. President, and since a judge can please only one and displease everybody else, plus their families, sweethearts and admirers, I never accept that job."

He said, "I'm sorry, my friend—you are the judge."

So, the beauties paraded in their evening dresses. The audience of two thousand cheered enthusiastically. Fortunately for me, one of the contestants was a blond Uruguayan girl of surpassing beauty, obviously the most beautiful there. I chose her, and it was a popular choice.

Next day Secretary Rusk made his speech—direct, hard-hitting, one of the best he had ever delivered. He had showed us parts of it, and we had each offered suggestions. Now speaking in a hall jammed with people, he bore down strongly. "We are here to consider the tragedy of Cuba," he declared. There were many elements in that tragedy. One, he said frankly, was the failure of the dictatorship which preceded Castro "to concern itself with the elementary needs of a people who had a right to be free."

The people were disillusioned, he said. They had placed so much hope on Castro at the beginning "of his resistance movement. . . . [But] now we see the Cuban people subjected to a regime which has committed itself to Marxist-Leninist doctrines at the very time when his answer to economic and social problems has proved itself to be brutal, reactionary and sterile."

Save for a murmuring from the Cubans, the hall was quiet.

"Wherever Communism goes, hunger follows," the Secretary declared. He read quietly from his speech, his words seeming the more emphatic for his lack of dramatics. He cited Communist China, "in the grip of a vast and terrible famine." He cited hunger in North Vietnam. "The techniques by which Communism seeks to subvert the development process are neither mysterious nor magical. Khrushchev, Mao Tse-tung and Che Guevara have outlined them in frankness and in detail." Step by step he detailed the process, finally reaching Castro and Cuba.

"Within the United Nations, the Cuban delegation has abandoned its brethren of the hemisphere to play the smirking sycophant for the Communist bloc." In thirty-seven votes taken on the most important issues of the General Assembly, a majority of the O.A.S. members, he pointed out, "voted together thirty-five times. . . . But, of these thirty-seven votes, Cuba voted thirty-three times with the Soviet bloc, and only four times with the O.A.S. majority."

Before he came to his indictment—knowing the audience before him—he referred movingly to his own youth. "Like millions of present-day North Americans, I spent my earliest years in what people would now call 'underdeveloped circumstances.'" To this audience of Latin American statesmen, many of them men of wealth and privilege, and all of them traditionally suspicious of rich, overfed Uncle Sam, the Secretary of State of the United States revealed that he had grown up "without public health or medical care; typhoid, pellagra, hookworm and malaria were a part of the environment in which Providence had placed us. Our schools were primitive. Our fathers and mothers earned a meager living with backbreaking toil. . . ."

Hearing him, I was never more proud to be an American. I confess there were tears in my eyes. How many of his listeners, I wondered, had thus come up through the ranks?

Now he struck: "With Communist help, Dr. Castro has built up the largest military establishment in Latin America. . . . The Castro regime has supplied Communism with a bridgehead in the Americas. . . . Every delegate in this hall knows in his mind and heart that those behind Castro hope to overthrow his government and every other government in Latin America. . . .

"The time has come for the American republics to unite against Communist intervention in this hemisphere."

He demanded: first, recognition that the alignment of Cuba with the Communist world is incompatible with the inter-American system; second, exclusion of the Castro regime from the functions of the O.A.S.; third, interruption of trade between Cuba and the rest of the hemisphere, especially in arms; fourth, individual and communal acts of defense against "the various forms of political and indirect aggression mounted against the hemisphere."

He concluded: "Our task today is not to let a petty tyrant who has appeared among us to divert us . . . but to put him in his place while we proceed with the great adventure on which we are embarked together."

Rusk, as he spoke, sat directly opposite Cuban President Dorticos, chewing on a pencil as he listened. When Rusk finished, the entire audience rose in a standing ovation—all save the Cuban delegates. They sat, Dorticos and Lechuga laughing openly, apparently over Rusk's designation in his last sentence of Castro as "a petty tyrant."

That night, however, Dorticos answered Rusk. It was a bitter, at times almost hysterical, four-hour address, from ten o'clock until two in the morning. Five months before, Che Guevara had spoken from a standing position, dramatically lifting papers from the table before him, and as dramatically letting them drop. He had been in complete command of himself. Dorticos, a heavy-set, heavily bespectacled man, spoke seated, shaking his finger at Rusk sitting directly opposite him, his voice rising shrilly, and with such vehemence, that he bounced up and down in his chair.

He denounced the United States again and again. It had forced this conference which would plunge the entire continent "into a colonial war of peoples against peoples." There had been "attempts before to crush our revolution," he shouted. "They have not succeeded." The United States had spoken of partnership, of concerted action, of consultation with her Latin American colleagues. With a sweep of his arm he indicated all the delegates present. "Were any of you consulted on this earlier occasion?" He pinpointed the Bay of Pigs, but did not name it. Echoing the slogans in the pro-Castro demonstrations throughout the hemisphere—to me, evidence of how clearly the demonstrations were initiated in Havana—he charged that the United States was preparing another invasion of Cuba, with this conference as a prelude. "This conference is designed to prepare the continental conditions for new military aggression against my country," he cried. He turned to his fellow Latin Americans: "You are casting us out at the command of the gringos of the North. For shame!"

In his long diatribe, Dorticos made the mistake of criticizing Punta del Este as the site of the conference. Why, he demanded, are we meeting in this rich-man's playground, isolated from the masses? "We are at a disadvantage here," he declared. "Our strength is with the people, and here the people cannot be heard." And scornfully: "In what kind of place are we meeting to make decisions affecting the entire hemisphere? In a gambling house!"

At this, Foreign Minister Martinez Montero of Uruguay raised his hand. "Please, please!" he exclaimed. A short man, he was nearly hidden by a table before him; it was some time before he caught the chairman's attention, while Dorticos put on his performance, bouncing and virtually screaming in his seat.

"I want to make a point of order," Montero said, when he was finally recognized. His voice echoed through the room. "My government has been criticized as the host government. Our facilities placed at your disposal have been criticized. I must point out that my country did not ask for this conference to be held here. We are a small country, a poor country, and we did not ask for this, we were requested to be your hosts." This was true. We had tried many countries, but they preferred not to entertain the conference, because they feared riots and demonstrations; and against these eventualities we knew Punta del Este was well protected.

"Because we wished to be a good neighbor, we accepted this obligation. We have tried to be a good host. We have entertained you as best we could with our limited finances. We have given you the best facilities we possess. To my Cuban colleagues I say this: When you come to pray or to contemplate, it does not matter the kind of church in which you pray, the kind of meetinghouse in which you gather. What matters is, do you come with honest purpose and admirable intentions?"

He concluded, and the hall broke out in thunderous applause. Dean Rusk turned around to smile at me, and Senator Morse at my side observed, "That little man grew two or three feet in that statement." I had to agree, although Foreign Minister Martinez Montero was the same man whose icy voice I had heard over the telephone in conversation with Ambassador Clulow when the latter defied him in voting yes on December 4 and so made possible this very conference.

Dorticos continued his speech, but whatever spell he had been able to cast, was broken.

Now came the intensive struggle for votes.

A story appeared in *El Dia*, the principal newspaper at Punta del

Este. It read, "Ambassador Morrison turned in his expense account for the day: Breakfast, $1.50; Taxi in the morning, $2; Lunch, $2.50; Afternoon taxis, $3; Dinner with the foreign minister of Haiti, $5,000,000."

Haiti's position had worried us from the very first day. Bob Woodward and I, and others, held a long series of meetings with Foreign Minister René Chalmers of Haiti, a dark, elegant gentleman with graying hair. We agreed on several important Alliance projects. One dealt with Haiti's airport, which is small, badly laid out, has only one runway, and that too short to accommodate jet planes. Haiti's tourist potential was high, but though virtually every other Caribbean country could handle jet planes—Jamaica, Puerto Rico, the Dominican Republic, even Barbados and Curaçao—Haiti, in the very center of all this, could not.

We committed ourselves to expedite the enlargement of Haiti's airport. It was a perfectly honorable arrangement, but rumors held that this was a *quid pro quo*. Mr. Chalmers is not a talkative man. When, on our caucus, we passed our final resolution around and he silently signed his name, I looked at Bob Woodward and breathed a sigh of relief. Uncertain Uruguay had fallen into place a little while before. We had, at least, our basic fourteen votes.

The key to the one more vote that President Kennedy wanted so badly—the key to the "soft six"—was Argentina, difficult, unpredictable, vacillating Argentina. Secretary Rusk concentrated on her delegation every resource we had. But, as I have indicated earlier, here we were involved in a long and complicated chess game, the first moves of which had been made months before. And here we saw exhibited some of the most extraordinary political maneuvering —now you see it, now you don't—that I have known.

The week before we left for the conference, two gentlemen had arrived in Washington from Buenos Aires. They were Deputy Foreign Minister Oscar Camilion, number two man in the Argentine Foreign Office, and Carlos Ortiz de Rozas, number three man. Dick Goodwin had seen them during his stopover in Buenos Aires at Christmas. I had no idea what their influence was on President Frondizi. We knew that Foreign Minister Miguel Angel Carcano was our friend and wanted strong action on Cuba. But as for his two aides, Camilion and Ortiz de Rozas, I was suspicious, especially after I saw a cable from our embassy in Buenos Aires, headed by Chargé d'Affaires Henry Hoyt, expressing doubt as to their sincerity and their basic attitude toward the United States. Dick Goodwin's feeling was that they were our friends. Some of us believed they belonged to the Frigerio, anti–United States, pro-Castro faction in Argentina—which, to me, meant they were not our friends.

The Camilion–de Rozas team, waiting in Washington to see Mr. Kennedy (they did not succeed in this), made it clear that if we wanted Argentina's vote at the forthcoming conference we must not press for sanctions against Cuba; this would be too harsh. It would—here echoed the words of Brazilian Foreign Minister San Tiago Dantas, as reported by Dick—punish the people of Cuba, and the Argentine people had no desire to do this. Instead, suggested Messrs. Camilion and Ortiz de Rozas, let us drop the idea of sanctions, and propose, instead, to oust Cuba from the inter-American system. It was, on the face of it, a lesser penalty and Argentina would find it possible to vote for this.

My own reaction, after some thought, was, Fine! If we could actually remove Cuba (something that had not been done in the seventy-two-year history of the Pan American Union) and brand her an outlaw, isolate her in the hemisphere—this would be acceptable, if it meant Argentina's vote. Mr. Kennedy desperately wanted that fifteenth vote. It could even mean Brazil's vote, too.

However, what about the reaction of the other thirteen nations we already counted on to support sanctions? They might not wish to compromise even to this degree. Guatemala, bitterly anti-Castro, as are all the Central American countries, and menaced immediately by neighboring Cuba, was against it. This is a trick, they warned.

But after canvassing others and working to persuade them—these labors lasted into and throughout most of the conference here—we finally reached an agreement. To achieve fifteen votes and possibly more, our delegation would push for ouster, not sanctions.

I confronted Camilion and Ortiz de Rozas in the lobby of the Casino. "It's done," I said. "We've sold the idea to the others. We can now say to you that fourteen countries are ready to move."

Messrs. Camilion and Ortiz de Rozas were suddenly remote. "We'll try it on our government. We're discussing it."

I stared at them, almost openmouthed. "Try it? Discussing it? But we understood that was your position—to oust Cuba rather than attempt sanctions. You suggested it to us. What is there to discuss? Isn't this what you proposed?"

They were maddeningly vague. I told Secretary Rusk later,

"We've been led down the garden path. We've moved to their position, and they're no longer there."

It seemed only too clear that they had deliberately misled us. At the last moment they would withdraw their support for the ouster, and we would suffer a dramatic and humiliating defeat. They had moved us from the strongest action—sanctions—to lesser action—ouster—and by pulling away (Haiti at this moment was still outside the fold), we would not even have fourteen votes for ouster.

So well did they play their game that until the very last day of the conference we believed we might still win Argentina. On the last day Foreign Minister Angel Carcano walked into our caucus to give us Argentina's final decision. The moment I saw his face I knew.

Señor Angel Carcano, with great restraint, showed Secretary Rusk a letter he had received from President Frondizi. It said, simply, that he was to abstain on the resolution to oust Cuba. The Camilion–de Rozas team had flown to Buenos Aires—it is only fifty minutes by air from Punta del Este—obtained the letter themselves, and brought it back to Angel Carcano. Left to his own wishes, he would have voted yes. Now he had to abstain.

Thus, in the end, because we had retrieved Haiti, we managed the fourteen votes to oust the Castro government. I still believe that had the Camilion–de Rozas team not shunted us to ouster, holding it before us as one holds a carrot before a mule, only to snatch it away, we might have pushed through our original hope: fourteen votes to impose economic and diplomatic sanctions against Cuba. Yet it should be pointed out that ouster was, in itself, a tremendous achievement for the O.A.S., so punishing to Cuba that Argentina would not vote for it.*

Dick Goodwin, who thought he had been succeeding, was greatly put out. So sure was he of Argentina and the possibility of others of the "soft six" falling in line that he had predicted to some corre-

* If we had had any doubt of its effectiveness, the violent reaction from Havana settled that. Castro cried, "The O.A.S. is unmasked for what it is—the Yankee Ministry of Colonies! . . . Uncle Sam went to Punta del Este with a bag of gold in one hand and a bloody dagger in the other!" President Dorticos, who had taken over his foreign minister's duties at the conference because of its importance, asserted: "You will not succeed in erasing us from the Americas' geography. We may not be in the O.A.S. but socialist Cuba will be in the Americas."

spondents that we would have as many as twenty votes—unanimous, save for Cuba—for ouster. He had conscientiously sought to win Argentina. But he chose not to believe the cables from our embassy characterizing Camilion and Ortiz de Rozas as basically unfavorable to us.

So bitter was the Cuban delegation that when the final vote was taken, they boycotted it. When we met on the morning of January 31, they had already left Punta del Este, silently—far more silently than they had arrived.

Although the ouster of Cuba—her exclusion from participation in the inter-American system—was passed by a two-thirds vote, fourteen votes, with only Cuba voting no and six other countries abstaining, three other resolutions, all aimed at Cuba, were passed unanimously—that is, 20 to 1. These included barring Cuba from the Inter-American Defense Board, denouncing international Communism, and favoring the Alliance for Progress. Nineteen voted to form a committee to help countries seeking aid against Communist subversion; seventeen voted that Cuba had voluntarily placed herself outside the inter-American system; and sixteen voted for a resolution calling upon all Latin American countries to refuse to engage in arms traffic with her.

In his report to the people of the United States, broadcast from Washington a few days later, Secretary Rusk said:

"The Foreign Ministers unanimously recognize that the struggle against Communism in this hemisphere is not merely a question of defense against subversion but of positive measures as well—economic, social and political reforms and development . . .

"The roll call of votes on these resolutions provided a dramatic demonstration . . . that Cuba stands alone in the Americas. No other nation voted with its delegates in opposition to any of these resolutions . . .

"The hemisphere has taken a long stride forward."

En route to Montevideo to board Air Force One, waiting to fly us back to Washington, I spoke with Emilio Oribe, Uruguay's chargé d'affaires in Havana, and one of the best informed diplomats on developments in the Cuban capital.

"This is a major defeat for Castro," he observed. Fidel, he said, had gone to the Havana airport to see his delegation off to Punta del

Este. He had made a little speech to them. "I know you will come home triumphant," he had told them. He considered the possibility of sanctions ridiculous; the idea that he would be expelled he also considered highly unlikely. That now he *had* been ejected—branded an outlaw by his own Latin American colleagues—that friends he had counted upon were not friends—that not a single Latin American country voted "no" on any resolution—this was a crushing blow to him.

It was Emilio who told me later of a bizarre episode in Havana reported to him after he had left his post there some months following the conference. Only five Latin American nations then still maintained embassies in Havana. Scores of Cubans had fled to these for political asylum. Nearly four hundred persons had taken refuge at the Uruguayan embassy.

So large a number posed a problem, for the embassy residence itself could accommodate only about twenty. Emilio had requested the Uruguayan embassy in Washington to purchase several large tents from United States Army surplus in Miami, and several hundred feet of serpentine wire, and these had been flown to Havana, the tents set up in the garden of the Uruguayan embassy there, surrounded by the wire, so that a fenced-in compound had been created. Here, at one point, some 388 persons were living.

One day, as reported to Emilio, those in the embassy heard considerable turmoil outside. They looked out. It was midafternoon of a hot Havana day. There stood Castro himself, in the street, bodyguards with tommy guns on either side of him, and he was exchanging insults with the refugees, who had crowded up against the fence to shake their fists and scream at him.

He had driven up in his car with his bodyguards and had gotten out in the middle of the street, and now he stood there, in his olive-green uniform, his head thrown back, shouting at them, "You're a bunch of dogs, swine, pigs!" He abused them with every kind of insult. They shouted back, "You no-good rat, you Communist stooge, dog, assassin!" Then he shouted still more at them, they shouted still more at him. It grew worse. Nearly all the refugees were out of their tents now, some who were living in the residence had come out as well, shouting, screaming, shaking their fists at him, and Castro with his bodyguards was no more than twenty-five or thirty feet away. The refugees picked up stones, pebbles from the garden, clods of earth, and began throwing them at Castro. They landed about him, and on the roof of his car.

The embassy was guarded by members of the Cuban militia, armed with rifles. When the people began throwing stones and other objects, Castro's bodyguards stepped forward, pointed their tommy guns at the refugees. Castro shouted, "I will begin firing."

At this moment the embassy guards rushed to the defense of the refugees. It was their duty to guard the embassy and to prevent even more serious trouble. They lined up in front of the fence, members of the Cuban militia, rifles aimed at Castro's bodyguards, Castro's men with their machine guns aimed at them.

So they stood for perhaps a minute. Castro suddenly made a gesture of disgust and entered his car; his bodyguards turned around, got in, and they drove off.

Hearing this story, and later, reading newspaper accounts of it, I thought, How does one explain it? This was the man in charge of the destinies of a nation of six million people.

We flew to Washington; then to the White House grounds to be received by Congressional leaders and Cabinet members. President Kennedy, smiling broadly, came out to the landing pad. He looked at Rusk, pale and white, having been so much in conferences, at the others, equally wan, then at me (I was tan as an Indian, having been in the sun every siesta), and he said, "Well, there was a lot of work done at Punta del Este but you sure as hell didn't do any of it!"

In the laughter I protested indignantly, "Mr. President, it was summertime down there, and I went water-skiing every day on my lunch period."

The President grinned. "A likely story," he said, and went down the line greeting the others.*

---

* Mr. Kennedy never ceased to surprise me. A few minutes later he said, "You have mighty long arms, Chep." I looked at him questioningly. "One's working at Punta del Este, the other's back in New Orleans, where your man came out first in the mayoralty race." Adrian Duplantier, the only one of three candidates I had endorsed, had won the first primary. I thought, how alert this man is! With all the cities in the United States, he had at his fingertips the facts of the New Orleans municipal elections—who was running, whom I had endorsed, who had won.

13. SOME THINKING ALOUD

It may be helpful to the reader at this point, in the immediate aftermath of the foreign ministers meeting with its tug of war in our own delegation, if I pause briefly and think aloud on the subject of my role as ambassador to the O.A.S. and why I found myself repeatedly disagreeing with some of Mr. Kennedy's top aides on our Latin American policy.

I am not an economist, I am not a social philosopher, and I do not consider myself a pundit in Latin American affairs. But I do believe that I have a feel for my Latin American colleagues and their problems, both in their home countries and vis-à-vis the United States, and that it was in this capacity, and as a politician with experience in the field of human relations, that I was appointed by Mr. Kennedy.

I was overwhelmed by Jack Kennedy. As few Americans in my time, it seemed to me, he "got through" to our Latin American friends, high and low. They appreciated him immensely. I once told him that though he had been elected by little more than 50 per cent of the vote in this country, had he been running for office in Latin America, he would have received 90 per cent of the popular vote. No other candidate in our national elections registered so vividly in their minds; his appearance, personality, mental and physical traits spoke directly to them as perhaps no one since Franklin D. Roosevelt. This handsome, vigorous, personable, highly intelligent young North American and his Spanish-speaking wife—serenely beautiful in the gentle, dark-eyed tradition of Latin beauty—were in a class by themselves. Kennedy became a banner under which the United States could proceed to improve its image below the border. I knew this, I felt this, I was sure of this. It was Kennedy as against Castro, "Kennedyismo" as against Fidelismo—two vital personalities around whom people could rally and to whom they could give their hearts as well as their political allegiance.

Yet these very qualities in Mr. Kennedy tended to pose certain dangers. Because he had tremendous intellectual curiosity, because he sought the original rather than the routine approach, he enjoyed surrounding himself with such men as Dick Goodwin, Arthur Schlesinger, Walt Rostow and others. They had helped give style and excitement to his campaign. Now they helped give style and excitement to his administration.

But brilliant as they were in theory, they were, in my judgment, impractical in the grass-roots area of international politics; and when they were brought into the White House and began at once handling major Latin American matters—though they knew little about Latin America—the one drawback added to the other could only result in trouble.

Politically they were what I term romantic theorists. As they studied Latin America from afar, they were intrigued by the so-called democratic left, which is comparable with the A.D.A. (Americans for Democratic Action) in this country. They believed that what we needed in Latin America was a democratic, or non-Communist, left that was friendly to the United States. This, they believed, would enable us to capture the Latin American masses because the democratic left, steering a course between the hated oligarchies of the right and the Communists, promised social and economic reform without revolution.

When Goodwin and Schlesinger spoke with their colleagues of the democratic left in Latin America, the latter said, in substance: We dare not drive Brazil and Argentina away. We must find a meeting ground. The politicians who can help us find it, with whom we can meet and speak a common language, are Frigerio in Argentina, San Tiago Dantas in Brazil.

This is not to say that these two gentlemen are members of the democratic left; rather, that those of the democratic left in Argentina and Brazil, plus other Latins, had decided to place *their* faith in Frigerio and San Tiago Dantas. In my opinion, these sentiments expressed to Goodwin and Schlesinger represented bad advice, reflecting the kind of politically naïve attitudes which lead the democratic left to allow the Communists to take advantage of it. When leaders of the democratic left are given power, in their zeal to grant civil liberties they allow all political parties to operate openly —including the Communists. While I recognize that this is what true political suffrage means, it presents a situation that only mature democracies or outstanding democratic leaders can cope with. Otherwise, the result can destroy the society which tolerates it.

Thus, President Romulo Betancourt, a member of the democratic left, knew how to handle the situation in Venezuela. He survived all Communist attacks—Venezuela has long been a principal target of the Communists, because with its oil royalties and its poverty it has been held up as a symbol of capitalistic exploitation—and kept order in his country. But President Juan Bosch, another member of the democratic left, was unable to handle matters in the Dominican Republic. There the government was infiltrated by Communists, there was a rapid drift to the left, and finally the military had its excuse to move in and take over.*

I believed that too many members of the democratic left in Latin America, and their supporters in this country, underestimated the Communists and the Castroites.

This difference of opinion between some of Mr. Kennedy's advisers and myself in the field to which I was assigned, meant from the very beginning of my service a clash of viewpoints. These men in the White House, close to the President, who believed in them and was stimulated by them, moved much as they wished. When they did so they set up another friction, for they quite often ran counter to the views of most members of the Congress.

The Congressmen were practical people responsive to public

* The democratic left is a rather complex subject, and the reader will find more about it in Chapter XVIII.

reaction. As a practical matter, a President, a governor or a mayor must depend upon his legislative body. Though he begins by being excited by those in his campaign entourage—his speech writers, idea men, the free souls, the unattached—as time goes on, he learns that he cannot enjoy the luxury of following their advice, because frequently it brings him into conflict with his legislators.

I had seen this happen repeatedly, on lower levels, in my own experience. As an elected public official who had to consider the people's attitude on issues, I could not fall into this romantic category. In New Orleans I had been compelled to be practical. Now, in Washington, I reacted in the same manner, and so did members of the Congress. They too had no wish to court the Frigerio and San Tiago Dantas groups, who sought to keep Argentina's President Frondizi and Brazil's Foreign Office neutral when such neutrality was against our interests.

Goodwin, convinced that we must back Quadros, maintained that we should not disagree with Brazil. In short, we should go to Punta del Este not prepared for a showdown on the Castro question, but rather, we should follow the advice of the Brazilian and Argentine neutralists.

What disturbed me was this entire *accommodation* to an element opposed to us, yet using us to bring President Kennedy into a posture of neutrality. The Congressional leaders and I were urging him to take a strong position—not to be a bully, but to go to Punta del Este saying: "I want full diplomatic and economic sanctions imposed on Cuba. I want a security program to stop Communism in this hemisphere. I want a strong, hard program, because that's what the American people want."

Kennedy was a great leader. He had begun not only with the idolized image I have referred to earlier, but he had impressed the Latins as a strong man. He had acted forthrightly in the Berlin crisis. He had increased the strength of the American military to cope with rising East-West tensions. I wanted him to move with the same strength and decisiveness in Latin American affairs. But here he was, thwarted, cautioned, held back by those around him. It was not the picture of John F. Kennedy to project to the world. Undoubtedly he could not help thinking, Perhaps my advisers are right and my instinct to be tough is wrong . . . So I had seen him in our

White House meeting—not decisive, yet wanting to be; wanting to take a strong line, yet unsure.

I believe that eighty per cent of the time of the United States delegation at Punta del Este was spent trying to find a formula by which Argentina and Brazil could support us, and we could at the same time show our own people and the world that we had at last taken concrete action on Castro.

Thus my dismay at the thought that the Argentinians and Brazilians might have been allowed to infer that Kennedy would be satisfied if they remained neutral. And my additional dismay when we learned that Camilion and de Rozas had shuttled between Washington and Buenos Aires playing the same tune to their officials. Representative Paul G. Rogers, Democrat, of Florida, speaking in the House three days after our return, summed up our situation: "The stage was set for compromise even before the drama had begun, and the ground was nearly cut off from under Secretary Rusk and the United States delegation even before they reached Punta del Este."

This cleavage between our two points of view existed, it seems to me, more sharply in the early days of the Kennedy administration. As time went on, and as he listened more to the Congress, sought its votes, heard its viewpoints, the influence of Mr. Kennedy's aides waned. It was members of the Congress who finally insisted that Goodwin be removed from the White House. Changes were made. Bob Woodward was relieved of his position as Assistant Secretary of State for Inter-American Affairs and became ambassador to Spain. Edwin M. Martin was brought in with the admonition to keep Goodwin in line.

Today Goodwin is back in the White House, essentially as a speech writer. He is superb in this capacity. He is credited with devising the term "Alliance for Progress." I do not wish to disparage his abilities in any way. He is a remarkably gifted young man. It is unfortunate, it seems to me, that he went too far too fast: some seasoning could so easily have prevented the blunders and, so far as I was personally concerned, have made my own service, not only at this time but in the days to come, less frustrating.

14. KAISER—AND FREE ENTERPRISE IN LATIN AMERICA

One of the main theses in the speeches I made now, in the strategic months following Punta del Este, to promote the Alliance was the importance of free enterprise. Industrialization was a must for Latin America. Some of its nations had virtually no industry; and only industry could be used as the springboard to catapult these people into the twentieth century. Only industry could provide a living wage for millions. Here private enterprise had to play an all-important role. Unless governmental planning was matched by private initiative, unless the savings of Latin America found its way into productive investments and reinvestments to build up industry which in turn built up the economy, the Alliance could not succeed.

I felt strongly about this. I had seen at first hand what could be done; I had been present at the birth of one of the most successful United States free-enterprise projects in the hemisphere—the great Kaiser automobile complex, which today in Argentina and Brazil generates more than $300,000,000 worth of business a year, 70 per cent of which flows into the pockets of the Argentinian and Brazilian people themselves.

In Argentina, Industrias Kaiser Argentina—known as IKA—supplies more than 50 per cent of the country's transportation needs. It employs nearly 10,000 persons directly and some 40,000 indirectly. Most important, only 28 per cent of it is owned by the Kaiser interests, and 72 per cent is owned by Argentinians. Save for a few North Americans, it is a completely Argentine enterprise, from executives and engineers to dealers, clerical help and mechanics.

In Brazil, its companion—Willys-Overland do Brasil—does over $10,000,000 worth of business a month. It is owned predominantly by Brazilian stockholders, is operated as a Brazilian enterprise, and utilizes Brazilian materials and labor.

No one can compute the measure of good done the people of Brazil and Argentina as a result of the jobs created, the roads built, the schools, churches and playgrounds constructed, the money poured into the economy on all levels by these vast enterprises, begun in 1954, about ten years ago.

Kaiser's Latin American story begins, interestingly enough, in New Orleans, four years earlier, in 1950, when Henry Kaiser, about to locate one of his giant aluminum plants in my city, decided against it. It was a blow to us. I telephoned him the moment I learned the news, and found him in his office in Oakland, California. He came on the line.

"You don't know me, Mr. Kaiser," I said. "I'm Chep Morrison, Mayor of New Orleans. I understand you've turned us down on your aluminum project, I'd like to talk to you about it."

He answered, in friendly enough fashion: "I appreciate your calling me, Mr. Morrison, but I can cite six good reasons why we can't locate in your town." The price of natural gas was exorbitantly high, Louisiana had a gas use tax, and so on. It was quite a catalogue.

"I don't want to waste your time, Mr. Kaiser," I said, "but you give me forty-eight hours to tackle those six reasons, and then let me come out to Oakland and tell you what we can do."

Kaiser said politely, "If you wish, come ahead; but I've already chosen a site in another state, and I'm afraid I can't reconsider."

I called together the Chamber of Commerce, gas producers, state and city officials—and a number of key legislators, to repeal, if necessary, the use tax—and when I flew out to Oakland two days later, I brought a proposition with me. Kaiser did reconsider. Four months later, a 200,000,000-pound aluminum reduction plant was under construction in New Orleans. Today it has doubled in capacity and has the largest private-industry-owned power plant in the world.

The acquaintance thus struck up, ripened. Mr. and Mrs. Kaiser and Corinne and I became good friends.

In June 1954, Corinne and I were guests of Kaiser and his wife, Alyce, at Lake Tahoe. While we were there, Walter P. Reuther, President of the Auto Workers Union, and a committee of Detroit leaders came out to urge Kaiser not to shut down his automobile operation at Willow Run. It was a lost cause. The dozen or so other Kaiser enterprises in the United States—aluminum, steel, engineering and cement—were flourishing, but in Detroit the Kaiser-Fraser Corporation's losses were substantial. Kaiser had determined to close down; his tools and equipment, worth nearly $30,000,000 would become, in his words, "secondhand junk" the day he quit. And he was unhappy about going out of the automobile business.

As I listened to him, lights began to pop in my head. We were sitting about his swimming pool, in bathing suits, and I said, "Henry, do you mind if I come up with an idea?"

"Shoot," he said.

As he knew, I was an enthusiast about Latin America. The one thing Latin America wanted—needed—was an automobile industry. It had none, except a few assembly plants to put together automobiles manufactured elsewhere—Volkswagens, Mercedes-Benzes and Fords. "Think of it, Henry: two hundred million people in Latin America without an automobile industry. In some towns, a twenty-year-old automobile is considered a new car. Why don't you take your thirty millions' worth of tools, your trained personnel, your experience, and transplant it all to Latin America?"

Kaiser catches fire slowly, but when he does, it is as though he lit the flame himself. "Why not go down and look around," I suggested. There were three possible markets: first, an area embracing northern Argentina, Uruguay and southern Brazil; second, Venezuela, Colombia, Ecuador and Panama; and third, Mexico and Peru. These areas, the most advanced, had countless potential car buyers. "If nothing develops, consider it a vacation for you and Aly," I said. "I can promise that you'll be royally welcomed by the presidents and chiefs of state. They'll be honored to have you."

I did not know then that Kaiser had determined long ago not to expand beyond the United States. In his youth he had been commissioned to build a road in Cuba. A political figure demanded a bribe. Kaiser indignantly refused, and he decided then that he would never again operate outside his own country.

Listening now, he asked, "What about financing?"

"I'm a supreme optimist," I said. I was sure he would be able to call on local capital. His reputation was his bond; the story of Kaiser's achievements in World War II—building a ship a day—had made him a legend everywhere.

The more he thought about the idea, the more excited he grew. He decided to go, but insisted that Corinne and I join him. Little more than a month later, Mr. and Mrs. Kaiser, William Weintraub, his advertising counsel, and Mrs. Weintraub, Robert Elliott, his press-relations aide, and Corinne and I were on our way.

I sent my trusted Mario Bermudez down beforehand to alert our New Orleans honorary representatives in the various capitals and to make other arrangements for what turned out to be a 24,000-mile trip through nine countries in search of industrial sites.

We had no idea, then, that we would see not only industrial but also political history made.

The afternoon we arrived in Brazil—Friday, August 20—we had an appointment at four o'clock with President Getulio Vargas. We arrived at a moment of high crisis. Days before two gunmen had attempted to assassinate Carlos Lacerda,* the newspaper publisher, who had violently attacked Vargas on grounds of graft and corruption. Lacerda's bodyguard, a popular young Air Force officer, was killed; Lacerda had been wounded, not seriously. An inquiry had been set up by the military, which was not under Vargas's control. Lacerda had publicly accused Vargas's son, Luthero, a member of Congress, as the man behind the attack. In the public mind President Vargas, a controversial figure to say the least, was also implicated. The entire nation hung on the outcome of the inquiry. The stock market rose and fell according to the odds on President Vargas's guilt, as did the price of the cruzeiro.

---

* The same terrible-tempered and incorruptible Lacerda, Governor of the State of Guanabara, who was to have so much to do with the ousting of President Janio Quadros in 1961, and President João Goulart in 1964.

I thought, This is hardly an opportune time to call on the President. This seemed even more apparent when we arrived at Catete Palace Friday afternoon, to find it surrounded by angry crowds brandishing signs: "GET OUT VARGAS, YOU MURDERER!" "GET RID OF VARGAS!"

But President Vargas himself, when we were ushered into his ornately beautiful office, was calm, apparently riding out the storm with ease. He had lived through many upheavals. A revolution put him into power in 1930; he was elected President in 1933; he was cast out by a military junta in October 1945; he had worked himself back to be elected President again in 1950. He had ruled by dictatorial decree from 1937 to 1945; he had survived an assassination attempt in 1938. Now, in his seventies, he seemed supremely sure of himself.

Accompanied by Oswaldo Aranha, Jr., son of the distinguished foreign minister of Brazil, we found President Vargas, a short, pudgy man with twinkling black eyes under a high forehead, a strong face—a man who looked as though he knew some secret we did not—seated at the head of an enormous mahogany table. Beside him he had an interpreter; in front of him on the table, a copy of the Portuguese edition of John Gunther's *Inside U.S.A.*, open, it developed, to a page dealing with Henry Kaiser. "Mr. Kaiser, I know you through Mr. Gunther," he said, speaking strongly and forcibly in Portuguese. He read aloud from the book. "Is this all true?" he asked. When his words were translated, Kaiser chuckled. "It may be somewhat exaggerated," he said.

Kaiser explained our mission. He wanted to look about Brazil, which offered a tremendous market for his automobiles. "We have the know-how, we have the tools, and if we locate here we would want the Brazilians to own the majority of stock in our company."

Vargas smiled, a warm, contagious smile. "Excellent," he said. Most foreign companies sought to own their enterprises wholly. Brazil's sad history had been one of foreign enterprises entering, exploiting the land, its resources and its people, drawing out millions, leaving little behind. Kaiser's proposal was, in effect, a forecast of the Alliance for Progress itself; a partnership, in which the country would be associated in the enterprise.

President Vargas observed that a local newspaper that morning reported that Ernest T. Weir, of Weirton Steel, had opposed a United States Export-Import loan to expand Brazil's largest steel mill at Volta Redonda—the only American-type steel mill in the country. Mr. Weir thought it unwise to loan money to Brazil to expand a steel industry that would take orders away from United States producers.

Kaiser said emphatically, "I will issue a press statement saying I think Mr. Weir is shortsighted in this instance, if he has been correctly reported. I am also a steel producer, not as large as Weirton Steel, but I don't think we should deny the development of industry in a Latin American country." If the Brazilians produced enough steel for their needs, they might not buy any steel from the United States, but with the money earned by industrial development, they might buy other American products. "I think we'll all do better if Brazil has a stronger economy."

President Vargas extended his hand—it seemed incredible to me that in this tense moment, with pickets parading downstairs, he could sit and chat so calmly—and said, "In this country, Mr. Kaiser, you will have the wholehearted support of us all." As we left, he turned to one of our party—Herbert Moses, editor of *O Globo*, Brazil's most important newspaper, and New Orleans's representative in Rio—and said, "Do please call me next week. There are a number of things we have to talk about."

I remembered his words in the light of what happened later.

Our last stop in Brazil, before entering Argentina, was in São Paulo, Brazil's great industrial city. Here an automobile distributor cautioned Kaiser against going into Argentina. As a result, at the last moment Kaiser turned to me and said, "Chep, I don't want to go into Argentina. Peron's a dictator; I'm told our rooms will be wired with microphones, they'll ransack our luggage when we're out, it's a Gestapo state—"

"Look, Henry," I said, "you mustn't do this. We're not here to endorse Peron. We're here to start an industry that will be good for everyone concerned."

Kaiser shook his head. Both Bill Weintraub and I expostulated. Kaiser had announced he was coming to Argentina; arrangements had been made, the most elaborate; reception committees were waiting. Regardless of how he felt now, for an American industrialist of his stature to walk off the program at the last moment would be highly embarrassing to him, to us, and to the United States.

"No," he said. "You go ahead. Aly and I will stay here until you come back."

I took a stand. "I'll carry out this program for you, Henry, but as Mayor of New Orleans I have certain obligations. I don't think any of us is ready to shout 'Hurrah!' about accepting Peron's hospitality, but I'm on a spot. I have to repay his courtesies. If you do this to me, I can be of no use to you in the future. I'm not working for Kaiser on this trip; I'm giving you my time because I think it's good for New Orleans and good for Latin America. You just can't do this."

Kaiser looked at me; and again, for the second time in our acquaintance, he reconsidered.

Few receptions I have seen matched the one arranged for us in Buenos Aires. Huge signs at the airport saying "WELCOME, KAISER!"; a red carpet stretching from our plane to a reception area; a welcome by high government officials; the road to the city lined for miles on both sides by cheering crowds waving small American flags; and when we reached our hotel, the Plaza, another enormous electric sign, across the street, saying "WELCOME, KAISER!"

It was interesting to see how a dictatorship, to impress the public, made it appear that our party was much larger than it really was. Each of us was given a limousine and an aide to ourselves; each lady, a private car and a lady in waiting. Our suites at the Plaza were piled high with flowers, bouquets and wreaths, from every imaginable labor union and industrial organization. For each of the ladies, from Peron himself, a huge plastic box containing twelve dozen American Beauty roses, with his card attached.

That night a reception was held for us at City Hall, to give us the keys to the city, and later, an opera, dedicated to Henry Kaiser, at the magnificent Opera House. Kaiser refused to go to either. As we entered the Opera House, an hour late, the lights went up. All eyes turned to us in the royal box. In Kaiser's absence, I stood up and clasped both hands over my head in greeting.

Later, at our hotel, I pleaded with him. He had, after all, come this far; he had to go through with the program laid out for us. "Here were twenty-five hundred people waiting for the guest of honor—and the guest of honor was not there. I had to tell them you were ill." Kaiser said, "I'm sorry, I'm really sorry, Chep." But he was stubborn.

Next day, Saturday, a luncheon in his honor had been arranged at the exclusive Jockey Club at the race track, and he reluctantly agreed to attend it. After lunch, as we watched the races, the mayor's aide approached: "The mayor thinks it would be an excellent idea if we went to the cycling races and surprised President Peron, who is there."

Kaiser refused. I felt that nobody surprises a dictator; obviously, Peron wanted us to come there. We went—but without Kaiser, who returned to the hotel. At the cycle races Peron greeted me. He recalled (either he remembered, or was reminded by an aide) that I had been there in 1949 as head of a mayors' delegation on a good-will tour of Latin America. It was on this tour that he gave me my much-discussed decoration. As we were about to leave, Peron extended an invitation: he hoped Kaiser would join him, with us, for Sunday lunch tomorrow at his hacienda. I cannot imagine that he was not aware of Kaiser's attitude.

When we returned to our hotel, Bill Weintraub and I prevailed on Kaiser to come to the luncheon the next day. At Peron's home to greet us Sunday were two thousand blue-shirted boys massed together singing "The Star-Spangled Banner." Outside his chalet stood a striking Mercedes-Benz convertible.

"What a beautiful car!" Kaiser exclaimed.

"Yes," said Peron. The two men had apparently at last found something they could agree upon. When I had introduced each to the other, Peron had been his magnetic best—few men I know have mixed such extraordinary charm with such utter ruthlessness—but Kaiser had been distant. Now Kaiser warmed up. Peron added, "The Mercedes-Benz people gave it to me." He turned to Mrs. Kaiser. "Why don't you drive it?" And before they knew it, Mr. and Mrs. Kaiser had been ushered into the front seat, Peron and I were in the back, and off we went, with Mrs. Kaiser driving.

When she brought the car back to where it had been, Peron leaned forward, pulled the key out of the ignition, and dropped it into Mrs. Kaiser's hand. "It is yours, my lady."

She gasped and turned to me. "What do I do now, Chep?"

I explained that in Latin America, if one greatly admires an object it is customary for the owner to present it as a gift to the admirer. Here Bill Weintraub suggested, "Why don't you say you'll send him a Kaiser car from the States?"

"Under those conditions I'll accept it," she said. "Tell him we thank him."

At lunch Kaiser took me aside. "Chep, if we're going to talk business with this man, let's start on it now."

I conveyed this to President Peron, who, in great good humor, waved a hand airily. "Later," he said.

Next morning at 8 A.M. we met at the Casa Rosada—the Executive Mansion—with Peron, his advisers and experts. We had played; now it was time to work. We got down to business. Here, as it turned out, Peron and Kaiser were like two old gloves together, without benefit of interpreter save me.

As the discussion went on, I noted with interest that each time a figure or estimate was brought up, Peron hesitated, glanced at a dark, silent man at the end of the table, then made his decision. This mysterious consultant had been introduced to us as Jorge Antonio. A few years earlier, Antonio had been a $30-a-month male nurse in the Army, at one time caring for Juan Duarte, Evita Peron's brother and Peron's private secretary. When Evita died in 1952, Juan took over her enormous Social Aid Foundation, to which all workers "contributed" one day's wages a year.

Later, Juan died (some believe he committed suicide when accused of gigantic graft), and now, some years later, Jorge Antonio, his erstwhile nurse, was reputedly worth millions, holding national franchises—automobile imports and the like—which made him the virtual economic czar of Argentina.

I had seen the extraordinary spectacle of Evita Peron disbursing money from her Social Aid Foundation to her *descamisados* ("shirtless ones"). Corinne and I had met her during my 1949 trip, at a reception given by Ambassador James Bruce at the American Embassy in Buenos Aires. *Time* Magazine had printed a cover story describing her as the onetime radio entertainer and later mistress whom Peron had made the second most powerful person in Argentina.* I saw a beautiful, petite woman, who looked almost childlike, far younger than her thirty years, with a soft olive complexion, blond

* She was, for all purposes, Secretary of Labor, Minister of Public Health and Housing, Director of Social Welfare, and top public-relations adviser to her husband, and in the opinion of many, politically more shrewd than he. At one time she was proposed as a candidate for Vice-President.

hair and enormous brown eyes. I said, "You're a lady I've read so much about."

She said, with a quick, nervous smile, "I suppose you read about me in *Time* Magazine." She made a grimace. "They shouldn't write such terrible things, so untrue."

She took us with her that evening, direct from the reception, to visit a *tránsito,* or house in which vagrants spend the night. These, under her charge, fed and housed from 100 to 150 persons each; there were at least a dozen in the country. As she led us about, she spoke rapidly, excitedly, with great intensity, almost frantically: I had the impression of someone running downhill, unable to slow down. She told us about her nightly radio programs: "I go on the air at six o'clock. I speak to millions of people, to give them hope and courage. I tell them they will get what they desire regardless of where they happen to be." She took us to a huge warehouse filled with her private Care packages. People wrote for what they wished, she said, and she saw to it that they received it. Each box carried a photograph showing her in a sweater, the wind blowing her hair back, with the lengend, "*Hasta el último del país* (I'll be with you in every corner of the country)."

Next night she invited Corinne and me to the Labor Ministry to see the distribution to the poor, which took place each evening after her broadcast. An attendant took us through three large waiting rooms filled with people. Evita met us in a fourth room; she was dazzling, in a Parisian evening gown complete to furs and diamonds, as though on her way to a state reception. As she led us to a large table and asked us to sit behind it, on either side of her, Corinne asked, with a smile, "Isn't this an unusual dress to wear for work?" Evita replied with great seriousness, "Oh, the people want to see me dressed this way. It opens a world of glamour for them. No matter how poor they are, they would rather have me like this than in a sweater and skirt. So I dress up for them every night."

At either end of the table sat an assistant; before Evita lay a large leather portfolio. She gave a signal; the doors opened; people poured into the room. Then, one by one, they were ushered forward to the table to confront her.

The first was a bedraggled woman with a baby in each arm and three children under five tugging at her dress. As she made her way toward us, tears began to stream down her face. She broke out in an almost hysterical plea: her husband had left her, she had no food, no money, she had waited days to see her sainted Evita.

Evita spoke rapidly to one of the assistants at the end of the table; he scribbled a notation on a pad; the woman was to go to Transito Number 1 and receive a food package. He passed the note to Evita, who initialed it with an "E," circled in ink, lifted the cover of the portfolio before her, extracted two 50-peso bills (about $15) in such a way that the woman did not see the money, folded them inside the note, and handed the note to the woman. The latter kissed Evita's hand, then opened the note. Her eyes widened as she saw the pesos; she burst into tears, hysterically kissed Evita's hand again, the children all kissed her hand, everyone in the room sobbed, and the woman and her children were ushered out.

The next applicant was a legless man on a wooden dolly, who pushed himself along the floor with his hands. When he came before us, his chin was on a level with the table. "I've waited to see you a long, long time," he stammered. "I've always dreamed of having artificial legs. You wrote me that you would get them for me." Evita spoke to one of her two assistants; he wrote on the pad, tore it off, gave the slip to Evita; she countersigned it, reached into the portfolio, extracted another two 50-peso bills, slipped them into the folded note and handed it to the man. Again the opening of the note, the glimpse of the money, tears, the kissing of her hand, the people all weeping as he pushed himself out of the room.

This went on and on. She seemed driven, tireless. I watched her closely. Was she sincere? Was this only a dramatic performance without heart, a way she assuaged her guilt for looting the treasury of Argentina? What was the truth here? She seemed completely involved in what she was doing. She listened intently to each unfortunate before her, and as she gave out the folded slips of instructions with the money hidden inside them, she kept up an intense, breathless commentary, almost whispered to me. "Isn't this terrible. . . . This does my heart good. . . . Yes, yes, you poor man, I weep for you. . . . How good to have this power, how wonderful to be able to do this, to give them hope, my *descamisados*. . . ." She seemed almost on the verge of tears herself.

Now Evita was dead, her brother Juan was dead, and the powerful Señor Antonio, Juan's onetime nurse, sat glowering at the table as Peron and Kaiser discussed the establishment of an automobile industry in Argentina. What was becoming shockingly apparent to me as the conversation went on—unless my understanding of the Spanish was at fault—was that Antonio was something more than Peron's financial adviser, and that he was apparently opposed to allowing Kaiser to start operations unless he, Antonio, was cut in for a share. I reported my impression to Kaiser.

Kaiser had never paid money under the table and he did not propose to do so now. This was a replay of the frustrating road-building experience of his youth. His face reddened and he rose. "Gentlemen, I'm sorry, if you will excuse me, I will return to my hotel and catch the afternoon plane out. Let's forget everything we've talked about. I will not be party to this kind of dealing."

We left. By the time we reached the Plaza, an urgent message from President Peron awaited Kaiser. The negotiations resumed, without Jorge Antonio present; the deal was consummated.

Kaiser's Latin American operation—his first outside the United States—opened the door on his international activities. Today there are Kaiser enterprises in twenty-one foreign countries.

The first Argentine-built Jeep came off the assembly line of Industrias Kaiser Argentina on April 27, 1956—thirteen months after the foundations of the Kaiser plant were laid at Córdoba, Argentina.

IKA had been formed in January 1955, after a six-month survey. It was financed by both United States and Argentine capital. Thirty-two per cent represented machines and tools Kaiser brought down from the States. Twenty per cent represented an investment of machine tools by the DINFIA, a division of the Argentine Air Force, the coordinating agency set up by the government; and another twenty per cent came from public sale of stock on the Buenos Aires exchange—it had been oversubscribed in two hours—in April 1955. Additional capital needed to build the plant came through a loan from the Industrial Bank of Argentina.

The statistics we were given that Monday morning, August 23, 1954, amazed us. Argentina had practically no automobile transportation—one vehicle for every fifty-six persons, compared to one for every three persons in the United States.

During our meeting I had watched Peron with interest. Handsome, poised, the picture of vigor, eloquent on the platform, this onetime army colonel, like Huey Long, had come to power with a welfare program—soak the rich, help the poor. This had enabled him to break through. I thought, Most backward countries must experience this stage, sooner or later; somebody, whether a Peron or what, has to get it off the ground. Father Salcedo, a priest of legendary accomplishments for his people in Colombia, once told me: "When men and women are poor and helpless and cannot read or write, someone must lead them until they can manage things for themselves."

It was difficult for us, reared in a democracy, to understand the support—the near deification—such men as Peron developed in their countries. The good thing was that the country going through this stage rarely returns to the old feudal regime; there is an improvement, but at tremendous cost. In Peron's case, it meant not only a rigid, all-pervading dictatorship, but almost bankrupting Argentina. Peron nationalized industry; he socialized the country without considering the problems of capital. He and Evita raised and reraised wages; the result was catastrophic. When government operation is characterized by skill and honesty, it does well. But where there are inept, poorly trained public employees and a tradition of graft and bribery, government operation can be a nightmare. This is what Argentina suffered under Peron. It led ultimately to his overthrow in September 1955, little more than a year and a month after we saw him.

Perhaps the best testament to the courage and integrity with which Kaiser established his industrial complex was given shortly after Peron's overthrow. When Peron fled into exile in Paraguay (and Antonio was shipped to an island in Antarctica), Industrias Kaiser Argentina and all other foreign companies were interdicted by the new government until they could prove the honesty of their operation. IKA was the first to be given a clean bill of health. Many others have yet to be released.

We left Argentina early Tuesday, well pleased. En route to Caracas, Venezuela, we stopped for forty-five minutes at Rio airport in Brazil. It was in chaos. We looked about us, aghast. People were wandering about as if in a state of shock, tears streaming down their faces; police were everywhere. Kaiser was about to go into the men's lounge, when a policeman roughly pushed him away. Mario Bermudez, a Colombian, who speaks Spanish and Portuguese fluently, rebuked the guard. "Here, what are you doing? This is a distinguished American—"

The policeman, nearly hysterical, blurted out, "Vargas has killed himself!"

Then we saw the headlines.

What had happened since Friday afternoon, when we last saw President Vargas? The military inquiry into the assassination attempt upon Lacerda had moved swiftly. The culprit turned out to be neither President Vargas nor his son, but the chief of Vargas's own bodyguard, who had hired the gunmen to carry it out.

This was too close to home. The Brazilian Cabinet met in emergency session all through Monday night. At 4 A.M. the chiefs of the Army, Navy and Air Force called on President Vargas. He received them in his pajamas. They demanded his resignation. Vargas agreed—here stories differ—to take a ninety-day leave of absence, with Vice-President João Café Filho replacing him as Acting President.

Vargas retired to his bedroom. At 7 A.M. a shot was heard. The old man had gone into his bedroom, had sat there and written a dying declaration until nearly 7 A.M. and then, sitting on the side of the bed in his pajamas, he had blown his brains out.

The letter he left was a moving piece of demagoguery:

"Once again the forces that are coordinated by the interests against the people have unleashed themselves anew upon me. . . . They seek to gag my voice, prevent my action, so that I cannot continue to defend my people. After decades of domination and exploitation by international economic and financial circles, I made myself chief of a revolution. I won. I instituted the work of liberation, a regime of social liberty for all. . . .

"Now I can give my people nothing further but my blood. I choose this way always to be with you. I gave you my life. Now I offer you my death. . . ."

It profoundly impressed the people. It was printed in the newspapers, read repeatedly over the radio. The very crowds that had been clamoring for his removal, who had cheered signs reading "GET OUT VARGAS, YOU MURDERER!" completely about-faced. Overwhelmed by his death, by his act, by his eloquent testament, they demonstrated before the United States Embassy and had to be driven away; they marched on Lacerda's newspaper, *Tribuna da Imprensa* and tried to sack Lacerda's office, to overturn and burn his trucks—a sharp, violent reversal by the people. It impressed me.

Standing there in that chaotic airport, I thought, How emotional, how sentimental, how easily swayed the people can be. Vargas, the criminal of twenty-four hours before, was now the glorified hero, the martyr.

Tragic though Vargas's death was, what remained in my mind as we returned to the States was the vision of the industry Kaiser had created. He had introduced a major new industry into the two largest countries in Latin America, one whose tangential benefits spread into every part of their economies. Automobile manufacture is the most far-reaching of industries; it supports so many others—textiles, rubber, glass, metal, paint. In the United States it is said that one out of every six persons employed, works directly or indirectly as a result of the auto industry.

Kaiser's formula, it seemed to me, could be followed in Latin America by others who can join vision with private enterprise, and in doing so, help allay the Latins' distrust of North American big business. The formula means not economic colonization, but economic development; not exploiting, but sharing. For Kaiser it meant putting to work tooling that no longer had great usefulness here. He employed local people in each of his enterprises—locally owned advertising agencies, local entrepreneurs. He had brought down originally 150 supervisors and engineers. When I visited Argentina not long ago on an Alliance for Progress check-up, I found that only thirty Americans remained in that vast enterprise. The others had been replaced by Argentinians as they learned skills and gained experience.

I think of IKA as a pilot plant: it has since gone into airplane manufacture, engineering, heavy construction, home building, credit unions, trade schools. Its success offers a challenge to all other American businessmen with resources and imagination. Henry Kaiser could not have known back in 1954, when he set up, in his own gruff, stubborn way, the companies that bear his name, that he was striking a path along the very lines that nearly a decade later were to be blueprinted in the Alliance for Progress.

15. THE CRITICAL MONTHS

There was no doubt of it: as the Alliance for Progress swung more fully into motion, it became abundantly clear that, though some cynics said Cuba's ouster at Punta del Este in early 1962 had been a Pyrrhic victory, it had been a major triumph for the West. Events proved it. Like a World Series contest, the score by which games were lost or won was unimportant; it was the victory that counted. The dividends from the Punta del Este victory began almost at once and were to continue for a long time.

I am convinced that the nine months following Punta del Este, climaxed by the October 1962 missile crisis, marked the turning point of our Cuban dilemma. From Punta del Este on, we grew steadily stronger, as O.A.S. attitudes hardened, and Fidel Castro's prestige dropped correspondingly, until ultimately he was to be revealed as little more than a tool to be used—or temporarily disregarded—by the Soviet Union in its power struggle with the United States.

Castro's descent was marked in stages. Three days after the Punta del Este conference closed, President Kennedy had announced a virtually complete embargo on United States–Cuba trade to reduce Castro's ability "to engage in acts of aggression, subversion and other activities endangering the Western hemisphere." Before the end of the week Argentina broke off diplomatic relations with Cuba —Argentina, who had refused to side with us.* A few weeks later Ecuador followed suit. She was the fifteenth country to close its embassy in Havana. The trend was clear.†

How seriously Cuba regarded her isolation was emphasized on February 14, when Ambassador Lechuga strode into the O.A.S. Council and proceeded to take his seat at the table. He was not recognized to speak, but began at once to make a bitter statement, and he refused to be silenced by the chairman, Zuleta Angel of Colombia. "This is illegal, this is shameful," he concluded; then he picked up his papers and, followed by his two aides, stalked out of the room, never to return.‡

A few days later, he was informed that his diplomatic visas and those of his five-man staff were no longer valid. The Cuban embassy in Washington was closed. Lechuga and his associates left the United States.

The first major dividends of the Cuban ouster had been paid. I could not know then that these were to lead inevitably to the crucial hour—one of the most crucial in our time—when the strength and moral support crystallized at Punta del Este were to prove beyond value to us.

In the spring of 1962 I added up a kind of Alliance for Progress balance sheet—not in specific terms as to the number of schools opened in Ecuador, or the degree of tax reform achieved in El Salvador, but in terms of six successive successes in our labors, social and political, in the Latin American field:

1. The signing of the Charter of Punta del Este, August 17, 1961, which laid the groundwork for the Alliance for Progress.

2. The decision of the O.A.S. Council, by a two-thirds vote, on December 4, 1961, to call a foreign ministers meeting under the Rio Treaty, to cope collectively with the Cuban problem.

---

* The Army, Navy and Air Force, furious because Argentina had abstained, forced Frondizi to take this step.

† In May 1964, Brazil broke off relations with Cuba. Only four countries now remained who recognized the Castro regime: Chile, Bolivia, Mexico, Uruguay.

‡ At the United Nations, Cuba, with the Soviet Union at her side, fought for days to have the world organization declare her ouster illegal—and lost.

3. The resounding success of President Kennedy's visit to Venezuela and Colombia, December 12 through 15, 1961, where the cause of the Alliance was advanced when he was welcomed by the largest crowds in those countries' histories—and this in spite of every attempt by Communist groups to make his visit a failure.

4. The first real test of popular sentiment toward the Alliance for Progress as reflected in the first national elections held since its formal ratification—those in El Salvador and Costa Rica. In both countries the winning parties were those firmly committed to the Alliance, the losing parties were those against.

5. The settlement, after thirty-one years of dictatorship, of the Dominican Republic problem.

6. Our success in ousting Cuba from the inter-American system.

There was, I thought, a seventh: the growing recognition—it was to be frighteningly underscored by the Cuban missile crisis a few months later—that Communist subversion in one state was always made to appear a domestic problem, so that other states were reluctant to treat it as a violation of the principle of nonintervention. We were slowly moving toward the recognition that subversion is intervention; that we could fight it effectively only if we recognized, too, that it is aggression, however indirect—aggression aimed at a nation's security. From infiltration of propaganda to the infiltration of agents, to the infiltration of weapons, the distance, one from the other, was not too far.

I thought these successes the more significant because in the year just passed we had begun from so far behind—in the wake of the Bay of Pigs disaster—when our prestige in Latin America had been at its lowest.

I was busy and I confess I loved it. I was interested in helping to push through the Inter-American Defense College,* in helping to establish more national commissions for the Alliance throughout the hemisphere to tell our story,† in maintaining an exhausting speaking

* A major O.A.S. project to bring together military officers from all nations of the hemisphere for seminars and lectures on a full range of topics in the fields of economics, political science and military theory. I will discuss this later.

† In some countries the commissions were so well organized they were able to take full-page advertisements explaining Alliance achievements.

schedule explaining the Alliance here at home,* and at the same time keeping pace with events in our own Inter-American Bureau of the State Department. Here, again, the brilliant and free-wheeling Dick Goodwin was very much in evidence.

What happened now was that Foreign Minister Carlos Martinez Sotomayer of Chile—one of the six nations that had refused to vote with us at Punta del Este—announced in Santiago, the Chilean capital, that Deputy Assistant Secretary of State Goodwin was to lead a United States trade mission to Chile. They expected it momentarily.

This was startling news. Thirteen countries had sided with us to oust Cuba; but it was Chile—who had not—to whom we were now reportedly sending a mission offering AID loans and other credits.

Dick vehemently denied that any such promise had come from him, or that he had made any such arrangements. But the Chilean press was full of it.

We discussed the matter at our department meetings. Both Fowler Hamilton, AID world director, and Teodoro Moscoso, director of the Alliance AID program, who should have been consulted if such a mission was contemplated, were concerned.

Now came a mournful cable from Ambassador Charles W. Cole in Santiago. News that no such mission was forthcoming had been badly received. There had even been demonstrations before the United States Embassy. Promised or not, the Goodwin mission must be carried through. This, from Ambassador Cole, a calm, conservative diplomat and former president of Amherst College, had to be respected.

---

* My calendar showed sixteen speeches in April, fifteen in May, and fifteen in June, before organizations ranging from chambers of commerce to university student bodies, and from military leaders to women's clubs. These requests to speak came through the State Department and the O.A.S. I spoke in Pittsburgh during May at the Duquesne Club, shortly after United States Steel had capitulated to President Kennedy and retracted its steel price increases. My host was the president of National Tube Company, a subsidiary of United States Steel. I had to bring greetings from Mr. Kennedy. My host said, "Don't feel too badly, Mr. Morrison. Our chairman, Mr. Roger Blough, went to the White House the other day. He came back to our board meeting and said, 'When I went to see President Kennedy I wished that I had been going to see the Pope instead, because then I would only have had to kiss his ring.'" This calmed down the situation and I proceeded with the speech.

Each time I came to an O.A.S. Council meeting I met the sardonic comments of my colleagues that the way to get favorable action of the United States was to rebuff her publicly.

Finally it was decided that a trade mission would be sent to Santiago, headed by Ted Moscoso. Again, a cable from Ambassador Cole. Mr. Goodwin had better be part of the mission, for it was his name that carried magic to the people of Chile. In the end, Moscoso led a United States task force, which included Dick Goodwin, to Chile to study Chile's economic needs and, in Moscoso's words, "the possible methods of aiding Chile through the Alliance for Progress." There was fear that inflation and other domestic troubles might result in an extreme-left, and even Communist, victory in the elections scheduled for next year. At the same time the Communists in Chile denounced the Moscoso-Goodwin trade mission as a camouflaged attempt by the United States to persuade Chile to break relations with Cuba.

So matters stood as we reached the first anniversary of the Alliance for Progress. It was clear that reverberations from Punta del Este* were still sounding through the hemisphere not only in Chile, but in Argentina. There the struggle between President Frondizi and his pro–United States anti-Castro military leaders had intensified. On March 18, Argentina had held its elections. Frondizi, forever the neutralist, and overestimating his own power, had lifted a ban on the Peronista party—supporters of Peron, who was now living in Madrid—and had given them the ballot.† When the votes were counted, the Peronistas had scored about 35 per cent, elected nine governors and more than forty members of parliament. The

* Quadros returned to Brazil on March 7 from his round-the-world trip, to be wildly greeted by his followers shouting "Revolution!"—but nothing happened. He ran for governor of São Paulo later and was defeated in his comeback attempt.

† The Peronistas had been outlawed in November 1955 by a military junta two months after Peron had been forced to flee the country. Frondizi, a lawyer, had been elected February 22, 1958, in the first free elections in more than a dozen years. A highly capable man, a master of maneuver, his reign was plagued by the fact that his election was partly due to the Peronista vote, and the problem of what precisely to do with this element, how to walk a tightrope between his adviser Frigerio, who spoke for it, and the military, who feared it, led him to the intricate political dance with which the reader is now familiar. In the end, he tumbled off the rope.

chiefs of the Army, Navy and Air Force, already smarting over Frondizi's abstention on the Cuban ouster, demanded that he resign. He refused, and the military put him under arrest and then placed him on a plane that took him to a nearby island.

That night I had been a dinner guest in Washington at the home of French Ambassador Hervé Alphand and his beautiful wife, Nicole. Their parties are among the finest in the capital, and I was in excellent mood when I came home and turned on the 11:30 P.M. news broadcast—to hear the first bulletins of the Argentine crisis. I immediately jumped back into my car and drove to the State Department, five minutes away. There, in the Operations Center, a room clattering with teletype machines, the Argentine story was spelled out, and I watched long into the night.

Next morning at eight-forty-five Edwin M. Martin, who had succeeded Bob Woodward as Assistant Secretary of State for Inter-American Affairs two weeks before,* opened our staff meeting. On the agenda was the reading of a statement condemning the action in Argentina. It had been prepared for President Kennedy to read at his 11 A.M. television press conference. It declared, in effect, that we condemned the military coup; the action was unconstitutional; it was in conflict with the Alliance for Progress; and the United States was therefore suspending AID relations at once with Argentina.

I had come to the meeting with a copy of a cable from our ambassador in Buenos Aires, Robert M. McClintock. He had wired Washington: "Please make no public statement with respect to developments here because you will make it impossible for me to deal with the transitional government."

The statement scheduled to be sent up to Mr. Kennedy was read aloud. There was a silence. As I sensed the mood, most of those present concurred. "But what about Bob McClintock's cable?" I

---

* Ed Martin was an experienced career officer who had been until now Assistant Secretary of State for Economic Affairs. He had occupied high economic posts, but none having much to do with Latin America. His appointment was described by one Washington commentator as a move "to end simmering differences between 'career men' and 'Kennedy men'" in the Latin American Bureau, since he was an intimate of Undersecretary of State George Ball, who was close to Kennedy.

asked, and quoted the salient passages. The response was, in essence: We've seen it, but we don't agree with it.

"But Bob McClintock is *there* and we are *here*. He's saying don't do it, and you're going ahead and doing it!"

I knew Ambassador McClintock. Mature, thoroughly experienced, married to a Chilean, he traveled intimately in Latin American circles and knew the continent as few others. His experience included a post in the Middle East, where he had been our ambassador to Lebanon; he was at home in every kind of intrigue, Levantine or Latin. At the same time he was rather dogmatic, had no hesitancy about venturing strong opinions and made enemies easily. The Department of State was, after all, made up of human beings, and their reactions to Bob's pronouncement, in the unequivocal language he used, could also be strong. Obviously, what he had in mind now was that the Argentine military would be around a long time, a transitional government would be set up, and any statement of condemnation by us would hamstring anything we wanted to do in Argentina, one way or another; we would simply put ourselves in a strait jacket.

There were strong voices for sending the statement up to Mr. Kennedy, although others agreed with me that no judgment should be made so precipitously. But when our meeting ended, it was clear that the statement would go to the President.

I went back to my office, dejected. Then something Dean Rusk had said on our return from Uruguay popped into my head. He was pleased with the liaison done with the four Congressmen. Would I continue that relationship and "make them feel they're part of what we're doing in Latin America?"

I looked at my watch. It was 9:30 A.M. There was little time to act. Mr. Kennedy would go on the air at eleven o'clock, and I myself was due at an O.A.S. Council meeting at ten-thirty. I telephoned Senators Wayne Morse and Bourke Hickenlooper. Their reaction echoed mine. Both men at once called upon Senator Fulbright, Chairman of the Senate Foreign Relations Committee. Twenty minutes after I had phoned them, Bourke called me back. "We have an appointment with the President and the three of us are going over to the White House. We hope we'll convince him."

When I drove to the O.A.S. a few minutes later I brought a pocket radio with me. At eleven o'clock I left the meeting long enough to go into the adjacent lounge, and turn it on. The first question asked Mr. Kennedy was about the Argentine crisis. The President replied in effect: We're in touch with our embassy in Buenos Aires. I don't wish to make any statement at this time as to what our attitude will be.

As it turned out, condemnation would have been most unfortunate. The military in Argentina had brought about the severance of relations with Cuba. As a result, Argentina moved to a strong position against Castro, supporting our stand—something we had not been able to achieve with all our maneuvering and politicking through two Punta del Este meetings and the crowded months between.

Although the military pulled the strings in Buenos Aires, a constitutional succession resulted. José Maria Guido, President of the Argentine Senate, a member of Frondizi's party and the man next in line for the presidency, became President.

With this underlined was a facet of Latin America today which I considered most important and which deserves more attention. This is the fact that not all military coups are take-overs by the extreme reactionary right and lead inevitably to rigid, antidemocratic military dictatorships.

Argentina had been an example of this in March. In April, El Salvador proved another. In a military coup, Colonel Julio Rivera took over the palace. Then he removed his uniform, donned a business suit, and proceeded to be elected President in an honest, democratic election. It became true again two months later in Peru, where again the military, after a coup, removed itself and surrendered power to the civilian elected authority. The military *could* be a force for stability.

More important, there was developing in Latin America, as the military drew its officers less from a narrow aristocratic class and more from the reservoir of middle-class university students, a type of nonpolitical military that would play a significant role in the hemisphere's future.

It seemed to me that if the O.A.S. could help to develop and strengthen the nonpolitical military in Latin America, this would constitute a tremendous achievement. We had the machinery. In 1957 the Inter-American Defense Board had approved the idea of a military college whose students would be Latin American officers and whose courses would deal not so much with military conquest and traditional military autocracy, but with economic, political and social factors involved in hemispheric defense. The majority of their instructors and lecturers would be sociologists, diplomats, governmental experts, international civil servants; a minority would be members of the professional military. They would study the inter-American system, the need for collective democratic action, strategic concepts of war, counterinsurgency; their curriculum would be similar to that of the United States National War College, the NATO Defense College, and the Imperial Defense College of Great Britain.

Though approved, the college had never been established. To turn the idea into reality—to set up such a college, preferably in the United States and still more preferably at Fort McNair, in Washington, near our own Army War College—became one of my major projects.

If we could orient Latin American military officers toward democracy, train them in a United States military environment, they would not only return home more friendly to the West but more likely, I thought, to emulate our own nonpolitical military.

This was important, because at least one half of the American republics were ruled directly, or from the wings, by generals and colonels. The reader who has come this far knows with what regularity governments are overthrown and presidents are sent into exile by military juntas.*

As an active Reservist—in 1960 I was President of the Reserve Officers Association of the United States—I was fascinated by the role of the military below the border. Among unfinished business brought up at our delegation meeting one morning shortly after the second Punta del Este conference was the Inter-American Defense College. I realized with something of a shock that this had been projected nearly five years earlier. Nothing had been done about it. Why not move on it now, on the heels of Castro's defeat? I discussed it with friends on the Inter-American Defense Board—the organ of the O.A.S. charged with planning common defense meas-

* As of this writing, nearly eighty *coups d'état* have taken place in the last thirty years or so. In the past two years alone they occurred in Argentina, Peru, Guatemala, Ecuador, the Dominican Republic, Honduras and Brazil; and one was attempted in Venezuela. These countries represent almost three fifths the population of Latin America.

ures for the American republics—and especially with Major General H. H. Fischer, chairman of the United States delegation to the Board. We agreed it was high time. If the military in Latin America was a major touchstone to the hemisphere's emotional health, wasn't it important to teach their military leaders of the future how democracy works, and the place of the military in a democratic society? Would not their role in the future be less concerned with repelling military invasion, and more concerned with maintaining stability at home? Would they not find themselves more involved in civil mobilization and less in military action with guns, tanks and armies?

I spoke to President Kennedy about it. "Go ahead, Chep," he said. "By all means see what you can do." The sum of $1,500,000—two thirds the estimated cost of such a college—had been earmarked. It was to be released if and when the Latin American states approved the idea of the college and voted their commitment, $750,000, or one third the cost. This was the hurdle.

I began a campaign among my O.A.S. colleagues and discovered resistance led by three countries—Mexico, Brazil and Venezuela.

Each of these had a deep-seated distrust of the military. Their diplomats feared that an Inter-American Defense College would help create an officer elite, precisely what they had been fighting against through the years. It would inculcate, they feared, theories of government in young military officers tending to make them politically ambitious, and even more eager to take over civilian regimes. From a purely nationalistic point of view, they resented the idea of sending their most promising officers to the United States to be under our influence.

I tried to persuade the three ambassadors—Vicente Sanchez Gavito of Mexico, José Antonio Mayobre of Venezuela and Ilmar Penna Marinho of Brazil. One day I prevailed upon Vicente to join me in a stroll through the beautiful grounds of Fort McNair. Here, on the banks of the Potomac, was the great Industrial College of the Armed Forces, and here the almost legendary Army War College, both fronting on the same tradition-rich parade ground. I pointed out a splendid brick barracks building we could use, and what had once been the Walter Reed Hospital, a building that could easily be remodeled into bachelor living quarters for forty officers, with a mess hall and a parking lot. Not far away stood a commandant's house, overlooking the Potomac. Our top military leaders—nonpolitical colonels and generals—were stationed here and at nearby Fort Myer. The first classes would be small, perhaps sixty, but the students would live on the same post with such men as General George H. Decker, General Maxwell D. Taylor and their associates; they would meet them at the Officers' Club and spend time in their company. Was this not an admirable environment to help shape them into professional soldiers of highest caliber rather than politically ambitious officers?

Vicente, brilliant in law, a cynic in politics, looked about, and said, "Chep, give the names of those first sixty students and I'll pick your presidents in Latin America for the next ten years."

"You're wrong, Vicente," I said. "But even if that happened, they'd be good presidents, with a first-class training and they'd know how democracy works—which is more than you can say for the average military academy graduate in Latin America or Europe, where many of them go now."

He was not convinced.

Ambassador Mayobre of Venezuela, an outstanding economist, also disliked the idea, as did his colleagues. One said to me, "You put sixty generals or sixty admirals or whatever in Fort McNair for five months, and you will breed every kind of a coup in them."

Just the opposite, I argued. Our State Department and Department of Defense experts were even now preparing a model curriculum designed to direct students away from military seizure and toward democratic processes.

He said, "Give them a diploma from such an institution of higher military learning and they will think themselves superleaders. More medals on their uniforms, more shine on their boots . . ."

Venezuela would not come along. Indeed, Ambassador Mayobre protested to President Kennedy in person that I was "pushing too hard." His arguments did not change Mr. Kennedy's mind. The President telephoned me later. "You must go ahead with it," he said. In Mr. Kennedy's opinion, the Inter-American Defense College would play an important role, and he wanted to see it come about.

Brazil's Ambassador Ilmar Penna Marinho, too, remained unconvinced. I knew our difficulty lay in its Foreign Office, headed by the omnipresent San Tiago Dantas. Brazil's War Office wanted the college, but it was San Tiago Dantas who instructed the Brazilian ambassador, so there was little hope in that direction.

On June 8, the voting took place in the O.A.S. Seventeen nations were in favor; three opposed it. We began construction and remodeling at Fort McNair. The Inter-American Defense College was under way.

On October 9, 1962, with Secretary of State Rusk as principal speaker, the college was officially dedicated. Six months later I attended the first graduation exercises. A group of us lunched with the Commandant, Major General Thomas V. Van Natta. He told us of the school's success to date, and added an interesting footnote about three Brazilian students in the first class.

They had arrived two weeks late. It was said that the Brazilian Foreign Office held them up to give them an orientation course before being sent to the United States. Van Natta said it appeared to him that they had arrived well-armed with "a party line." Other students quoted them as saying that the United States highly exaggerated the Cuban matter; we wished only to push our own imperialistic designs. They were generally suspicious, on guard. But after eighteen or twenty weeks, their courses, their discussions with their lecturers, their bull sessions with fellow students and what they saw and experienced had worked a remarkable change of attitude. They had arrived anti–United States; they left pro–United States. They learned about Cuba, for example, not from North American propagandists, but from such authorities as Dr. Portell-Villa, former dean of the history department of the University of Havana. Their lectures on other hemispheric matters were given by equally distinguished figures. Of the seventy-two lecturers, only twenty-four came from the professional military. The others included nineteen professors from academic institutions; ten persons occupying high government positions; ten officials from international organizations; six representatives of the diplomatic corps in Washington; and three leaders of private industry. Twenty-three of those who lectured to them were prominent non–United States personalities, mostly from Latin America.

In addition, they had practical instruction. On weekends they joined other students on guided tours of Washington. They saw the United States Congress in action. They visited the Pan American Union and heard the free interchange of opinion in the O.A.S. Council. They took side trips to New York, an hour's plane ride away, to observe the United Nations General Assembly and Security Council at work. Their education went far beyond textbooks and lectures.

Now, every half year, a new class of one hundred Latin American officers—the cream of their countries' military talent—graduate, with a greater measure of hemispheric understanding, a greater comprehension of democracy, better equipped to cope with the problems of maintaining stability at home.

I thought, as I left Fort McNair, that if Vicente should be right and the presidents of Latin America for the next decade will be chosen from among the graduates of this college, I would not be disturbed. And when I read, in early 1964, of the ouster of President Goulart by the prodemocratic military of Brazil, I felt, once more, how important the Inter-American Defense College can be for our hemisphere. That the threat of the hammer and sickle could be removed from a country representing almost one half the population of Latin America—and this by a prodemocratic military—I considered a real turning point in hemispheric history, as important as many a major battle.

16. L.B.J. AND MY FRIENDS THE AMBASSADORS

It was early October, Astronaut Walter Schirra had just orbited the earth six times, the New York Yankees were playing the San Francisco Giants in the World Series, and on the other end of my telephone was Lyndon B. Johnson at his LBJ Ranch in Texas.

"Mr. Vice-President," I was saying, "we're taking these ambassadors to Texas to see the country and participate in a seminar at San Antonio, and I wondered whether you couldn't do something for them—say, maybe host them at some affair."

Johnson's hearty voice came back, "Sure, Chep. Tell you what—bring 'em out to the ranch and we'll have a real Texas barbecue."

Which explains how it came about that on Friday, October 12, 1962, the ambassadors and alternates of fifteen countries trooped into the LBJ Ranch some sixty-five miles from Austin to partake of Texas hospitality while the Vice-President of the United States, expansive in shirt sleeves, presided over a huge barbecue in his back yard.

The trip had resulted from an invitation sent by Mrs. Lois Parkhouse of the Development Office of Trinity University, San Antonio, who wanted a group of Latin American ambassadors to participate in a seminar on hemisphere problems. Because of the success of an earlier trip when I had taken a number of my Latin American colleagues to New Orleans, I thought this an excellent idea—not only the discussion on Latin America before nearly two thousand students there, but also the occasion for my O.A.S. colleagues to see as much as possible of the interior of the United States. It had always seemed regrettable to me that most of them had rarely gotten beyond the Washington–New York City circuit. They saw here reflected an interest in international affairs—a liberal, sophisticated interpretation of world events—which led them to believe that the average American was almost as interested in Vietnam, or Berlin, Buenos Aires and other cities of the world as he was in his own home town. Like it or not, as an American from the Southern and Southwest provinces of my country, I knew this was not true. Even New Orleans had been atypical in its concentration on Latin America. The ambassadors should see and feel the temper of the United States at the grass-roots level. Then they might better appreciate the difficulties in promoting the Alliance in this country as well as in Latin America. It could only help us all if they knew more about the United States.

Once the invitation had come from Trinity University, the idea snowballed. The World Affairs Council of Dallas, hearing of it, wanted to know whether the ambassadors could extend their visit to include Dallas, where a program would be built around them. When this word reached Fort Worth, civic leaders there extended an invitation. It was then that I telephoned Lyndon Johnson; and when the White House promised to provide us with a plane, we were on our way.

For the ambassadors, the high point of the trip was the visit to the LBJ Ranch. Two planes picked us up in San Antonio Friday morning, October 12, and took us directly there. The Vice-President and Lady Bird awaited us on the landing strip of the ranch, she in a fresh farm-housewife outfit, he in rough khaki slacks, tennis shoes and a monogrammed cowboy shirt. "Gentlemen, I'm proud to have you at the LBJ Ranch," he said, as I introduced them in order, according to protocol. "We're just home folks and we say come aboard and be one of us."

A large motorcart took us to the nearby rambling wooden ranch-house. Here, over cool drinks, the ambassadors relaxed. Johnson was an exceptional host, gay, warmhearted, completely outgoing. He had even seen to it that about two dozen swim suits of various sizes were on hand for those who might want to take a dip in the pool. Later, helicopters flew us about, to give us an idea of the ranch which spread over some four hundred acres.

When we returned, Johnson said, "Come on, Chep, let's bring 'em all back here and get their signatures on the blocks." This was a feature of the ranch. In the garden, blocks of wet, soft cement awaited us. Each of us signed his name in the cement. About us were scores of blocks signed by world celebrities who had visited here through the years.

After lunch, Johnson bestowed an honorary citizenship in the State of Texas upon each ambassador, presenting each man with a certificate already made out in his name. They received these with proper ceremony while a photographer recorded the event for posterity. A touchy moment came when Johnson presented Ambassador Antonio Carrillo Flores of Mexico his certificate. There has been a long-standing and often bitter feud between Mexico and Texas over a disputed piece of territory. Antonio, a jolly and always friendly man, took it in good spirit when Johnson said, with a grin, "Mr. Ambassador, I'm afraid you'll never be able to go home and run for office now, after having been made an honorary citizen of Texas."

After the presentation, a school bus—apparently part of the ranch equipment—drove up, we all got in, and the Vice-President, standing next to the driver, a microphone in his hand, played the tour director, describing the farm buildings as we passed by and giving us a little history of the area. We came in sight of the cattle barns. "We have to stop here," said Johnson, all enthusiasm. "We had a calf born this morning. You must see it." The bus stopped. We looked over at the cows and baby calf. "Look at 'em," he said, proudly. "Fine stock, I tell you; the best in Texas."

Later we flew back to San Antonio, to Trinity University. Johnson spoke. He talked of his youth as a poor boy, when all he wanted "was a picture on the wall, a rug on the floor, and a little music in the house."

As I watched my colleagues, it was obvious that they were charmed, completely won over, by the warmth and simplicity of this Texas rancher who had risen so high in his country's political favor. Watching Johnson, I could not help thinking he is a man of moods. Here he was the tireless, superbly energetic man and host, the master politician. But I recalled him in one of his more difficult days during his campaign for the Vice-Presidency in 1960.

He had been the only major candidate on the Democratic ticket to come to Louisiana. A Gallup poll in my state indicated that John Kennedy was then a two-to-one choice over Richard Nixon. A few weeks before the election I spoke by telephone with Bobby Kennedy. There was a question as to whether his brother should campaign in Louisiana.

I said, "Let's let the man go where he really has a fight. He has it made in Louisiana. But I think it would be fine if the vice-presidential candidate could come instead. We'll put on a big show for Senator Johnson." So it was agreed, and I, as mayor, handled the arrangements.

Johnson arrived by train about five o'clock in the evening—a weary man. He had been making whistle-stop speeches all the way, and at each stop had been harassed by professional hecklers. They were on hand, too, to give him trouble when his train arrived in New Orleans. Our arrangements committee had prepared for this by setting up a dummy platform, with a band, about a hundred feet before the place the train would really come to a halt. The hecklers at once took over the dummy platform. When the train came into the station, it continued beyond the bandstand and the hecklers. All they got was the steam from the Pullman car as it halted. The people at the second receiving stand made a human wedge so that L.B.J. never saw the hecklers or their banners: "L.B.J. UNTRUE TO THE SOUTH" and "L.B.J. IS FOR INTEGRATION."

I had promised Bobby to put on a big production, and it was waiting for Johnson: a carnival and a parade of perhaps 100,000 people. One of the carnival organizations loaned us the floats they were to use in a Mardi Gras a few weeks later, and these were put to use in the Johnson parade. I knew people would come by the thousands—in New Orleans you have only to say "parade" on Canal Street to have them show up—to see the floats, to get the throwaways, doodads and other trinkets showered upon them. I was determined to make a real occasion of this one visit by Lyndon Johnson, who was accompanied by Lady Bird and Luci Baines.

When it was obvious how tired Johnson was, I took him to the anteroom of my office in City Hall, where he could rest on a couch. "Go in there and catch some sleep, Senator," I said. "We're going to have a big evening."

He lay down and sighed a long sigh. "I've had a rough day," he said. "I was heckled all along the way."

"You never even saw them here," I said. "The press didn't see them either. All they'll report is that you just had a grand reception in New Orleans." I told him about the subterfuge.

He grinned at that. "I'm grateful to you," he said. Then he closed his eyes and tried to doze off. I tiptoed out.

Within five minutes he was up, looking for his aides.

"Why don't you go back and get your rest?" I asked.

Reluctantly he went back. Again, a few minutes later he was up. Obviously, he could not rest. Ten minutes later he was dictating to a secretary two speeches he was to give.

After a buffet supper we began our parade. The crowds were all I had hoped for, but Johnson was not too happy about it. He refused to ride in one of the floats. Our committee had thought that appropriate. Instead, Luci Baines did, and she seemed to have a gay time distributing the little gifts and favors to the crowd.

Johnson sat in the back seat of a convertible with me, Lady Bird in the car following. He was slumped down in his seat, his big Texas hat on his head, his spectacles on his nose. He was anything but the dynamic candidate.

We were deep in the parade now, with thousands of people on all sides of us, cheering and applauding.

In desperation I said, "Mr. Senator, why don't you get up and sit on the back of the seat here so people can see you?"

He shook his head. "This driver is starting and stopping—I might fall off."

I said, "I'll wrap my arm around your ankles and hold you. But please sit up here where the people can see you. You've got a hundred thousand folks out there that want to look at you and want to look at you real close."

He got up reluctantly and sat down gingerly on the back of the seat. I held his ankles. The people continued to cheer.

I said, "Senator, take off your hat."

He took it off and handed it to me.

I said, "Take off your glasses, too."

Meekly, he took off his glasses.

I said, "Wave to the people."

He waved to the people.

I realized his weariness, his lassitude, but it was almost impossible not to catch the contagion of the gaiety of the crowd.

When he spoke, first at the statue of Simon Bolivar, the liberator of South America, then before the annual banquet of the Press Club of New Orleans in the Municipal Auditorium, both speeches were enthusiastically applauded. We dined later at Brennan's, one of New Orleans's most famous restaurants, but he was still out of sorts, fussing at his aides, and not enjoying himself.

I said to myself when the day was finished, Can he be the politician I thought he was? I'm just a bush-league politician but, by God, I don't care how tired I am—it can be an eighteen-hour day—if I see a hundred thousand people all cheering, applauding, happy to see me, I come to life!

Fortunately, the ambassadors to the O.A.S. saw him when he was enjoying himself, host in his own home, his own state. On the plane returning to Washington two days later, there could be no doubt of it: Johnson was the hero of their journey.

I think of this Texas jaunt as significant not only because it allowed the Latin American diplomats to see, close up, the man who today is President of the United States, to know him as a warm, friendly, unaffected human being, a man among men whom they recognized as such, and whose character, as a farmer, as a rancher, and as head of a family, they appreciated, but also because of the political lessons taught on this brief, five-day trip.

For the first time they discovered, I believe, the deep-seated hostility of prominent persons, at the grass-roots level, to the entire Castro-Cuba issue. They spoke with, listened to, and spent time with an extraordinary number of persons in San Antonio, Dallas and Fort Worth. They attended the International Livestock Show in Dallas and a huge civic barbecue in their honor at the Amon Carter ranch at Fort Worth; they mingled with the students at Trinity University; they attended the Texas-Oklahoma football game. All this was important, for it gave them a cross section of opinion they might never get as graphically in Washington or New York.

Nor had they ever seen the conservative newspapers of medium-sized cities in the interior reflecting the parochial interests of the rural American. They might see dozens of front pages in these towns—and hardly any comparable to the front pages of *The New York Times* and the Washington *Post*. If this shocked or alarmed them, or gave them pause for thought, it was good. It yielded them a far more rounded picture of this country.

The missile crisis was little more than a week away—we returned to Washington the night of Sunday, October 14—and I cannot help thinking, or at least hoping, that this experience had an effect on their thinking and on the reports they sent back to their home countries.

17 CRISIS

It began days before. It was climaxed at 3:45 P.M., Tuesday, the twenty-third of October.

This day, October 23, 1962, a historic day for the world, was also, for me, the most important day in my service so far as ambassador. It was the culmination of efforts by high United States government officials in many directions: the launching of the Alliance for Progress at Punta del Este; the removal of Cuba from the inter-American system at the second Punta del Este meeting; the breaking-off of diplomatic relations with Cuba by Argentina and Ecuador; the activities of the O.A.S. in many fields; the work of its public-information commissions throughout the hemisphere; the personal diplomacy of President Kennedy, including his visits to Colombia, Venezuela and Mexico; the skillful labors of Dean Rusk, Douglas Dillon and their experts; the undramatic, unpublicized day-to-day duties of our embassies below the border. All these worked together toward this denouement, the confrontation, at last, of the United States and the Soviet Union over the problem that had haunted Mr. Kennedy from the first days of his administration: Cuba.

This day the Organization of American States was to meet at 9 A.M. in Washington, the Security Council of the United Nations at 4 P.M. in New York. It was Mr. Kennedy's hope that Ambassador Adlai Stevenson could go before the nations of the world and declare that the twenty free republics of the Inter-American system had voted unanimously to back the President of the United States in his ultimatum to the Premier of the Soviet Union and had unanimously approved his determination to use armed force, if necessary, to meet the Cuban threat.

Mr. Kennedy had spoken Monday night—the night before—to the nation over television. He had called for the quarantine of Cuba. He had asked the foreign ministers of the Latin American countries to meet in extraordinary session to render their verdict on the action he was taking. The eyes of the world were upon us. Would these nations, with whom we had labored so long through these strategic months, to persuade them to take an ever harder line toward Cuba—would they now support not only a United States quarantine of Cuba, but our right to take military action against her? If they would not, we risked the accusation that after all our protestations of consultation and partnership, the United States had returned to the unilateral, big-stick policy which we had spent so much time, energy and money to expunge.

I had arrived in Washington from Mexico City at 8 A.M., after an all-night flight, and hurried to my office to see the latest cables. Feverish canvassing had been going on by our embassies in Latin America. We could count on the fourteen nations who voted with us at Punta del Este; add Argentina and Ecuador, and we had sixteen. Four still remained: Brazil, Chile, Mexico, Bolivia. They still recognized Castro; despite all reasoning, they had refused to vote with us against Cuba.

A few minutes before nine o'clock I joined Secretary Rusk, and we walked into the O.A.S. Council room. Rarely had the stately Pan American Union been the scene of such activity. Washington was tense. Across the street from the Russian Embassy stood an eight-story office building. On virtually every window, huge drops of blood had been painted. Outside the Embassy, diplomatic cars, chauffeurs at the wheel, waited. The ambassadors from the Iron Curtain countries had been summoned there through the night and were now consulting behind the heavily draped windows. Down the street, at the White House, men conferred as the world stood on the brink of war. Three blocks apart, in this lovely city of Washington, men were meeting on a matter—melodramatic as it sounds, it was true—of life and death.

Hours before—was it only the afternoon before?—I had sat with Secretary of the Treasury Dillon in his suite at the Maria Isabel Hotel in Mexico City listening to President Kennedy in his historic eighteen-minute speech in which he announced our discovery that Soviet Cuba was now the site of offensive missiles aimed at the United States and that this country was proceeding with a series of actions to counter this.

Dillon and I and our delegation, bound for the Second Annual Review of the Alliance for Progress opening in Mexico City, Monday, October 22, had left Washington the night before, Sunday night, as though no crisis were brewing. Our departure was a camouflage to buy additional time for Mr. Kennedy in which to arrive at the decision he had to make. Had we canceled our trip it would have forewarned our enemies. The mere fact that Secretary of the Treasury Dillon, one of the key men in the Cabinet, and the United States ambassador to the O.A.S. were going off, as scheduled, to an economic meeting in Mexico, helped to abate the crisis atmosphere spreading through Washington. Our only recognition of the situation was that we went a day later than planned.

We were originally to have left Washington Saturday noon. Then Dixon Donnelley, Dillon's aide, telephoned that we would leave Sunday at 2 P.M. instead. Then, a call again: we were now leaving Sunday at 6 P.M.

Although I did not know the exact nature of the emergency, I knew there was an emergency. The President had cut short a speaking trip to the West. The story given out was that he had a cold. Vice-President Johnson had been called back to Washington from Texas. The Cabinet was in continuous session. We had postponed our take-off for Mexico because the Cabinet had not finished whatever it was discussing, and until then Dillon could not be spared.

We were at the plane at six o'clock. Dillon was not yet there. We waited. At six-thirty a limousine suddenly loomed out of the darkness and drove almost to the very steps leading to the plane. Dillon emerged, unsmiling, entered, and we took off.

Donnelley had said to me, moments before, "We may come back tomorrow. We may not even unpack our bags."

In this tense, uncertain atmosphere we landed in Mexico City and began at once our sessions with the O.A.S. finance ministers assembled at the Maria Isabel Hotel. After lunch Dillon took me aside. I had exchanged few words with him on the plane; he had been obviously preoccupied and tired. Now he said, "Chep, please be prepared to return to Washington immediately after the President speaks at 5 P.M. I'll have a radio in my suite and we'll listen to it there." By 5:20—that is, 7:20 P.M. in Washington—I would know, said Dillon, that the President had called for the O.A.S. to meet in extraordinary session at 9 A.M. tomorrow. I was to attend the meeting. This meant flying through the night and arriving in Washington an hour before it began.

I could not leave before the President spoke. White House instructions were strict: nothing was to be said or done to cause alarm. Even in the States no one knew precisely what the President would speak about; it was announced only that he had asked for all network facilities to address the American people "on a matter of great national urgency."

I went to my room and packed, then went downstairs to the afternoon session. At 4:50 P.M. Dillon and I quietly left the conference hall for his suite. The meeting of the finance ministers was adjourned a few minutes later so they, too, could hear Mr. Kennedy.

Sitting there with Dillon and several members of the American delegation, listening to that familiar voice speaking with such gravity, I confess I felt shivers up and down my spine. "This government, as promised, has maintained the closest surveillance of the Soviet military build-up on the island of Cuba. Within the past week, unmistakable evidence has established the fact . . ." I am one of that patriotic type that stands at attention when it hears "The Star-Spangled Banner." The solemnity with which the President spoke, the finality of his words, shook me. This was an ultimatum. There could be no turning back. We *were* in a crisis: we were taking a step that could bring on a nuclear war. And once Mr. Kennedy finished his speech, the matter was no longer in our hands. Then it depended upon the man to whom it was directed—Khrushchev. If the man was mad, unstable, pushed from behind . . .

Moments later I was on my way to the plane. When I arrived next morning at Dulles Airport, the State Department driver who awaited me was somber. "Just like war," he said heavily. "The lights have been on at the State Department for the last seventy-two hours."

Then came the race to my office, a study of last-minute cables, a quick staff meeting, and the entrance with Secretary Rusk into the O.A.S. Council chamber.

However critical the situation, the formalities had to be observed. President Kennedy had requested a meeting of the O.A.S. as the Organ of Consultation. The ambassadors took their seats; a resolution was offered that we transform the Council into the Organ of Consultation, empowered to act on behalf of the foreign ministers on the highest level. It was passed. I relinquished my chair to Secretary Rusk and took the chair behind him. The same procedure—almost theatrical under the circumstances—simultaneously took place at several other locations about the huge, circular table. In most instances the foreign ministers were unable to reach Washington on such short notice and the O.A.S. ambassadors in this emergency became their countries' acting foreign ministers.

Mr. Kennedy had asked for a sea and air quarantine of Cuba. He had pointed out that the Communists had lied. What they had said were defensive weapons were offensive weapons; what they had said were defensive bases were in truth missile bases armed with rockets that could strike any of our cities; the presence of Soviet troops—not mechanics and technicians, but soldiers—had now been confirmed.

In the few minutes before the gavel sounded I had a chance to visit each of the twenty places around the table in a last-minute check. I was on first-name terms with every man seated there. At one time or another I had partied with them, danced with their wives and sweethearts, been host to them, a guest at their homes, brought them to the Mardi Gras in New Orleans. . . . If any dividends were to be paid in this rather special person-to-person diplomacy I had been carrying on, now was the time. I went from position to position; the information in our cables, sent through the night by our ambassadors in the Latin American capitals, was correct. O.A.S. Ambassador Vicente Sanchez Gavito of Mexico—one of the doubtful four—had not yet received instructions from Mexico City. My friend Vicente, who had always been on the opposite side of the table from us on Cuba, was doubtful about the United States resolution invoking the Rio Treaty. This was, in effect, asking the

Latin American states to endorse the United States invasion of another Latin American state—a dangerous, dangerous precedent. "But Vicente," I remember saying, "when you're directly over the target and it's bull's-eye time, someone has to press the button. This is it. What more can you ask for? How can we turn the other cheek at this?" He only shook his head dubiously.

I knew, however, that his colleague, Antonio Carrillo Flores, Mexican Ambassador to the United States, and one of those who had been on our trip to the LBJ Ranch, was favorable. At a dinner party in his home after Mexico had abstained on the Cuba ouster, Antonio had told me he thought Mexico gained nothing "from this neutral attitude toward Communism." To be sure, it was Vicente, the O.A.S. ambassador, who would cast his country's vote, but his home office would base its final decision—and its instructions to him—on information and opinion it received from all its ambassadors. Antonio's favorable attitude would play a role.

Here, then, was Mexico, divided. The same was true of Brazil. The ambassador to the United States, Roberto Campos, supported our resolution. Ilmar Penna Marinho, the O.A.S. ambassador, had always struck me as an enigma. A career man, remote and noncommittal, he simply awaited instructions. It was difficult to infer whether he had or had not recommended the United States resolution to his government. Campos, a distinguished economist, a brilliant, outgoing man, who could be witty in eight languages, came to our meeting red-eyed from lack of sleep. He had been on the telephone to President Goulart of Brazil several times before dawn, discussing the issue with his leftist chief executive.

Our major United States resolution was a demand to invoke Articles Six and Eight of the Rio Treaty, to brand Cuba as an aggressor, to authorize the member nations of the O.A.S. to take whatever steps necessary—including the use of force—to remove this threat to the peace. Another paragraph of the resolution called for a UN inspection team to go to Cuba and verify the removal of the missile sites.

This resolution was far from words only. The United States, as a sovereign power, could move as she wished against any country for her self-defense. But if the Latin American states would not consent, Cuba would not be branded an aggressor. If we then moved against her, we would be the aggressor. It was essential to receive the O.A.S.

vote—equally important, perhaps even more important, that it be unanimous, for this meant a solid Latin American wall against Khrushchev—a factor in world public opinion he could not disregard.

First to speak when the meeting opened was Ambassador Roberto T. Alemann of Argentina. He supported President Kennedy completely. Argentina, so long wooed, would vote in favor of the whole resolution.

Surprisingly enough, Chile spoke second. That morning we had had a cable from Ambassador Charles W. Cole in Santiago reporting that Senator Allende, leader of the powerful FRAP, the Socialist–Communist coalition, had declared in the Senate that Kennedy lied: there were no offensive weapons in Cuba. Chile, too, had abstained on the Cuban ouster. Nonetheless, Cole predicted the Chilean Foreign Office would support us. Yet, to see this come about—to see Chile rise and say that though they had been neutral at Punta del Este, this was an entirely different matter, this was a matter of deceit, and they therefore supported the United States resolution—this was immensely cheering, reducing as it did our four neutrals to three. In addition, it gave me an idea on how to win one of our most difficult votes, that of Bolivia.

At ten o'clock a brief recess was declared as we sought to gain time during which ambassadors without instructions might receive them.

At this moment five countries were still uninstructed: Uruguay, Colombia, Brazil, Mexico and Bolivia. To have any of these abstain for technical or mechanical reasons on an issue of such importance was not only exasperating but criminal.

In the next ten minutes word came that Mexico and Brazil appeared to be coming our way. President Kennedy had twice spoken on the telephone to President Lopez Mateos of Mexico, then traveling in the Far East, first in Manila, and then in Hawaii. Meanwhile, President Goulart of Brazil was reported veering toward us.

Emilio Oribe, who months before had been Uruguayan chargé d'affaires in Havana, and had reported to me the bizarre tale of Castro and the Cuban refugees hurling epithets at each other, was now his country's acting ambassador to the O.A.S. Though he supported us personally, he had to obey instructions. Without them, he had to abstain. "And I don't think I will get them," he said, unhappily. "Our elections are only two weeks off and most of the members of our Council of State are campaigning in various parts of the country. How can we get them together in so short a time for a vote?" I thought, A ridiculous situation! A country with a nine-man presidency, and all nine scattered through the provinces! Not only was their machinery of government clumsy; in an emergency, it was impossible to obtain an immediate decision.

But Bolivia, I felt, would be our toughest vote. She had abstained at Punta del Este; she was one of four Latin American countries still maintaining diplomatic relations with Cuba.* Still, I knew that Bolivia's two ambassadors—Enrique Sanchez de Lozada, its chargé d'affaires in Washington, and Emilio Sarmiento, its O.A.S. ambassador, were friendly. Yet, in addition to Bolivia's reluctance to take a hard line toward Cuba, another hurdle faced us—the difficulty in communicating with La Paz. It had only been a matter of hours since President Kennedy's speech precipitated the issue before us, and I knew from experience that sometimes it took a day or more to get through to La Paz by cable or telephone. If Emilio Sarmiento received no instructions he would be forced to abstain—which was tantamount to voting no, for it deprived us of an all-important yes vote.

I turned to Secretary Rusk. "Mr. Secretary, if you don't mind, let me concentrate during this break on Bolivia. I'll just live with them, I won't let them out of my sight."

"Fine," said Rusk. "Go ahead."

What follows is a bit of history that has never been told. Chile's announcement of support, made just before we recessed, was noteworthy because it meant a neutral coming to our side. But it bore special importance for us in relation to Bolivia. Chile and her neighbor Bolivia, who have a history of territorial disputes with each other, were now engaged in a bitter controversy over the Rio Lauca, a small river which had its source high in the mountains of Chile, but which flowed through Bolivia for more than a hundred miles before emptying into the Pacific Ocean. Chile, desperately needing irrigation, and maintaining that one half of the waters of the Rio Lauca belonged to her, had built a tunnel diverting almost that amount of water to her own arid land. This issue, virtually unknown

---

* On a visit to La Paz, the Bolivian capital, in April 1963, a friend reported to me that he observed placards everywhere celebrating the second anniversary of the United States defeat at the Bay of Pigs. What astonished him was a legend in small type at the bottom of these placards: "Printed by Government Printing Office."

to the rest of the world, had led to riots; there had been attacks on the Chilean Embassy in La Paz; the two countries had actually broken off diplomatic relations over the dispute. They had finally brought it before the O.A.S. for adjudication. Bolivia was still trying to get O.A.S. action against Chile.

I sought out Emilio Sarmiento, the Bolivian ambassador. I put the matter directly to him. Chile had just declared in our favor. "Emilio," I said, "you know and I know that this vote should have no connection with the way the United States stands on the Rio Lauca matter. The trouble is that the average United States citizen won't see it that way. He's going to see it as a clear-cut problem: Should the United States side with Chile, who voted with us in the missile crisis, or should we side with Bolivia, who sided with the Russians? You know what the answer's going to be. Congress is going to be deluged with mail demanding that the United States side with Chile, and I just can't answer for the consequences when Congressional demands begin to hit us at the State Department."

Emilio listened, in silence. Might it not be advisable therefore, I suggested, for Emilio to inform his foreign minister in La Paz at once of Chile's action? I wanted Foreign Minister José Fellman Velarde of Bolivia, whom I recalled as a cantankerous man who had given us trouble at Punta del Este, to have this information. I knew his government would not want a further setback over the Rio Lauca; it could mean its overthrow.

Emilio agreed he would try to telephone Fellman. We went to the nearest telephone, in an anteroom immediately adjacent to the Council chamber. There, after much pleading on our part, A.T. & T. passed a small miracle: somehow it gave us a line to La Paz; and at ten-thirty Emilio was explaining the situation to his foreign minister. "Yes," he was saying in Spanish, "Chile has already announced it will vote in favor. We must act. . . ."

I thought to myself, standing next to Emilio as he argued with his foreign minister some 4,000 miles away, How deeply an extraneous matter can involve itself in a major policy decision!

If we had passed a minor miracle by reaching La Paz quickly, there our magic ended. Connections with the Bolivian capital are notoriously bad. One's voice fades, grows stronger, suddenly vanishes. Emilio was now pleading for instructions. "I must have them by three o'clock, Washington time—that is when we shall vote," he was saying. He knew that to obtain instructions meant a Cabinet meeting in La Paz, "but I must have a decision."

Foreign Minister Fellman must have asked how Emilio expected the vote to go, for I heard Emilio, an optimist like myself, reply, "*Unanime.*"

At this moment the phone failed. Emilio obviously could not be heard at the other end for he began repeating "*Unanime,*" each time more loudly, until he was actually shouting.

The door to the Council chamber was open: I had not shut it, so that I would be able to hear the gavel when the meeting was resumed. You must see this scene: the Bolivian ambassador shouting into the telephone; a sudden cessation of conversation in the adjoining Council chamber, so that Emilio's voice rang out clearly, "*Unanime! Unanime!* A unanimous vote!"

Actually, as of this moment the vote was not yet unanimous. We had no official word from Mexico or Brazil. But everyone in the chamber could hear Emilio shouting to his foreign minister, ". . . a unanimous vote!" The psychological impact must have been tremendous. They were not checking each other. They undoubtedly thought to themselves, Perhaps it *is* unanimous.

Then the connection failed completely. A frustrated Emilio hung up. He turned to me. "Chep, my friend, I don't think I will receive my instructions by three o'clock. They will debate and debate and reach only one decision—that they cannot reach a decision. This will take all day. I'm afraid I will receive no instructions."

I said, "Then I ask you not to abstain but to vote with us—to support the majority. Emilio, you and I know that it is in the best interests of all of us—that it is the right and just thing to do."

Emilio nodded. "Yes," he said. Then he was silent for a moment. I realized the dilemma he faced. His government was at this moment struggling with a most difficult decision: for though the majority of the Bolivian population was anti-Communist, there was a small but highly organized and extremely vocal Communist minority which might attempt to topple the government if it took this stand against Cuba. I was convinced that Emilio anticipated that his government would in the end vote Yes, that it would take a calculated risk that it could withstand a possible Communist upsurge. But I realized that Emilio ran a great personal risk in voting without instructions: for though he was confident that President Victor Paz

Estenssoro would back him, still if the Communists did set off riots in Bolivia and if the reaction was too strong, the President might be forced to dismiss him—which would mean virtually the end of his career in the Foreign Office.

I broke the silence: "Will you shake my hand and give me your commitment that you're going to support the United States if no instructions are received? And give me permission to tell the Secretary and the President that we have Bolivia's vote?"

Emilio shook my hand. We would have his vote. I admired him very much at that moment. "Emilio," I said, "if anything happens, you can count on me. I'll do anything I can to help."

Emilio and I patted each other on the back in an *abrazo,* and I returned to Secretary Rusk to report that unless instructions were received to the contrary by three o'clock, we had Bolivia's vote. And I was ready to wager ten to one that instructions would not come through by then.

"That's great, Chep," Rusk said.

"Just one more thing," I said. "I feel committed to help him get placed if he should be sacked."

Rusk smiled. "That's all right. If we can't get him a job in Washington, I'm sure you'll get him one in New Orleans."

The meeting was resumed at eleven o'clock, then recessed for lunch, without official word from the three neutrals or from Bolivia and Uruguay.

When I returned to my office to check cables and snatch a quick sandwich, I received a telephone call. It was Sanchez Gavito of Mexico. "I have good news for you and bad news for me," he said. He had received instructions to support our resolution, but, since he did not think it an appropriate one, "the news is bad for me."

When I returned shortly after two o'clock for the afternoon session, the Colombian ambassador approached me. He showed me a cable he had received: Vote for the resolution. By three o'clock, the hour of voting, we had Mexico and Colombia; we had an understanding with Bolivia; rumor held that Brazil was also with us; Uruguay still awaited instructions.

The minutes slipped by. No vote was called for. At three-thirty Ambassador Campos of Brazil strolled by and nodded. "We have it," he said. That left Bolivia and Uruguay still uninstructed. I checked with Emilio Sarmiento. "Have you received any instructions?" "No." "Are you ready to vote?" "Yes."

We started voting the resolution shortly after 3:35 P.M., paragraph by paragraph, the preliminary ones first. The telephone rang in the anteroom, and I saw Emilio Sarmiento rise and leave. We held up proceedings, waiting for him. When he returned he passed behind me on his way to his seat. "It will be well," he said.

The vote concluded. There were nineteen yeas. Uruguay still had not yet obtained instructions, so Ambassador Emilio Oribe took the floor, explained that he would not abstain, and asked permission to delay his vote until he received instructions from the Council of State. (When these arrived, they were for a yes vote.)

The vote, therefore, was unanimous for the United States.

President Kennedy's proclamation the next morning interdicted the shipment to Cuba of offensive weapons. It stated that the land, sea and air forces of the United States would "prevent" any such delivery. He based his authority on two pillars: a joint Congressional resolution of October 3, 1962, and the resolution of October 23, 1962, of the Organ of Consultation of the American Republics.

Later, I went back to Mexico City for the last four days of our Alliance review. It was a hectic week. The day I arrived the United States quarantine went into effect at 10 A.M. Our embassy in Mexico City kept us informed almost hourly: Now our ships were spreading out to patrol the sea lanes, our planes were on the search; Soviet ships were steaming toward Cuba . . . Now a Soviet freighter had been halted, now a second . . . Kennedy and Khrushchev were negotiating . . .

Saturday, October 27, as cables indicated that Khrushchev was capitulating, our conference closed on a high note. We had pledged one billion dollars to the Alliance in the first year. We had fulfilled the pledge and we could continue, in the words of Secretary Dillon, "on the same order of magnitude" in 1963. In ways too numerous to count, the Alliance, slowly, ponderously, but irresistibly, had gotten under way throughout the hemisphere.*

* One of our last acts at this meeting was to elect an interim committee to keep the work of the Alliance under constant survey and to make recommendations between annual reviews. Two men—immediately dubbed "the superwise men" of the OAS—were elected: Alberto Lleras Camargo, twice President of Colombia, and former President Juscelino Kubitschek of Brazil.

I left Mexico immediately afterward for a swing through several countries to check on the national commissions for the Alliance. I boarded my plane just as newspapers were headlining that Khrushchev had agreed to halt construction of Soviet bases in Cuba and to dismantle and remove Soviet missiles.

My trip, made on the very heels of the United States–Soviet confrontation, gave me an unparalleled opportunity to see at first hand the reaction on the scene—the more telling because I would see it in countries that still maintained diplomatic relations with Castro. Thus, in Rio, Ambassador Lincoln Gordon told me the story of his exasperating experiences with President Goulart. In view of Goulart's highly publicized ouster from the Presidency in the spring of 1964, it was a most interesting story. To persuade Goulart to change Brazil's policy was difficult. First he went along with the United States, and Brazil voted for our resolution. When there was a violent reaction from the extreme left, Goulart changed course and summoned home O.A.S. Ambassador Ilmar Penna Marinho—as if to intimate that Penna Marinho had disobeyed instructions; this, of course, was not true. To placate the pro-Castro element further, Goulart added that he had ordered a general of the Air Force to Cuba to investigate Kennedy's charges—an empty gesture, since only a few days later Khrushchev admitted Soviet guilt. Then, when it became obvious that public sentiment supported the United States, Goulart reversed his field again. Gordon told me: "Yesterday I was called to the Catete Palace for a reception. President Goulart was all cordiality. 'Let's drink a toast,' he said. I held up my glass. 'I make a toast to freedom and liberty' "—Gordon thought this most politic under the circumstances. But President Goulart went him one better. "No, no," he exclaimed. "I drink to a great American victory."

In Mexico I dined at the home of Pascual Gutiérrez Roldan, Director General of PEMEX, the government-owned oil and gas monopoly. "You would have expected demonstrations somewhere in Mexico," he said. "After all, this was the first time that Mexico voted with the United States on the Castro question." But nothing happened, anywhere in Mexico. "Wherever there's a filling station in this country," Pascual said, "I have employees. No demonstrations, not even in the remote areas." Evidently, the Communists were caught completely by surprise. They had nothing to offer, they were completely disheartened here as elsewhere. "Certainly there must have been Red elements who wanted to hold rallies, to protest the vote," Pascual said. "But the fact that they did not is amazing. They were virtually shell-shocked."

The Mexican cab driver who took me back to my hotel switched his radio off—he had been listening to the news—with his own pithy comment: "*Los Rojos se corrieran.*" Translated into the American-English vernacular, this was, "The Reds chickened out."

In Chile I found Communist reaction echoing that in Mexico. Khrushchev's retreat left the pro-Castro demonstrators very little to demonstrate about. Chilean diplomats and newspapermen with whom I talked agreed that Castro had suffered a crushing blow. As long as considerable numbers of Latin Americans persisted in seeing him as a bearded Robin Hood, effective counteraction against Communism was difficult. Now it seemed very clear that he was a Soviet pawn—Russia gave, and Russia took away, and no one consulted Castro.

When I returned to Washington in early November, my friend Emilio Sarmiento, the Bolivian ambassador, told me what had happened in his country. When his vote became known the extreme left, as he feared, took to the streets, rioting; then something occurred that had never before taken place in La Paz. Anti-Communists poured into the streets in even greater numbers, and won the day. If these events, if these reactions meant anything, they confirmed that what we had done was right; even those republics whose fear of United States "big-stick" intervention is almost on a paranoid level had accepted the action with extraordinary composure.

History will, of course, write its own assessment of the events preceding the crisis of October 23, 1962, the crisis itself, and its aftermath, which I was to see spelled out in the months to come. But I am convinced that the solid front of opposition—the unanimous stand against Khrushchev by the twenty free republics of this hemisphere—had much to do with the Soviet withdrawal. Had that opposition been halfhearted—had that wall shown cracks or signs of crumbling under Soviet-Cuban pressure—it is quite possible that Khrushchev would have pushed forward, gambling that he could widen the split in a divided hemisphere and win through.

18. THE MEN AND THE PROBLEMS OF TOMORROW

There are, in my opinion, perhaps half a dozen men who hold the future of Latin America in their hands. Here I stress again that I do not speak as an economist. I am a practical politician, who makes strong personal relationships and is affected by them. Among the strategically important men who have colored my views—with some of whom I may disagree, but all of whom I admire—are the following.

First among them—the first citizen of Latin America, to my mind, a man above debate, a man whose influence transcends borders—is Alberto Lleras Camargo, twice President of Colombia. He is a frail, scholarly intellectual with a tremendous appreciation of Latin America. He was the first Secretary General of the O.A.S., serving from 1948 until 1954. A brilliant speaker, he is a man of unprecedented value to the free world because of his ability to communicate with the people of all countries.

Lleras was president of the University of the Andes. He has been a leader of the Liberal party of Colombia, a powerful voice against dictatorship, and is perhaps the most learned man in government in Latin America. He was unanimously selected by the other Latin American states to be one of the two "superwise men" of the O.A.S.

He stands for the highest principles of democracy. In politics I place him left of center, not as far left as the members of the democratic left, a group I will discuss later. He believes in reform, but does not take the somewhat skeptical and slightly suspicious attitude toward private enterprise which marks the democratic left and its leader, José "Pepe" Figueres of Costa Rica.

What make Lleras special are his mind, his erudition, his tolerance, his character, and his remarkable skill in bringing together the far left and the far right.

In appearance he is a small man, thin and narrow of face, usually seen in an enormous black coat that all but engulfs him, wearing a black hat—a frail-appearing, sick-appearing man—the great little man of Latin America.

His purpose in life is the Alliance for Progress. He has been talking about it, in essence, for years, has lectured on it all over the world, and has insisted time and again that Latin America is not one entity but twenty different nations. He is pro-West and anti-Communist, and he believes that the United States must exert a strong leadership in Latin America. He maintains that the American republics must find a happy mean between total sovereignty and acceptance of United States leadership.

Were it not for this man, I do not think there would be an O.A.S. today. When the United Nations was founded in 1945, many believed the new world organization obviated the need for a regional association of American states. But Lleras with his eloquence, his finely reasoned arguments, brought to the attention of the UN the importance of preserving the covenants of human rights, the various declarations and treaties so laboriously developed through the years by the Pan American Union, the predecessor of the O.A.S. These would vanish if the O.A.S. vanished. In the end, the O.A.S. was saved.

In Colombia itself Lleras has played a most significant role. His country had suffered many fiery political wars. The Liberal party had been split by two factions, who virtually tore each other apart. In 1948 this culminated in the assassination of an eloquent Liberal leader, Jorge Eliecer Gaitan, an act which seemed only to intensify the political turmoil. For years thereafter the Colombian scene was one of violence and bloodshed.

Lleras was elected President in 1958 and soothed his nation. A year earlier he guided Colombia through a most unusual constitutional change which ended this period by establishing a sixteen-year truce. By its terms, the Liberal and Conservative parties alternate in holding the presidency each four years. But, in addition, the party in power must divide every post with the opposition.

Thus, if an Ambassador belonging to the Liberal party is sent abroad, he is accompanied by a deputy belonging to the Conservative. This applies to all appointed offices. If there are ten Cabinet posts, five are Conservative, five Liberal; and in each instance, the second man is a member of the opposite party. Lleras, a Liberal, elected in May 1958, was succeeded in 1962 by Dr. Guillermo Leon Valencia, a Conservative.

Lleras represents the new breed of Latin American presidents—scholarly, liberal, nonmilitary in background—in whom, I believe, will be found great hope for the continent's future.

Next to Alberto Lleras Camargo, I would place Juscelino Kubitschek of Brazil, the other "superwise man" elected by the O.A.S. Grandson of a Czech immigrant, a former President of Brazil, a man of vision who created Brasilia, pro-West, anti-Communist, he is, I believe, more of a politician than other outstanding leaders of Latin America. He will yield to expediency—that is, attack the United States in his speeches if by doing so he can win votes to enable him to continue with his own blueprint for Brazil.

To Kubitschek goes the credit, as has been pointed out in these pages, for originating the basic idea of the Alliance for Progress. His "Operation Pan-America," with its emphasis on economic and social reform based on self-help, was the forerunner of the Act of Bogotá, of 1959, in which President Eisenhower agreed to appropriate half a billion dollars to launch such a program in the hemisphere. The nations that signed the Act of Bogotá pledged themselves to commit their resources to these goals and to inaugurate the necessary reforms. Kubitschek's original concept was embodied in this agreement: Kennedy put it into effect with the Alliance.

It is true that there has been much controversy in Brazil over Kubitschek, including 1) the charge that he drove the country to the brink of bankruptcy by his vast expenditures, including the enormous expense of Brasilia; and 2) charges of graft in connection with the building of the city. But no matter what these charges are, the fact is that Kubitschek took a giant step toward opening up the vast interior of Brazil which will, I think, have a significant effect on the future growth of the nation.

He is a friendly, personable man—a warm human being of rare charm. He speaks a little English, is married, has children.

Surely Galo Plaza Lasso of Ecuador, onetime president, son of a president of his country, the man whose interpretation of the incomplete revolution now sweeping Latin America I quoted in my introduction, belongs among the first six. Though he was defeated in his last attempt to regain the presidency, losing chiefly because he was attacked as a rich, pro–United States candidate, he is one of the continent's great souls. A tall, impressive man of magnetic personality, he is the only Latin leader who can claim birth in New York City.

Galo Plaza comes from a prominent ranching family. His father, Leonidas Plaza Gutierrez, was President of Ecuador from 1901 to 1905 and from 1912 to 1916. Galo Plaza today is president of the Development Bank of Ecuador. He was educated in the United States; he was a star football player, and, so the story goes, when his father cut off his allowance because Galo's grades failed to equal his football prowess, young Plaza took to selling apples in the streets to obtain his tuition fees.

Like Lleras, he has a superb ability to communicate with the Latin American public, speaking with authority and conviction. His ideas, like Lleras's, are those of the Alliance. He has often been mentioned as a potential candidate for election as secretary general of the O.A.S. I think he would easily be elected, but he has said that he will take no part in seeking the position so long as the incumbent, Dr. José A. Mora of Uruguay, is in office. Nonetheless, Galo Plaza would enormously strengthen that post, in my opinion. (I shall have more to say on this subject later.)

Romulo Betancourt, former President of Venezuela, is a onetime Communist who is now vigorously anti-Communist. Betancourt is a short, rather stocky, bald man of tremendous energy. Each time I think of him I cannot help recalling a meeting between him and President Frondizi of Argentina. Here was the slim, professorial Frondizi doing an *abrazo* with the short, pudgy Betancourt; and as the latter leaned forward, his coattails peeled up to reveal a pistol on each hip.

Recalling that he had been the target of assassination attempts by the late Dictator Trujillo of the Dominican Republic, I could not blame him. In addition, Venezuela has long been listed as one of Castro's chief goals. In February 1964, the O.A.S. declared the Castro regime guilty of intervention against the Betancourt government.

Betancourt is the only Venezuelan president to complete his term —that is, to hand his powers over to a freely elected successor and not to be ousted or assassinated. He elected a successor from his own party, the Acción Democratico, in 1963.

Then there is my friend Miguel Aleman Valdes, of Mexico, a handsome man, over six feet tall, with a warm, contagious smile, a driving, vibrant personality. When he was elected President of Mexico in 1946, he was the first chief executive in decades who had not been an army general. He typifies to my mind the revolution in Mexico. He pushed social and economic reforms energetically. He encouraged the *ejidos,* or collective farm, system in Mexico, which makes his country far ahead of all its neighbors in land reform. To my mind the system is not as successful as it might be; for although the peasants received land, they did not receive with it the technical means, the knowledge and the stimulation, which would enable them to do much with the land. But the big estates were split up, the distribution of land to the *campesinos,* the farmers, did come about; and this, after all, was the very dream of the revolution begun more than half a century ago.

Aleman was succeeded in 1952 by Adolfo Ruiz Cortines, a minister in his cabinet. Ruiz Cortines was succeeded by Adolfo Lopez Mateos, another minister in the Aleman cabinet. The new president of Mexico, to be inaugurated in late 1964, Gustavo Diaz Ordaz, may also be described as an Aleman man. This means that we are still in the Aleman regime in Mexico—tribute to his vitality, vision and political strength.

Thanks to him and his vision in the years gone by, Mexico is now developing a middle class. Aleman stands for close friendship with the United States. He is one of the wealthiest men in Latin America, reputedly worth over eighty million dollars.

I believe these five men—the sixth is José "Pepe" Figueres, whom I will deal with later—hold the key to the future of Latin America. But there are others. Any discussion must include Raul Prebisch of Argentina, Latin America's best-known economist, and Felipe Herrera of Chile, its best-known banker.

Prebisch served from 1950 to 1963 as head of the United Nations Economic Commission for Latin America. He is the first Latin American economist to assert that economic theories designed for industrialized nations do not necessarily apply to underdeveloped nations. He has been called a pink, by some conservatives even a Communist. In my opinion, this is nonsense. He believes firmly in free enterprise, but also believes in government planning.

Prebisch was the economic genius behind Kubitschek's Operation Pan-America. As long ago as 1950 he advocated self-help measures. He has always maintained that Latin America must have land reform and a redistribution of wealth—not taking from the rich to give to the poor, but so utilizing and developing the assets of the hemisphere that its benefits could be distributed to all.

He has also been accused of being anti-United States. I do not think this is true. Prebisch holds that if Latin America is to prosper, it cannot depend economically upon the United States; it must be protected by favoritism clauses in trade relations, to be sure, but the goal should be a Latin America able to steer an independent economic course.

Prebisch today is secretary general of the United Nations Conference on Trade and Development, and one of the most powerful exponents of the common-market principal. He had a part in the Latin American Free Trade Association (LAFTA), which is made up of eight South American republics plus Mexico (Bolivia and Venezuela are not affiliated), and in the Organization for Economic Development in Central America (ODECA), which is made up of five Central American republics (all except Panama).

The LAFTA objective is to develop industry in one country that will not compete with that in another LAFTA country, and then, by lowering trade barriers, to create a common market of the 14,000,000 people in the nine associated countries. Prebisch points out that Central America similarly presents a fragmented picture—five segments of a market. He is laboring to bring them together into a market that will be advantageous to all, with a minimum of competitive production among the member states. This is economic planning on a high level.

Far more colorful, probably far better known in this country, is Felipe Herrera of Chile, president of the Inter-American Development Bank, each of whose governors represents a Latin American nation. Begun in 1960 with $800,000 capital, today that figure has more than tripled. The bank has made loans totaling nearly one billion dollars.

A lawyer as well as an economist, something of a prodigy—at thirty-one he was Foreign Minister of Chile—Herrera is perhaps the most eloquent continental spokesman for the political union of Latin America. He sponsored LAFTA; he also has encouraged the formation of the growing Central American common market; and he speaks everywhere on the inevitability of a United States of Latin America.

A onetime Socialist, Herrera left the party when he backed an austerity program to fight inflation in Chile. I believe he represents the new look in Latin America; he is personable, friendly, a genius for detail, a man of the high caliber so badly needed by the continent. He was chosen to handle the Social Progress Trust Fund for the United States, when Alliance funds appropriated by the United States were extended. This fund is the very heart of the financial assistance extended to Alliance countries.

Among other men, some of whom may emerge as leaders of tomorrow, we must consider:

Roberto de Oliveira Campos of Brazil, a world-renowned economist, a former ambassador to Washington, and now minister of planning in his country. He has been President of the Development Bank of Brazil, and is often considered a prospective head of the Economic and Social Council of the O.A.S. because of his wide knowledge in the field of economics. A brilliant man, a superb speaker, witty, excellent company.

I attribute to Campos main credit for freeing Brazil's difficult vote on October 23, 1962, during the missile crisis. He finally took it upon himself to assume responsibility. After he acted, a minister in President Goulart's cabinet demanded his removal. But Campos survived. He is a man of the future.

Ambassador Gonzalo "Chalo" Facio of Costa Rica, former Chairman of the O.A.S., a follower of José Figueres, is a man who bears watching. He has undertaken assignments in the United States to translate the aims of the Alliance and explain the problems of Latin America to our people. These tasks he has accomplished with great skill.

He has no illusions about Castro. He has constantly voted anti-Communist. He is politically ambitious and looks forward some day to the presidency of Costa Rica. A man of great ability, he may well achieve that post.

Among perfect diplomats I would cite Dr. Roberto Alemann, Argentine Ambassador to the United States, economist, publisher, and a first-rate thinker. He was his country's finance minister at the first Punta del Este, and made a tremendous contribution. He is, incidentally, one of the handsomest men in diplomatic life. When I conducted a group of my O.A.S. colleagues on a tour of Hollywood studios not long ago, Roberto was thought to be a leading man, waiting to take his place before the cameras. He is cool, balanced, in full command of a situation—the sort of man who, in my book, will be among those who will lead the Latin American countries in the days to come.

There are also the spokesmen, the leaders, the high priests of the left—Communists, pseudo Communists, fellow travelers, Castroites. Among them, General Lazaro Cardenas of Mexico; Francisco Julião, lawyer and leader of the 25,000,000 peasants in the nine states of Brazil's bitter, poverty-stricken northeast; Juan Lechin Oquendo, Vice-President of Bolivia, who led the strike of tin miners and held a number of United States nationals as hostages; Senator Salvador Allende of Chile, the pro-Castro leader of the FRAP (a coalition of Socialists and Communists which has caused much alarm through Latin America), and a candidate for president. Each of these men play roles of lesser or greater importance depending upon the regime in power in their respective countries.

Among nationalist leaders who seek to move their governments into a position of less dependence upon the United States are former President Adolfo Lopez Mateos of Mexico. He is an eloquent exponent of Mexican neutrality.

Dr. Arturo Umberto Illia, elected President of Argentina in July

1963, is at this moment a question mark. He canceled a number of foreign oil concessions which had done much for his country's economy, enabling her to be self-sufficient in oil and gas. But he is regarded as moderate, middle-of-the-road, well oriented to the West. Before his election he was a rather obscure country physician.

I have left for the last in this roll call one whom many would put among the very first. This is José "Pepe" Figueres, of Costa Rica, whose name has appeared at intervals in these pages. Economist, political philosopher, sage and teacher, leader of his country's National Liberation Party, a onetime President of Costa Rica, he is a controversial figure. Many consider him the greatest statesman of Latin America. Others fear him. Whatever the case, he is unquestionably one of the most original thinkers—and one of the most effective—in the hemisphere.

Son of a Spanish immigrant to Costa Rica, he became a wealthy plantation owner, a colonel in the army and, in 1953, president of the country. For five years he led Costa Rica, making her one of the most advanced republics in Latin America.

Figueres's greatest impact, however, has been as leader of the democratic left, or non-Communist left, or anti-Communist left. This political grouping—it is sometimes called a "third force"—threads its course left of center between the extreme right and extreme left. I have referred to it briefly in Chapter XIII.

The democratic left had its inception in the late 1940's, when Colonel Figueres organized a force of Latin Americans to fight dictatorship, first in his own country, then elsewhere on the continent. A number of Latin political leaders—some of them exiles, many of them distinguished—joined him from other Caribbean countries. There gathered such men as Juan José Arevalo, former President of Guatemala; Luis Muñoz Marín, perennial Governor of Puerto Rico; Juan Bosch, former President of the Dominican Republic; Romulo Betancourt, former President of Venezuela; Victor Haya de la Torre of Peru; President Francisco J. Orlich Bolmarcich of Costa Rica; President Victor Paz Estenssoro of Bolivia; deposed President Ramon Villeda Morales of Honduras; Fidel Castro of Cuba in his earlier years—all, at one time or another, were under Pepe Figueres's influence.

In the thirties, some were Communists or Communist sympathizers; today all but Fidel Castro are stanchly anti-Communist. They are firmly opposed, of course, to dictatorship; they also distrust the military; they are committed to social and agrarian reform.

The democratic leftists maintain that they, rather than the reactionary right, are the Communists' chief enemy. Since the democratic left promises reform—and reform is the all-powerful weapon in the Communist arsenal—the democratic left asserts that the Communists recognize it as their principal competitor for the allegiance of the Latin masses.

Figueres organized a political-action school in San José, attended by many members of the democratic left, and at which some of its leaders taught. There are followers of Figueres's philosophy in every Latin American country. They have frequent contact with him, correspond with him, and carry his political interpretation to their neighbors. This philosophy—in addition to its emphasis on reform and its anti-Communist basis—stresses that the Latin American states cannot develop in the United States image, but must do so in their own—and this despite what the United States may think, or wish, or fear.

In the controversy over Figueres and what he stands for, many Latin American conservatives view him as the leader of a dangerous cause. They consider him a socialist. I do not. Although he is a well-known anti-Communist, the complexity of his thinking has led some to think of him even as a Communist.

Basically, as I understand it, Figueres believes that the concentration of wealth in the hands of a few is an evil that keeps the vast numbers of poor in an endless cycle of poverty. His solution, however, is not violent revolution, but a gradual approach, using progressive taxation plus the redistribution of idle lands now owned by the wealthy. He believes government should accomplish what free enterprise can not. I have said that he is skeptical and slightly suspicious of free enterprise; yet he recognizes it as one of many forces that can operate for good. But chief among these forces, he preaches, is government.

In its beginnings the democratic left, because it was a sworn enemy of dictatorships, and because the United States was then doing business with dictators—they were the rule almost, rather than the exception—became identified as anti-United States. Actually, it was then the United States State Department that they opposed. Many elements in the New Deal of President Franklin Roosevelt sympathized with the Figueres group, not only because of its antipathy to Communists, dictators, and the military, but because as a "third force" it promised social reform without revolution. In this direction, many of Roosevelt's men—and, years later, Kennedy's men—believed, lay the path to be taken by Latin America's millions if we were to avoid an ultimate blood bath below the border.

Laudable though the aims of the democratic left are, to me this orientation possesses a major weakness in Latin America—namely, that when in power its theories are all too often betrayed by reality, the reality of the determined Communist designs to obtain power through subversion and political turmoil.

Because the democratic left in Latin America believes that it can use the Communists, and outdo them in achieving social change, it frequently becomes an easy target for them. Witness the regime of Juan Bosch, the poet, scholar and theorist, who was the first freely elected President of the Dominican Republic in more than thirty-eight years. He came to power in December 1962, in an honest, non-violent election following the long, arduous labors of the O.A.S.—familiar to the reader of earlier pages of this book—to bring the Dominican Republic back into the community of free nations.

Bosch caught the imagination of the masses of his country. He was tremendously popular, intelligent, personable, eloquent; a political romanticist who wished only good for the Dominican Republic. At his election the United States was delighted. This was especially gratifying because, for a critical time, the Dominican Republic might have become another Cuba on our doorstep. To newly elected President Bosch, therefore, we sent a virtual blank check to help him carry out his promise to build a democratic showcase in the Caribbean—the more important because it would provide a dramatic contrast to Castro's Cuba, in ever greater difficulties, next door.

But Bosch believed that he could deal with the Communists. No Dominican, he said, need be in exile because of his political beliefs. He allowed them back—the very people Balaguer, months before, at the urging of Mr. Kennedy and the C.I.A.—had kept out of the Dominican Republic. These people spoke Bosch's language—social reform, literacy, human equality, social justice—but they were

Communists. They used his romantic mind and vision to push their programs of slowly abolishing the military, of forming a Castro-style militia with total allegiance to Bosch. They infiltrated the educational system, the communications media, and other key areas, toward the same end: the building of a strong central government.

The generals saw this creeping socialism as a threat to their power. They were not alone in their apprehension. With full support of the conservative Dominican business community, they ousted Bosch in September 1963, after little more than seven months in office. He fled to Puerto Rico and took refuge in the governor's mansion of Muñoz Marín, a colleague of the democratic left.

Another example of the democratic left's belief that it can outdo the Communists at their own game was seen when Venezuela—under Romulo Betancourt, a distinguished leader of the democratic left—became one of the few countries to oppose and delay the O.A.S. action of July 3, 1963, approving a security program to fight Communism and calling for a ban on the movement of funds and people to Cuba. In the end, the O.A.S. voted, fourteen to one, in favor of this action—an action I consider one of the most important taken by the inter-American system.

The United States was deeply disappointed at Venezuela's behavior—perhaps "quixotic" is the kindest word to use in describing it—which seemed designed to cut off one's nose to spite one's face. I can only assume that Betancourt's success as president, despite all the Communist designs upon him, made him feel he could act as he did.*

Time and again one finds such instances where the democratic left fails to keep pace with reality. Its vulnerability to Communist infiltration is understandable. Were Latin American society literate, democratic in tradition, with a love and belief in the constitution, the democratic left would be an unqualified asset. But where unstable governments exist, and peoples to whom a constitution means

* I recall at the time of the July 3 vote speaking with Governor Muñoz Marín, one of the least romantic of the democratic left, and a major force in it. "Here your good friend Betancourt opposes this," I said. "It simply doesn't make sense to me. Venezuela has been a Communist target for years. She should cheer and say, 'Let's stop this Communist subversion and aggression.'" Muñoz said, "Well, Romulo believes he can fight these fellows better in the open, and doesn't need the hand of the O.A.S. to stop them."

little (in Latin America, constitutions come and go, and rare is one that has any tenure), where political thinking suffers from lack of maturity, where there is no true comprehension of the meaning of freedom and personal liberty which alone supports a constitution—in such cases the democratic left, high though its aims, is easily subverted.

This is an explanation of what took place in the Dominican Republic. And Bosch's ouster underlines the dilemma before us: how to work with the democratic left, how to help strengthen it, yet not open the door to the Communists. This poses complex problems to those of us in the United States interested in Latin America and wanting to do what is right and helpful.

For example, when Bosch was deposed, the reaction was violent here and in Latin America. Below the border, Governor Muñoz telephoned President Kennedy. So did President Betancourt of Venezuela. Both demanded that United States Marines be sent to the Dominican Republic to reinstate Bosch. Here at home, Senator Morse and Senator Ernest Gruening, Democrat, of Alaska, echoed them, calling for United States intervention.

President Kennedy immediately cut all political ties with the junta ruling the Dominican Republic. However, our own conservatives—and such Democratic Congressmen as Representative Selden, Chairman of the House Subcommittee on Inter-American Affairs—applauded Bosch's downfall. Within weeks, they said, the Communists would have had sufficient control of the government to launch a Castro-like Marxist revolution in the Dominican Republic—the very denouement we had been fighting with every means at our command ever since Trujillo's assassination.

This faction pointed out the apparent contradiction in the liberal arguments of nonintervention and self-determination when it pertained to Castro—and how it made a complete turnabout and demanded United States military intervention when it pertained to Bosch. In short, those who had advocated a hands-off policy on Cuba now called for big-stick diplomacy in the Dominican Republic.

This was September 1963. Two months before, in July 1963, President Arosemena of Ecuador had been ousted by a military overthrow, one of the accusations against him being that he was sympathetic to Communism.

Then, in October 1963, the military in Honduras overthrew President Villeda Morales, charging that his successor in that month's elections would be "soft" on Communism. In April 1964, the military in Brazil overthrew President Goulart, charging that he had brought the country to the brink of Communism.

So the debate continues. Each time a government in Latin America—socially progressive or reform-minded—falls to the military in the name of anti-Communism, we see again a replay of this special problem of the democratic left. For, given its head in the Latin America of today, it seems often to move directly into the lion's mouth.

My own view is that the answer must be sought in many directions: a more mature democratic left developing in countries where, in time, we shall also find developing a better understanding of, and faith in, personal liberty and the institutions of democracy; an increasingly socially conscious, nonpolitical military; and the economic and social reform brought about by the day-to-day achievements, on an infinite number of levels, of the Alliance for Progress.

In these directions, I think, lies hope for the future.

19. THE CLOSING OF A MISSION

As I sit in my office, thinking over my service, I am reminded of Costa Rican Ambassador Gonzalo Facio's characterization of the Alliance for Progress: "In essence, the United States government is underwriting the social revolution that Latin America so desperately needs. . . . The Latin American countries are taking the bold, difficult steps to achieve peaceably and democratically the reforms which throughout history have been accomplished by revolutions of blood and violence."

I think this is as good and succinct a summation as possible.

We know the scope of the problem. We are not dealing with a single entity called Latin America, but with twenty different countries, each sovereign and each jealous of its painful, hard-won sovereignty, each with its special social and economic pressures, its psychological fears, which have made each nation as sensitive—often as difficult to deal with—as if it were a troubled human being.

For this reason I accept the fact that we are both respected and disliked. I accept the fact that Latin American states will never again be as subservient to the United States as in the past. I accept the fact that young, independent men are coming to power, and often for them to acquire the right kind of political image in their own countries, it is necessary for them to announce their opposition, in one way or another, to the United States or to United States policy. But I maintain that we, the free Western world, are winning.

If I were asked to make recommendations for our attitudes and policies in the future, on the basis of my own experience in Washington and in Latin America, and growing out of what I feel is the right thing to do, I would stress the following:

1. We need a flexible Latin American policy, one that can cope with sudden turns, twists and explosions in the political course of any country. Our attitude toward these violent upsets—these all-too-often military *coups d'état*—should give us freedom to judge each on its merits. During the end of my tenure the White House and State Department had both moved in this direction, the result, I think, of our unhappy experience with Peru in the summer of 1962.

That July a military junta headed by General Juan Perez Godoy took over the country. At the request of our Ambassador, James Loeb—an outstanding member of the democratic left in this country—we refused to recognize the new government. He asked emphatically that we suspend relations, and we did. We immediately cut off all aid. *The New York Times* observed that Uncle Sam was now playing "the role of tough policeman of Latin American democracy." But a month later, Mr. Kennedy reversed himself, recognized General Perez's regime, and reinstated our aid program. Such flip-flops in foreign relations are humiliating and do us little good.

I believe that our approach should be sufficiently flexible to avoid such a situation. We should not assume that all *coups d'état* are bad, or, conversely, that all are to be recognized at once. We should maintain a cautious, hands-off policy until we see the trend in the country.

It goes without saying that I am against military take-overs. They are inconsistent with the Alliance for Progress, with the Preamble we hammered out with such labor. A military take-over is not a decision by a free people, nor does it reflect representative democracy.

Yet—and here I speak again as a practical politician—we must pursue what is best for us. We have frequently supported dictators. I do not think we can summarily sever relations with a country that is our partner in the Alliance, and with whom we have complex financial and economic agreements. We have pledged ourselves to work together; and if one of our partners goes amiss, I do not think we should slap them with the American dollar. We should continue our aid; why should the people be penalized?

I believe that we must take our patient where we find him, keep him in the family, and then try to move him toward democracy through the collective moral force of the inter-American system. After appraising the situation, we must attempt to obtain a commitment from the ruling junta for the earliest date free elections can be held. Here we, the United States, have bargaining power and should use it. A military junta, when it takes power, wants, above all, United States recognition. This becomes its mark of respectability. If the seizure is autocratic, we can withhold recognition until such time as we are given a promise that free elections will be held at such and such a day.

There is a strong but unpublicized support in the Department of State for the kind of flexibility I advocate. During my service the Kennedy administration denied the State Department that kind of freedom. It simply said: All take-overs are bad. An example is the Argentine episode which I have cited earlier. I am sure that the statement which was prepared at that morning meeting denouncing the Argentine coup, and which Mr. Kennedy was scheduled to read at his eleven o'clock press conference, had been prepared because the State Department thought this was what the White House wanted—or, indeed, because the White House specifically asked for it.

Mexico believes, for example, that it should not pass moral judgment on any country. Mexico asks only two requirements in instances of take-over: 1) the nation under the new regime must honor its international commitments; 2) the group that professes to be in power must actually be in power. I recognize both the assets and the liabilities of such a doctrine. It is practical diplomacy. You deal with whoever is in power, unless he is the enemy. But it might be pointed out that we maintain relations with the Soviet Union, whose moral conduct we cannot be said to approve.

At the same time, I believe we must maintain open lines of communication with all groups throughout Latin America. This means not only the democratic left; but the military, the oligarchies —whatever groups are effective. Labor unions and national commissions for the Alliance are highly valuable in opening such communication between states. When the spokesmen of the oligarchies, the labor unions and the outstanding communication media sit down together, they represent a cross section of the country. When we maintain communication with such groups, we maintain communication with the country as a whole.

2. Through these pages the Alliance for Progress has been a basic theme. I am aware of the criticisms against it. The American public should realize that it is a long-range program, that it is not a give-away program, that it is in our own interests. Not only does it help us in the global struggle against Communism—if the reader wishes to learn the importance of the Alliance, let him see how the Communists attack it—but also in the development of the hemisphere. As the hemisphere prospers, we prosper. The work of the Alliance goes on, day by day, often in far-from-exciting fashion. The Alliance, reduced to its essentials, means not only a new well where there was not one before, it means shoes on children until then barefoot, decent living quarters for people living in incredible slums—it means *hope*. And the Organization of American States, in its smallest, least-publicized activities, is constantly laying a groundwork for better hemispheric relations, for better people-to-people relations. The value of this cannot be adequately measured, and is hard to dramatize. *But it goes on.*

3. We must advocate free-enterprise funds from all sources—not only from the United States, but also from Europe, from Japan, and from Latin America. I have mentioned a successful example of United States free enterprise—the thriving and mighty Kaiser complex in Latin America. There are many others today. I don't think we should be embarrassed to encourage United States investments below the border. It might be instructive for those who are interested to check on how much European capital—European free enterprise—helped to build the United States. British funds, particularly, flowed in tremendous amounts into United States railroads in the early years.

4. Let us accept differences of opinion, particularly those involving Latin national aspirations, even when they appear to take on an

anti–United States coloration. Mexico has every right to differ with us on foreign policy. I fought our accommodation to her attitude on the Cuban question because I did not want us to exchange our firmness and conviction for her neutrality on an issue relating to our very survival. But Mexico is not a United States satellite. The fact that we are not trying to make her one is the major difference between the free world and the Communist world. The second Punta del Este meeting, at which we labored so diligently to win more votes to our side, was not a meeting of the Warsaw Pact. The fact that there were differences of opinion was extremely significant.

5. Let us continue the excellent program, inaugurated by Mr. Kennedy, of upgrading our State Department and its personnel. A survey made of the State Department in the mid-40's by Dr. Henry M. Wriston, now President Emeritus of Brown University, resulted in bringing career civil service people into the Foreign Service. This strengthened it considerably. Mr. Kennedy has continued this program, and Mr. Rusk has been particularly effective. The Secretary is to be congratulated for placing increased emphasis on Latin America. Today top young career people are assigned to Latin American posts; that section of the Foreign Service was once considered almost the stepchild of the State Department. In my recent trips through the continent, I was constantly impressed by the high caliber of the personnel of our embassies in the Latin American capitals. They were thoroughly professional. My own personal staff was absolutely first-rate, and I am indebted to them for more than I can express in these pages.

6. The O.A.S. Here, I am convinced, much can be done. Perhaps the most pressing need is to strengthen its secretariat and increase its prestige. It can best be strengthened by electing as secretary general a man who can translate the ideals of the inter-American system to the peoples of the hemisphere. We desperately need as secretary general a man who can serve the O.A.S. in a capacity similar to that in which the late Dag Hammarskjöld served the United Nations.*

* One night in Acapulco, having cocktails with two well-educated Mexicans, I was stunned when I realized that neither knew what I meant by the O.A.S., or O.E.A., as it is called in Spanish. They had not heard of it.

The present secretary general of the O.A.S. is Dr. José A. Mora, of Uruguay, a willing, charming and erudite gentleman, who is an unquestioned friend of the United States. But he sees his function as comparable to that of a chairman of the board. I disagree most strongly with this concept. The secretary general of the O.A.S. should be a leader—one who points the way, a man of such prestige in his own right that, like Mr. Hammarskjöld, when a crisis erupts in any country of the O.A.S., he can fly to the scene, and the mere fact of his presence there helps put out the fire.

Such a man should be, in my opinion, a Latin American, known and trusted by the Latins, who possesses outstanding executive ability and who in his person symbolizes the Alliance. He must be dynamic, a man who can organize a program, find the people to implement it, appear on television and radio to talk to the people of the United States. One of my fears has always been that it will not be the Latin Americans who will fail to support the Alliance, but our fellow citizens, because they do not understand it, are unfamiliar with it, exhibit apathy toward it. Such indifference reflects itself in the Congress; and it is the Congress that votes appropriations for the Alliance. To help counter all this, the secretary general of the O.A.S. should be a public and powerful figure, who makes his position preeminently important because *he* is the secretary general.

Dr. Mora does not see himself playing such a role. On one occasion I called upon him to express the dissatisfaction of the United States delegation toward his appointment of a man to an important executive post in the O.A.S. The applicant had been recommended to Dr. Mora by Mrs. Mora, a lady whose hand reputedly lies heavy on the O.A.S. secretariat.

"I don't wish to tell you whom to employ," I said to Dr. Mora. But, I went on to observe, the State Department considered the man highly unqualified. As one of the nations of the O.A.S., we felt we had the right to express our view in an instance where we felt that hiring this man could harm the effectiveness of the Organization.

It was a most unpleasant task for me. Dr. Mora, a gentle and quiet man, lost his temper in one of the rare times of his life. "I cannot retract my appointment," he said indignantly. "If the United States is not satisfied with me, I am ready to resign." I was not, of course, in any position to accept his resignation. I could only withdraw. My observation that the appointee was completely unsuited for the job bore no fruit.

Toward the summer of 1963, my mail began to take on a new coloration. Mixed with letters from Latin America were those from New Orleans, in greater and greater number. Was I going to run for the governorship in 1964?

I had not yet made any announcement. When questioned, I replied, "If conditions are favorable, I intend to be a candidate." But I knew that I would run. If conditions were not favorable, I would do all that was humanly possible to make them so; but I would run again for an office I genuinely wanted and in which I hoped I could be of real service.

In the mail were letters from politicians and from rank-and-file Louisianians, writing to give me advice, or asking advice as to how they should handle local situations. They came, too, from uncommitted politicians who were feeling out potential gubernatorial candidates, to determine whom they would support.

And almost daily I received visits from Louisiana friends. The word they brought was encouraging—particularly the results of a confidential poll in which a cross section of Louisiana voters had just been interviewed, first, to "gauge the climate of opinion" in which the forthcoming race for the governorship would be held, and second, "to measure the relative acceptance" of potential candidates.*

I found the results fascinating. Most significant was the improvement in racial attitudes. When a similar poll had been taken four years earlier, on the eve of my second campaign for the governorship, 70 per cent of those questioned had said they would either "disobey the law" or "find a way to get around the law," in order to maintain segregation in the schools of the state. Now, only 54 per cent were prepared to do this.

I was delighted to find that most of my state's voters approved the record of the Kennedy administration. I had wondered, when I first accepted my appointment, whether "out of sight" would mean "out of mind," whether my absence from Louisiana and my exclusive immersion in Latin American affairs would work harm to any future

* "Attitudes of Louisiana Voters toward Possible Candidates for Governor," a survey made by Louis & Bowles, research consultants, of Southland Center, Dallas, Texas.

political hopes I might have. The poll indicated these fears had been groundless. What gratified me the most personally—in view of my endless and, I am afraid, boring insistence in the White House, at the O.A.S., and at our various conferences, on a "strong line" toward Castro—was this sentence in the poll's conclusion:

"The National Administration maintains majority approval in the State principally because of the President's firmness in foreign relations, especially his success in Cuba."

The poll pointed out that if I ran, I would receive "the great bulk of the Negro vote." Of six possible candidates, I received two thirds of the votes of the Negroes interviewed by the poll takers, and the other five candidates combined received only one third.

Then came two ominous sentences:

"The fact that Morrison is so strong among the Negro voters would tend to make him vulnerable in a run-off in which segregationist sentiment could be arrayed against him. . . . In the Northern part of the State the fact that Morrison is a Catholic would make voters doubtful or not in favor [of him]."

Against this was the fact that virtually everyone questioned had heard of me, and only two out of every five knew of John J. McKeithen, Public Service Commissioner, who, it developed, was to become my chief opponent.

Increasingly now, on my trips to and from Latin America—particularly those dealing with the establishment of more national commissions to tell the Alliance story—I stopped over in New Orleans to mend political fences and tie together loose ends.

The last months of my tenure in office were, in a sense, anticlimactic. For although much was accomplished—we consolidated positions taken earlier—little of it was dramatic. There are two cases in point.

One is the national commissions for the Alliance. From the first days of the Alliance we faced a Gargantuan task: how to tell the two hundred million people of Latin America about this vast new concerted effort and what it would mean to them. The United States had spent more than twenty million dollars to explain the Marshall Plan—the over-all blueprint for rebuilding Europe's economy after World War II—to the people of Europe, where the audiences to whom we spoke were generally literate. In Latin America, however, we were speaking to men and women half of whom could not read or write; and in some countries—such as the Dominican Republic

—surveys showed that only one in a hundred read a newspaper, one in a thousand a book!

Complicating our task was the fact that illiterate people live by hearsay. The word was out that millions of dollars were being showered on Latin America. That the Latin countries themselves contributed to the Alliance, that certain conditions had to be met, that this was a partnership, not a giveaway program—almost none of this filtered down to the average man and woman. The people knew only that money was being given away—where was their share? A colossal job had to be done, and one in which one or a dozen Pueblo Kennedys, however dramatic, could help very little.

As chairman of the O.A.S. Committee on Public Information, I had this as a continuing assignment, and I was involved in it until the end of my mission. During 1963 I made half a dozen trips below the border helping to set up in each country the national commissions so badly needed. When possible, these were composed of publishers, labor leaders, chamber of commerce officials and other public-minded men who knew how to use all communications media in each country—from television to village-square meetings—to publicize the Alliance.

A second case in point was the omnipresent Cuban problem, which now had clearly divided itself into two chapters. The first—the Soviet arms build-up—had been at least temporarily alleviated. I say temporarily, because no true inspection had been set up.

But the second chapter was basic, and continuing: the campaign to subvert the Latin American republics. How were we to meet this aggression—the transportation of agents, the movement of funds and propaganda throughout the hemisphere, with Cuba as a base?

In the spring of 1963, Assistant Secretary of State Ed Martin and I had been among several witnesses to testify before Congressman Selden's House Subcommittee on Inter-American Affairs, on "Castro-Communist Subversion in the Western Hemisphere."*

The testimony taken here, together with a report presented to the

* Ed Martin brought out a number of interesting facts. In 1955 a survey of Latin America reported ten dictatorships, most of them military. Today there were two. Citing Cuba's isolation as a result of O.A.S. action, he pointed out that a year ago one hundred ships of the free world had called at Cuban ports; today, in the same period, there had been twelve. Cuba's trade with the free world had reached $770 million; this year, it would be less than $100 million.

O.A.S. by the Special Committee on Consultative Security—the "watchdog committee" created at the foreign ministers meeting—led to a historic decision by the O.A.S. Council on July 3, 1963. By a vote of 14 to 1, we approved a security program which included a ban on travel to Cuba and other measures to fight subversion. Chile alone opposed it; Brazil, Haiti, Mexico and Venezuela—Venezuela, as I have pointed out earlier, under the democratic left leadership of Betancourt—abstained.

What this meant was that, in the course of time, flights between Cuba and the rest of the Latin American republics were to be reduced until at this writing only a few flights a week operate on these routes.

I think the July 3 decision by the O.A.S. was a most important one. During World War II a similar resolution—aimed at prohibiting the movement of Nazi propaganda and Nazi agents—proved 85 per cent effective.

Now, as I prepared to resign, I tried to consider our achievements in the Alliance for Progress. To do what I could had been my all-absorbing concern. Every man is limited in what he can do: he can only try to lead where he thinks he can lead, work in cooperation with others to further the common goal—and at the end, look at what has been done, and be as proud of it as though he had done it all himself, though he knows that his part was infinitesimal.

To attempt to present the reader with a bewildering array of statistics serves little purpose. But a summary, as of this writing, might include:

In the field of land reform, sixteen of the nineteen Latin nations within the O.A.S.—I can give no statistics for Cuba—had instituted programs. Venezuela had resettled 40,000 families on three million hectares.* In Honduras, over 4,000 hectares had been distributed to peasants. In Panama, plans were under way to distribute 20,000 hectares to 1,200 families. In Chile, 1,100,000 hectares were distributed among 6,000 families. The same story—thousands of hectares of land being distributed—held true in Argentina and Brazil. Bolivia and Mexico were continuing effective, well-established programs: Mexico, as the reader knows, had begun agrarian reform

* A hectare is about 2½ acres.

nearly fifty years ago. Colombia and Guatemala were enacting far-reaching legislation in this field, as well.

In tax reform, considerable progress had been made in eleven countries: Bolivia, Venezuela, Colombia, Peru, Argentina, Costa Rica, Uruguay, Mexico, El Salvador, Nicaragua and Guatemala. Guatemala, for example, instituted an income tax in 1963. Bolivia had increased tax collections in one year over 30 per cent. Brazil had proposed new legislation that would increase revenues by $70 million a year. To have such measures passed in many instances by the very persons most directly affected—and painfully so—was a real achievement, I thought. It meant introducing new concepts as to the obligation of the rich to their fellow citizens.

In housing, almost all the countries were formulating or carrying out regional programs to help citizens buy and build houses, to modernize the construction industry, to establish savings and loan associations. A particularly dramatic development took place in Costa Rica. A national housing institute obtained an Alliance loan at zero interest, added Costa Rican money, and built hundreds of houses, which it offers to workers for $900, payable at the rate of $4.50 a month, and no down payment needed. Picture Costa Rica, its rolling green hills near San José, the capital, then think of these little wooden homes, brightly painted different colors, each boasting a concrete front, a kitchen sink, free running water, a sidewalk, a gutter bottom, and fronting on a gravel street. Each house bore a sign, "Alliance for Progress," until sold. Now 20,000 more have been planned, so successful has this project been.

In eight countries specialized offices for education have been created. In others, those already in operation were streamlined for efficiency. School enrollment in nineteen countries rose at a higher rate each successive year.

On a wider scale, the signs were equally encouraging. All but one of the countries had earmarked more than 20 per cent of the national budget for *social improvements*; eight countries, as much as 30 per cent; two countries, 40 per cent. Again, the introduction—and acceptance—of concepts of civic responsibility that had been little respected before.

Every Latin American country now had committees working on Alliance over-all development plans. The scope was staggering, ranging from experimental agricultural institutes, where seed and fertility of soil were studied, to wide-ranging blueprints covering national health plans, swamp clearance, road building, development of hydroelectric power, rural welfare, and price and exchange controls.

In most countries, so much is done on an executive level, that new procedures have had to be devised for training civil servants, public-administration employees and other public officials. This has always been a crying need in Latin America.

By autumn of 1963, the United States, according to Undersecretary of State Averell Harriman, had fulfilled all its commitments under the Alliance by making available $2.3 billion to Latin America since August 1961. To be sure, there had been delays—these were inevitable in a program so vast, involving the mobilization of the resources of nineteen countries, the planning, establishing of priorities, the development of sound projects.

Item: Four million children were receiving nutritious free lunches through the Food for Peace program.

Item: Through a world commodity agreement, coffee prices had been stabilized, thus indirectly stabilizing the economies of eleven Latin American countries that depend on coffee as their principal export.

Item: Alliance benefits had been yielded directly to an estimated 35,000,000 people.*

Item: The Latin American countries themselves had committed more than $8 billion of their own funds in self-help economic and social development.

What had to be remembered, above all, was that this process—even the smallest steps taken by a tiny country—in terms of education, understanding, establishment of a better way of life, was an irreversible one. In the simplest, least dramatic terms, the child made literate would never again return to illiteracy. The village given a well providing fresh water would never again be content to do without fresh water. The man given a measure of dignity would never again willingly accept humiliation.

Here, indeed, one finds both an optimistic and a pessimistic interpretation of the future. Will there be more *coups d'état,* more

* For the reader interested in the overwhelming scope of Alliance activities, a good reference volume is the annual report of the Social Progress Trust Fund of the Inter-American Development Bank, published in Washington, D.C.

uprisings, riots, revolts, unrest? I think we shall have a rather steady diet of this for at least the next decade. The very boons brought to the people of Latin America by the Alliance stimulate such unrest. Better education, better communication, higher standards of living, a moment of free speech—these bring the average Latin American out of his isolated lethargy, it moves him from the inertia which has been his curse through the centuries. In the riots, the unrest, the violent changes, the intense nationalism which now and then becomes bitterly anti-American, we are witnessing the growing pains of freedom. Dissatisfaction with what has been; demand for something better tomorrow.

And we are encouraging it.

The Alliance for Progress has set into motion forces which are impossible to halt. They are moving in the direction of greater good for all. I have been proud to have played some small part in getting these forces underway.

On this note—that of the Alliance, the note on which I began my story—I end it. I resigned on September 13, 1963, bid goodbye to Mr. Kennedy, to my State Department associates, to my colleagues in the O.A.S.—I knew I would see them again and again, for if I now had behind me more than eighty trips to Latin America, surely I would make at least eighty more—and returned to New Orleans and to my family.

Before me was the race for the governorship. All omens were good. Twice I had tried before; perhaps the third try would turn the trick.

I thought, as my plane from Washington circled the city of New Orleans and I saw below all the places so familiar to me—the new City Hall and Civic Center, the complex of railway lines meeting in the giant Union Passenger Terminal, the Moisant International Airport Terminal, the buildings and projects that people said couldn't be done and were done—I thought, it was all worth while, and it gave me a warm glow. I was glad to be home.

INDEX

Acosta Yepez, Francisco, 180
Act of Bogotá (1960), 83, 154, 254
Agence France Presse, 161
Agency for International Development (AID) program, 35, 221, 223, 267
Aleman Valdes, Miguel, 17, 256
Alemann, Roberto Teodoro, 95, 244, 259
Alessandri Rodriguez, Jorge, 180
Allende Gossens, Salvador, 244, 259
Alliance for Progress, 21, 23, 25, 28, 34, 35, 36, 41, 67, 81, 97, 135, 144, 146, 149, 153, 161, 178, 179, 181, 192, 195, 202, 203, 207, 217, 218, 219–21, 222, 249, 250, 253, 254, 255, 267, 269, 271, 273, 274, 275–78; birth of, 83–92; Charter of Punta del Este (1961), 24, 92, 96, 98, 101, 135, 219; Food for Peace program, 35, 83, 277; Power Pact for Peace project, 94 n., 95, 106–11
Alphand, Hervé, 223
Aly Khan, 15
Americans for Democratic Action (A.D.A.), 199
Andrews Air Force Base, 70
Angelita (Trujillo's yacht), 142, 143, 148
Annapolis Naval Academy, 47
Antonio, Jorge, 211, 213–14, 215
Arango, Augusto Guillermo ("Bill"), 118, 119, 120, 133
Aranha, Oswaldo, Jr., 207
Arevalo, Juan José, 260
Argentina, 62, 82, 97, 103, 104–05, 108, 154, 166, 171–72, 174, 179–80, 192–95, 200, 202, 203–04, 205, 208–15, 217, 219, 222–25, 239, 244, 257, 259, 275, 276
Arinos, Afonso, 101
Army Policy Board, 145
Army War College, 226, 227
Arosemena Monroy, Carlos Julio, 180 n., 264
Associated Press, 178
Ayub Khan, Mohammad, 70

Balaguer, Joaquin, 97, 114, 115, 116, 119, 120, 123–26, 127, 129, 131, 134, 136 n., 137, 139, 145, 147, 150, 151, 152, 262
Ball, George W., 159–60, 223 n.
Barahona, Dominican Republic, 131
Barinas, Pedro, 122–23, 124, 127
Batlle Ibanez, Jorge, 171 n.
Baton Rouge, Louisiana, 54
Baudreaux, Peggy, 17
Bay of Pigs disaster, 27, 31, 34, 68, 96, 102, 190, 220
Beals, Carleton, 23 n.
Berle, Adolf Augustus, Jr., 28, 32, 74
Berlin crisis, 71, 81, 201
Berlin wall, 85, 90, 95
Bermuda, 148

Bermudez, Mario, 56, 57, 79, 94, 108, 206, 215
Berrellez, Robert, 122–23, 124
Betancourt, Romulo, 88, 130, 200, 255–56, 260, 263, 264, 275
Bissell, General Richard Mervin, Jr., 114, 116, 117, 122
Blough, Roger M., 221 n.
Blumenthal, W. Michael, 76
Boca Chica, Dominican Republic, 131, 138, 140, 142
Boggs, Thomas Hale, 28, 30, 33, 51
Boggs, Mrs. Thomas Hale (Lindy), 30, 51
Bogotá, Colombia, 83 n.
Bolivar, Simon, 30
Bolivia, 82, 154, 166, 179, 180, 219 n., 239, 244, 245–48, 251, 275, 276
Bolles, Edmund Blair, 95
Bomchil, Max and Zarita de, 95, 98
Bonafede, Dom, 186 n.
Bosch, Juan, 126, 200, 260, 262–63, 264
Bowdler, William G. ("Bill"), 119, 121, 123, 125, 127, 134, 150
Bowles, Chester, 166
Bradenton, Florida, 161
Bradley, General Omar Nelson, 58
Brasilia, Brazil, 73–74, 75, 76, 169
Brazil, 73–76, 81, 96–97, 101, 104, 108, 153, 154, 166, 168–70, 172, 173, 174, 179, 180, 193, 200, 201, 202, 203, 204, 205, 206–08, 215–17, 219 n., 227, 228–29, 230, 239, 243, 244, 247, 248, 250, 254–55, 265, 275
Bremen Port Command, 55
British Guiana, 167
Bruce, James, 62, 211
Buenos Aires, Argentina, 103, 209
Bulge, Battle of the, 55
Bundy, McGeorge, 31, 71, 165, 168
Bureau of Inter-American Affairs, 31–32, 116
Burkley, Dr. George, 69
Byrd, Harry Flood, 70

Cadon, Alberto Charles, 96
Café Filho, João, 216
Camilion, Oscar, 192–94, 195, 202
Campos, Roberto de Oliveira, 243, 248, 258
Caracas, Venezuela, 78
Carcano, Miguel Angel, 192, 194
Cardenas, General Lazaro, 259
Caribe, El, 127
Carrasco Airport, Montevideo, 78–79
Carrillo Flores, Antonio, 233, 243
Carter, Amon, 236
Castro, Fidel, 39, 67, 86, 87, 96, 100, 103, 104, 105, 130, 140, 147, 148, 151, 153, 154, 156–57, 166, 168, 169, 174, 178, 182, 184, 186, 188, 189–90, 195–97, 199, 225, 239, 244, 250, 251, 259, 260, 261, 264
Castro, Raul, 86 n.
Central Intelligence Agency (C.I.A.), 116, 122, 123, 124, 133 n., 167, 262
Chalmers, René, 192
Charter of Punta del Este, *see* Alliance for Progress, Charter of
Chayes, Abram Joseph, 159, 160
Chile, 154, 179, 180, 219 n., 221–22, 239, 244, 245–46, 251, 257, 258, 275
China, Communist, 149, 188
Ciudad Trujillo, Dominican Republic, 59, 62, 115, 119, 120, 128, 129, 145, 147, 150, 160
Clulow, Carlos Alberto, 89, 149, 155–56, 157–58, 170–71, 191
Cole, Charles W., 221, 222
Colombia, 57, 82, 96, 100, 147, 149, 152, 155, 179, 205, 215, 220, 244, 248, 252–54, 276
Communism and Communists, 23,

28, 34, 35, 39, 68, 80, 82, 85, 100, 104, 114, 115, 116–17, 122–23, 124–25, 127, 132, 148–49, 154, 157, 168, 170, 175, 179, 188, 189, 195, 200, 201, 220, 222, 242, 250, 251, 260, 261, 262–63, 264, 265, 269; intervention in Latin America, 166–67, 189, 220, 256
Congress of Panama, 30
Constanza, Dominican Republic, 126 n., 131, 135, 136
Conte Aguero, Luis, 87–88
Córdoba, Argentina, 214
Corro, Miguel, 133, 134, 145
Costa, Lucio, 74
Costa Rica, 147, 156, 166–67, 179, 220, 260, 276
Crescent City Democratic Organization, 55
Cuba, 23, 24, 31, 66 n., 81, 82, 83 n., 85–90, 96, 99–105, 125, 130, 144, 147, 148–49, 151–52, 153, 154, 156–57, 165, 169, 174, 177–80, 184, 188, 189, 190, 193, 194–97, 218–19, 220, 225, 229, 238–40, 243, 250, 263, 264, 274–75; Bay of Pigs disaster, 27, 31, 34, 68, 96, 102, 190, 220; Communist intervention in Latin America, 166–67, 189, 220, 256; embargo on, 218–19, 225; sanctions against, 165–66, 168, 170, 174, 179, 193–95, 218–19; Soviet missile crisis, 218, 220, 237, 238–51, 258; *see also* Castro, Fidel
Curtis, Colonel Henry Baldwin, 56

Dallas, Texas, 232, 236
Davis, Jimmie H., 30
Decker, General George Henry, 228
Defense Department, U.S., 228
Democratic left, the, 199–200, 253, 260–65, 267
Depression of the 1930s, 47
Dia, El, 191–92
Diaz Ordaz, Gustavo, 256
Dillon, C. Douglas, 36, 76, 79, 80, 83 n., 84, 87, 90–91, 93, 94, 100, 238, 240, 241, 249
Doherty, William Charles, 95
Dominican Republic, 41, 57–59, 62, 82, 97–98, 114–17, 118–28, 129–43, 144, 145, 146, 147, 148, 149–51, 152, 159, 160–61, 174, 179 n., 200, 220, 262–63, 264, 273–74; sanctions against, 130–32, 135, 136 n., 141, 142, 145, 147, 149, 150, 160–61, 167, 174
Dominican Revolutionary Party (P.R.D.), 126, 129, 132, 136
Donnelley, Dixon, 93, 240
Dorticos Torrado, Osvaldo, 177, 190–91
Duarte, Juan, 211, 213
Duplantier, Adrian, 197 n.
Duvalier, François, 179 n.

Echandi Jimenez, Mario, 167
Echevarria, General Rodriguez, 150
Ecuador, 82, 146 n., 154, 166, 167, 179, 180–82, 205, 219, 239, 255, 264
Education program, 276
Eisenhower, Dwight D., 60, 64, 78–79, 83 n., 254
Eisenhower, Milton S., 39
El Caribe, 127
Ellender, Allen J., 33, 61, 62
Elliott, Robert, 206
El Salvador, 56, 84, 152, 166, 178, 219, 220, 225, 276
Embargo on Cuban trade, 218–19, 225
Escalante, Manuel G., 95
Escudero, Gonzalo, 118, 119, 133, 145, 181, 182
Estrella Liz, Victor Rafael, 127–28
Export-Import Bank, 35

Facio, Gonzalo J., 259, 266
Fairbanks Morse Company, 107
Fellman Velarde, José, 246–47
Fiallo, Viriato A., 125, 132, 133 n.
Figueres, José ("Pepe"), 253, 257, 259, 260–62
Fischer, Major General Harvey Herman, 227
Food for Peace Program, 35, 83, 277
Fort Buchanan, Puerto Rico, 27
Fort Hood, Texas, 71
Fort McNair, 226, 227, 228, 230
Fort Myer, 228
Fort Polk, 71–73
Fort Worth, Texas, 232, 236
Fourteenth of June Party, 126, 129, 136
Franklin D. Roosevelt, U.S.S., 150
Free enterprise in Latin America, 203–17, 269
Frigerio, Rogelio, 104–05, 172, 180, 200, 222 n.
Frondizi, Arturo, 103, 104–05, 180, 192, 194, 201, 219 n., 222, 223, 255–56
Fulbright, James William, 61, 62, 224

Gabor, Zsa Zsa, 33
Gaitan, Jorge Eliecer, 253
Geyelin, Philip, 162
Girard, Stephen A., 107
Gomez, Marco, 138, 140, 141, 142
Good Neighbor policy, 152
Goodwin, Richard N., 13, 28, 31, 32, 37–38, 66, 93, 98–103, 104, 105, 112, 113, 162, 165, 166, 168, 169, 170, 172, 174, 180, 183, 184, 185, 186–87, 192, 193, 194–95, 199–200, 202, 221, 222
Gordon, Lincoln, 93, 250
Goulart Belchior Marques, João ("Jango"), 104, 168, 206 n., 230, 243, 244, 250, 265
Grad, Rosalie, 65
Graf Spee (German battleship), 80
Gruening, Ernest, 264
Guantanamo Naval Base, 102
Guatemala, 56, 82, 84, 90, 156, 157, 166, 179, 193, 276
Guerrilla warfare, 148
Guevara, Major Ernesto ("Che"), 13, 79, 86–90, 91, 99–105, 112, 148, 169, 172, 177, 180, 188, 190
Guido, José Maria, 225
Gunther, John, 207
Gutierrez, Donã Carmen, 108, 109–10, 111
Gutierrez Roldan, Pascual, 250–51

Haedo, Eduardo Victor, 79, 80–81, 83, 100, 106, 107, 109–10, 111, 171, 184, 188
Haile Selassie, Emperor, 64
Haiti, 57, 82, 84, 152, 166, 179, 192, 194, 275
Hamilton, Fowler, 221
Hammarskjöld, Dag, 270, 271
Harriman, W. Averell, 277
Hartwick, Toby, 145
Havana, Cuba, 196
Haya de la Torre, Victor Raul, 260
Hebert, F. Edward, 33
Hecht, Rudolph, 55–56
Hendrix, Harold Victor (Hal), 161, 186 n.
Herrera, Felipe, 257, 258
Hickenlooper, Bourke B., 167, 173, 182–83, 184–86, 187, 224
Hill, John Calvin, Jr., 121–22, 145, 148, 150, 161
Honduras, 166, 264, 275
Horsey, William L. F., 178
Housing program, 276
Hoyt, Henry Augustus, 192

Idlewild Airport, 148
Illia, Arturo Umberto, 259–60

Illiteracy in Latin America, 84, 274
Imperial Defense College, Great Britain, 226
Industrial College of the Armed Forces, 227–28
Industrias Kaiser Argentina (IKA), 203–04, 214, 215, 217
Information Service, U.S., 174 n., 185
Inside U.S.A. (Gunther), 207
Inter-American Conference (1954), 153
Inter-American Defense Board, 195, 225, 226
Inter-American Defense College, 220, 225–30
Inter-American Development Bank, 35, 258
Inter-American Economic and Social Council of A.O.S., 67
Inter-American Municipal Association, 62
Inter-American Municipal Organization Conference (1962), 111
Inter-American Peace Committee, 149, 152, 155, 166, 167, 168
Inter-American Security Organization, 187
Inter-American Treaty for Reciprocal Assistance, *see* Rio Treaty
International House, New Orleans, 43, 55, 56, 57, 94 n., 108
International Trade Mart, New Orleans, 43, 56
International Union of American Republics, 30

Jamison, Edward Alden, Jr., 68, 114, 168, 172
Johnson, Luci Baines, 235
Johnson, Lyndon Baines, 88 n., 106, 107, 108, 231, 232–36, 240
Johnson, Mrs. Lyndon Baines (Lady Bird), 232, 235
Jones, Sam Houston, 51, 54
Julião, Francisco, 259

Kaiser, Alyce (Mrs. Henry J.), 205, 206, 210
Kaiser, Henry J., 15, 107, 108, 204–11, 213–15, 217, 269
Kaiser-Fraser Corporation, 205
Keating, Kenneth B., 70
Keely, Charlie, 184, 186, 187
Keller, Lafayette, 48
Kennedy, John Fitzgerald, 22, 23, 24, 28, 31, 32–38, 40, 66, 69, 70–71, 72–73, 80, 82, 83, 85, 97, 98, 112–15, 116, 117–18, 124, 146, 150, 161, 162, 165, 166, 168, 169, 170, 172, 173–74, 175–76, 179 n., 180 n., 183, 185, 193, 197, 198–99, 201–02, 218, 220, 221 n., 224, 225, 227, 228, 234, 238, 239, 240, 241, 242, 244, 249, 262, 264, 267, 268, 270, 278
Kennedy, Mrs. John Fitzgerald (Jacqueline Lee Bouvier), 199
Kennedy, Robert F., 114, 234
Keough, Eugene J., 107
Khrushchev, Nikita S., 71, 85, 174 n., 188, 239, 241, 244, 249, 250, 251
Kubitschek de Oliveira, Juscelino, 73, 74, 75, 83 n., 169, 249 n., 254

Lacerda, Carlos, 104, 206, 216
Land reform program, 275–76
Laos, 31
La Paz, Bolivia, 82, 246, 251
La Romana, Dominican Republic, 135
Latin America, 23–25, 57–59, 81–82, 83, 84, 94, 96, 144, 147, 152–53, 168, 174, 178, 179, 199, 220, 225, 252–65, 266–72, 273–78; Alliance for Progress achievements in, 275–78; Com-

Latin America, *continued*
munist intervention in, 166–67, 189, 220, 256; democratic left in, 199–200, 253, 260–65, 267; free enterprise in, 203–17, 269; illiteracy in, 84, 274; military in politics in, 225–30, 264–65, 267–68
Latin American Free Trade Association (LAFTA), 257, 258
Lavalle, Juan Batista de, 147
La Vega, Dominican Republic, 135
LBJ Ranch, 231, 232–33, 243
Leche, Richard W., 50
Lechin Oquendo, Juan, 259
Lechuga, Carlos, 68–69, 90, 148, 151–52, 157, 177, 190, 219
Leddy, John Marshall, 93, 100
Lesseps, Ferdinand de, 22
Liebling, Abbott Joseph, 10
Lill, Winston, 17, 65, 75, 93
Lima, Peru, 146, 149
Lincoln, Evelyn, 33
Linder, Harold Francis, 93
Little Rock, U.S.S., 150
Lleras Camargo, Alberto, 147, 155, 249 n., 252–54, 255
Lobo, Fernando, 69–70, 76
Loeb, James Isaac, 162, 267
Long, Earl, 30, 51
Long, Huey P., 45, 48
Long, Russell B., 28, 33, 61–62, 71–72, 73
Lopez Mateos, Adolfo, 244, 256, 259
Lopez Molina, Maximo, 115, 127, 149
Louisiana State University, 45, 46, 47–48, 161
Luce, Clare Boothe, 60

Machado, José A., 147
Mahony, Pat, 14, 15, 17, 65, 142–43
Maldonado, Uruguay, 179, 188
Maneen, Diana, 161–62
Mao Tse-tung, 188
Marshall Plan, 38, 273
Martin, Edwin M., 93, 202, 223, 274
Martinez Montero, Homero, 158, 171, 191
Martinez Sotomayer, Carlos, 221
Mayobre, José Antonio, 149, 166, 227, 228
McClintock, Robert Mills, 223–24
McCloud, James, 95, 107
McGhee, George Crews, 146
McHugh, General Godfrey T., 69–70
McKeithen, John J., 17, 18, 273
Mercado, Luis R., 131
Merrigan, Larry, 160
Merrow, Chester E., 167, 183, 184
Mexico, 82, 153, 154, 156, 166, 172, 179, 180, 205, 219 n., 227, 233, 239, 243, 244, 247, 248, 250–51, 256, 268, 270, 275, 276
Mexico City, Mexico, 174 n., 240, 241, 249
Miami News, 161
Military in Latin American politics, 225–30, 264–65, 267–68
Miolan, Angel, 126, 132
Mississippi Shipping Company, 55
Moca, Dominican Repubic, 135
Montevideo, Uruguay, 77, 78, 101, 179
Moore, John Denis Joseph, 97
Mora, José A., 255, 271
Morales, Eduardo, 126–27, 160
Morales-Carrion, Arturo, 68, 93, 162
Moreiro Sales, 76
Morrison, Ben (brother of deL.), 46
Morrison, Corinne Ann (daughter of deL.), 17, 29, 40
Morrison, Corinne Waterman (wife of deL.), 29, 57, 62–63, 205, 206, 211, 212

Morrison, deLesseps S., achievements in Alliance for Progress, 275–78; ambassador to the O.A.S., 11, 12–13, 16–17, 66, 145, 198–202, 238, 266–78; appeal to women, 15–16; appointment to ambassadorship of the O.A.S., 27–41; Brasilia visited by, 73–76; bribe mystery, 159–61; campaign for governorship of Louisiana, 17–18, 61 n., 272–73, 278; corruption at the polls and, 48–50, 52–54; Cuban-Soviet missile crisis and, 238–51; death of, 9, 11; delegate to Latin America, 57–59; Dominican Republic investigation, 115–17, 118–28, 129–43; education, 45, 46, 47–48; election to Louisiana legislature, 51–54; enjoyment of life, 18–19; father-son relations, 45–47; Fort Polk reopened, 71–73; Inter-American Defense College and, 220, 225–30; Johnson and the O.A.S. ambassadors and, 231–37; journal entries, 146–58; Kaiser free enterprise and, 203–17; legal practice, 48, 51; Mayor of New Orleans, 45, 55–57, 66, 204–05; military career, 48, 54–55, 72, 226; political career, 10, 13–14; Punta del Este Alliance for Peace Conference, 83–92, 93–105; Punta del Este Foreign Ministers Conference, 165, 170, 177–97, 201–02, 219, 270; resignation from ambassadorship, 278; resignation prediction mystery, 161–63; Senate confirmation of, 60–65; titles, 42 n.

Morrison, deLesseps S. (Toni), Jr. (son of deL.), 17, 29, 40

Morrison, Mrs. E. S. (aunt of deL.), 51

Morrison, Jacob H. (father of deL.), 45–47, 178

Morrison, Jake (brother of deL.), 46, 51

Morrison, John Randolph (Randy) (son of deL.), 9, 11, 17, 29, 32, 40, 66

Morrison, Mary (sister-in-law of deL.), 51–52

Morrison, Virginia (sister of deL.), 46

Morse, Wayne Lyman, 32, 60, 61, 62–65, 167, 180–82, 183, 191, 224, 264

Moscoso, Teodoro, 88, 221, 222

Moscoso-Goodwin trade mission, 221–22

Moses, Herbert, 208

Mugica, Adolfo, 101, 103

Muñoz Marín, Luis, 260, 263, 264

Murphy, Robert Daniel, 146–47

Murrow, Edward R., 146

Nardonia, Pedro, 171

Nathan, Colonel, 56

National Association for the Advancement of Colored People, 60–61, 63

National Civic Union (U.C.N.), 125, 129, 134, 136, 137, 145

National Commission for the Alliance, 146

National War College, U.S., 226

NATO Defense College, 226

New Frontier, the, 28

New Orleans, Louisiana, 30–31, 43–45, 48, 55–56, 57, 63, 64, 201, 204–05, 234–36, 272–73, 278; *see also* Port of New Orleans

New Orleans *Times-Picayune*, 31, 122

New Roads, Louisiana, 45, 46

New York Times, The, 31, 162, 178, 267

Nicaragua, 82, 152, 166, 179, 276

Niemeyer, Oscar, 74
Nixon, Richard M., 64, 78, 120, 234
North Vietnam, 188
Nutter, Charles, 56

Office of Inter-American Political Affairs, 68
Office of International Relations, New Orleans, 57
O Globo, 208
"Operation Pan-America," 73, 83 n., 254, 257
Organization for Economic Development in Central America (ODECA), 257
Organization of American States (O.A.S.), 28, 29–30, 35, 36, 38, 41, 43, 67, 97, 114, 115, 130, 131, 134, 136 n., 144, 146, 147, 148, 149, 151, 153, 154, 155, 156, 157, 166, 167, 180, 184, 187, 189, 194, 218, 219, 225, 227, 229, 238, 241, 242, 243–44, 252, 253, 255, 256, 262, 263, 269, 270–71, 274, 275, 278
Oribe, Emilio, 195–96, 244, 249
Orlich Bolmarcich, Francisco José, 260
Ortiz, S. Salvador, 98
Ortiz de Rozas, Carlos, 192–94, 195, 202

Panama, 81, 205, 275
Pan American Union, 30, 66, 118, 193, 230, 239, 253
Paraguay, 82
Paredes, Antonio José, 134
Parkhouse, Lois, 231
Partido Dominicano, 116, 129
Patorno, Captain Nino, 51–52
Patrick, Ted, 107
Paz Estenssoro, Victor, 247–48, 260
Peace Corps, 83, 186 n.
Penna Marinho, Ilmar, 228, 243, 250
Peralta Azurdia, Colonel Enrique, 90 n.
Perez Godoy, General Juan, 267
Perez y Perez, Carlos Federico, 119
Peron, Eva Duarte ("Evita"), 62, 211–13, 215
Peron, Juan Domingo, 61, 62, 208, 209, 210–11, 213–15, 222
Peru, 81, 84, 146, 149, 152, 166, 179, 205, 225, 267, 276
Phillips, Richard I., 93, 146
Plaza Gutierrez, Leonidas, 255
Plaza Lasso, Galo, 25, 180–81, 255
Point Four program, 38
Portell-Villa, Dr., 229
Port of New Orleans, 10, 56
Power Pact for Peace project, 94 n., 95, 106–11
Poydras High School, New Roads, Louisiana, 47
Prado Ugarteche, Manuel, 117, 118, 134
Prebisch, Raul, 257–58
Pueblo Obrero President Kennedy, Uruguay, 109–11, 184
Puerto Plata, Dominican Republic, 135, 136–37
Puerto Rico, 57, 58, 130
Punta del Este, Uruguay, 36, 77, 79, 80, 177, 181, 190–91
Punta del Este Alliance for Progress Conference, 80, 83–92, 93–105, 106; Charter of Punta del Este, 24, 92, 96, 98, 101, 135, 219
Punta del Este Foreign Ministers Conference, 165, 170, 177–97, 201–02, 219

Quadros, Janio da Silva, 73, 74–76, 101, 104, 105, 168–69, 201, 206 n., 222 n.

Radio Caribe, Dominican Repub-

lic, 115, 127
Radio Clarin, Uruguay, 108
Radio Havana, Cuba, 69, 136, 151
Reuther, Walter P., 205
Rhadames Bridge, Dominican Republic, 119, 120–21
Rio Treaty (1947), 151, 152–53, 155, 156, 182, 219, 242, 243
Rivera, Julio Adalberto, 225
Roa Garcia, Raul, 153
Robichaud, Gerard A., 186 n.
Roca, Blas, 148
Rockefeller, Nelson Aldridge, 70
Rodriguez, Carlos Rafael, 177
Rodriguez, Echevarria, General Pedro Rafael Ramon, 150
Rodriguez Laretta, Horacio, 101, 104, 105, 172
Rogers, Paul G., 202
Roosevelt, Franklin Delano, 50, 54, 152–53, 262
Rostow, Walt (Whitman), 31, 88 n., 113, 165, 168, 170, 187, 199
Ruiz Cortines, Adolfo, 256
Rusk, Dean, 27–28, 29, 34, 36, 60, 61, 114, 150, 160, 165, 168, 172, 175, 180, 181, 183, 186, 187, 188–90, 191, 192, 193, 194, 195, 197, 202, 224, 229, 238, 239, 242, 245, 248, 270
Ryan, William, 178

Salazar, Gustavo, 108, 109, 110–11
Salazar, Santiago, 134, 137, 138, 142
Salcedo, Father, 215
San Antonio, Texas, 231, 232, 233, 236
Sanchez de Lozada, Enrique, 245
Sanchez Gavito, Vicente, 156, 227–28, 230, 242–43, 248
San Cristóbal, Dominican Republic, 135
Sanctions: against Cuba, *see* Cuba, sanctions against; against Dominican Republic, *see* Dominican Republic, sanctions against
San Isidro Air Base, Dominican Republic, 127, 133 n., 142, 149, 150
San Pedro, Dominican Republic, 135
Santiago, Dominican Republic, 122, 133, 134–35
San Tiago Dantas, Francisco Clementino, 169, 180, 193, 200, 228–29
Sanz de Santamaria, Carlos, 95
São Paulo, Brazil, 208
Sarmiento Caruncho, Emilio, 245, 246–48, 249, 251
Schirra, Walter, 231
Schlesinger, Arthur, Jr., 13, 28, 31, 66, 113, 165, 166, 168, 169, 170, 173, 174, 180, 183, 187, 199–200
Schwing, Judge Calvin, 46
Selden, Armistead I., Jr., 32, 167, 181, 183–84, 185, 186–87, 264, 274
Sentinels of Liberty, 87
Sevilla-Sacasa, Guillermo, 95, 157
Shriver, Robert Sargent, Jr., 114, 118
Silva, Gerson Augusto de, 101
Smathers, George A., 28, 166
Smith, Stephen, 114, 118, 161, 175, 176
Social Aid Foundation, 211
Social Progress Trust Fund, 258
Soviet Union, 85, 91, 148, 157, 174, 218, 219 n., 238, 239, 241, 242, 249, 250, 251, 268, 274
Space achievements: American, 231; Soviet, 85, 95
Special Consultative Committee on Security, 187
State Department, U.S., 66, 112–15, 117, 118, 133 n., 144, 155, 167, 221, 223, 224, 228, 267,

State Department, *continued*
268, 270, 271, 278
Stevenson, Adlai Ewing, 29, 39–40, 155, 166, 239
Stroessner, Alfredo, 39
Surinam, 73
Symington, James W., 93, 98
Symington, William Stuart, 93
Szulc, Tad, 162, 163, 178

Tavarez Justo, Manuel, 125
Tax reform program, 276
Taylor, General Maxwell D., 71, 72, 228
Telles, Raymond L., Jr., 166
Time magazine, 33, 45, 211, 212
Titov, German Stepanovich, 85
Today, NBC TV show, 108, 110
Tourreilles, Paco, 108
Trinity University, San Antonio, Texas, 231, 232, 233, 236
Trujillo, General Arismendi, 132, 135, 141, 145, 148, 149, 161
Trujillo, General Hector, 132, 135, 141, 145, 149, 161
Trujillo, General Pedro, 145
Trujillo, Generalissimo Rafael Leonidas, 58–59, 61, 62, 63, 97, 114, 115, 116, 120, 123, 126, 127, 130, 134, 135, 137, 143, 256
Trujillo, General Rafael Leonidas, Jr. ("Ramfis"), 116, 124, 127, 131, 132, 133 n., 134, 137, 138–42, 145, 147, 149, 150, 161
Truman, Harry S., 62
Tubman, William V. S., 64
Tucson, Arizona, 61
Tulane University, 51
Turbay Ayala, Julio César, 96, 147, 155
Turnage, William Vincent, 93

United Nations, 29, 66, 125, 151, 152, 174, 179, 219 n., 230, 238–39, 253, 257, 270
United Press International, 178
Upton, Thomas Graydon (Grady), 146
Urruela, Rafael, 57
Urrutia Aparacio, Carlos, 68, 90, 156, 157
Uruguay, 77, 152, 156 n., 157, 170–71, 179, 180, 192, 205, 219 n., 244–45, 248, 249, 276

Valencia, Guillermo Leon, 254
Van Natta, Major General Thomas V., 229
Vargas, Getulio Dornelles, 104, 206–08, 216–17
Vargas, Luthero, 206
Venezuela, 57, 82, 88, 89, 152, 161, 179, 200, 205, 215, 220, 227, 228, 255, 263, 275, 276
Villeda Morales, Ramon, 260, 265
Voice of America, 69

Washington, D.C., 144–45, 239
Washington *Evening Star*, 165
Waters, Colonel Adair, 56
Weintraub, William H., 106–07, 206, 208, 210
Weir, Ernest T., 207–08
Weirton Steel Company, 207–08
White, William S., 165
White Citizens Council, New Orleans, 63
Willys-Overland do Brasil, 204
Wilson, Simon, 93
Woodward, Robert F., 66, 93, 100, 113, 114, 165, 168, 172, 176, 183, 192, 202, 223
World Bank, 35, 146
World War II, 54–55, 80
Wriston, Henry M., 270

Ydigoras Fuentes, Miguel, 90 n.

Zuleta Angel, Alberto, 118–19, 133, 141, 145, 149, 155, 219